THE
BLACKWELL PHILOSOPHER DICTIONARIES

A Rousseau Dictionary

N. J. H. Dent

BLACKWELL
Reference

Copyright © N. J. H. Dent 1992

The right of N. J. H. Dent to be identified as author of this work has been asserted
in accordance with the Copyright, Designs and Patents Act 1988.

First published 1992

First published in USA 1992

Blackwell Publishers
108 Cowley Road
Oxford   OX4 1JF
UK

238 Main Street, Suite 501,
Cambridge, Massachusetts 02142
USA

British Library Cataloguing in Publication Data

A CIP catalogue record for this book is available from the British Library.

Library of Congress Cataloging-in-Publication Data

Dent, N. J. H., 1945–
    A Rousseau dictionary / N.J.H. Dent.
      p.   cm. — (The Blackwell philosopher dictionaries)
    Includes bibliographical references and index.
    ISBN 0-631-17568-7 (hb). — ISBN 0-631-17569-5 (pb)
      1. Rousseau, Jean-Jacques, 1712–1778—Dictionaries, indexes, etc.
    I. Title.   II. Series.
    Z2042.D46   1992
    848'.509—dc20   92-17607
                                                              CIP

Typeset in Baskerville 10/11pt by Acorn Bookwork, Salisbury, Wilts
Printed in Great Britain by T.J. Press (Padstow) Ltd, Padstow, Cornwall

This book is printed on acid-free paper

For my parents

Everybody knows that there is a great dispute amongst their leaders, which of them is the best resemblance of Rousseau . . . Rousseau is their canon of holy writ . . . he is their standard figure of perfection . . . We have had the great professor and founder of *the philosophy of vanity* in England . . . he entertained no principle either to influence his heart, or to guide his understanding, but *vanity* . . . It was this abuse and perversion which vanity makes even of hypocrisy, that has driven Rousseau to record a life not so much as chequered, or even spotted here and there, with virtues, or even distinguished by a single good action.

Edmund Burke, *Letter to a Member of the National Assembly* (1791)

For many of them, the Stoics, for instance, positively reject and condemn compassion. On the other hand, my foundation is supported by the authority of J.-J. Rousseau, who was undoubtedly the greatest moralist of modern times. He is the profound judge of the human heart, who drew his wisdom not from books but from life, and intended his doctrine not for the professorial chair but for humanity. He is the enemy of all prejudice, the pupil of nature; he alone was endowed by nature with the gift of being able to moralize without being tedious, for he hit upon the truth and touched the heart.

Arthur Schopenhauer, *On the Basis of Morality* (1841)

Contents

Preface

The main focus of this Dictionary is on Rousseau as philosopher (however uncomfortable he might have been to bear that name). Whilst I do not at all neglect his achievements in literature, music, etc., I have not given as much prominence to these as I have to his ideas in the areas of social, political and moral philosophy. This is in part because I think Rousseau's enduring importance rests on this work and not on the other aspects of his output; in part, because my own training is as a philosopher and I am, therefore, more at home with these elements in his thought. I have also tried to give some idea of Rousseau the man, and of the context in which he lived and worked. But I feel it necessary to say that I am not a scholar of eighteenth-century France, nor am I, in any strict sense, an exact scholar of Rousseau's work, in the sense in which for instance M. Cranston and R. Wokler are, and the late R. A. Leigh was. (They are much more in addition, of course.)

In have received generous assistance on certain points from Professor Basil Deane and Dr Colin Timms of the Music Department at the University of Birmingham; Dr Peter Jones of the History Department; Dr Ceri Crossley of the French Department; and Professor Frances Young and Dr Iain Torrance of the Theology Department. I should like to record a more general debt to Peter Nicholson of the University of York, who has been, as always, unstinting with his help and thoughtful interest.

The bulk of the Dictionary was compiled during a period of study leave that I enjoyed in 1990. Such leave is only possible because colleagues are prepared to shoulder a heavier burden of work during that time, and I wish to express my thanks to them. I am grateful to Sue Bowen for typing, and to the publisher's copy-editor for turning my clotted prose into something more readable. And I could not have written this book without the continued loving support of my wife, Stephanie.

N. J. H. D.
Birmingham
December 1991

Introduction and notes on the use of the Dictionary

The purpose of this Dictionary is to provide in an accessible form sufficient information about and discussion of Rousseau's principal works and ideas to enable the reader to acquire a comprehensive sense of the man and his achievement. The main body of the book breaks down the material concerning Rousseau and his works into two broad categories: entries on his principal ideas; and entries on his principal books and essays, or groups of works (for instance, theatrical pieces). I have not attempted to cover absolutely everything that Rousseau wrote, but I have included some of his more minor pieces in order to give a more rounded picture than concentration on the 'great' works alone would yield.

There is little in Rousseau's work that is non-controversial. Even the attempt to state what he held as simply as possible often requires a good deal of contentious interpretation. It must not be supposed, then, despite its being a work of reference, that this book achieves some dispassionate and impartial standpoint. However, where I have been aware of making particularly disputable claims, I have alerted the reader.

The structure of the Dictionary as follows:

Entries concerning works. Where the work is best known under an English title I have provided the entry under that head, but given the French title in brackets. Works whose title begins with *The* or *Le/La* are located by their first differentiating word. Where the title of a work does not appear as the entry head, this is because that work is, in my view, minor and is therefore treated under a generic head. For example, a discussion of *Le Lévite d'Éphraïm* appears in the entry, **poetry and miscellaneous prose**. The Index indicates the location of such pieces.

In virtually every case I say something about the genesis of the work, the circumstances under which it was written, and the reception it received. I give also an account of its character and principal features, and attempt to identify what is of value and interest in it. Where appropriate, the entry also contains reference to books or articles that discuss the work.

Details concerning publication dates, translations and so on are given in the Bibliography. The square-bracketed number in the entry head indicates where in the list of individual works by Rousseau (pp. 254–9) this one is cited.

There is, inevitably, some overlap and repetition between entries on the works and entries on the ideas. I have tried to make each entry more or less self-contained, so that the reader is not obliged to hare about the whole book following up cross-references. But, in order to avoid excessive duplication, I have sometimes made cross-references, which need to be pursued. I hope I have found the right balance over this.

Entries concerning ideas. I give an explanation of the idea, an indication of the place that it occupies in Rousseau's thought overall, a discussion of what is difficult or controversial in it, and an indication of its importance. I specify where in Rousseau's writings the principal presentation of the idea is to be found, and cite books or articles that provide a useful treatment of it. As with entries on works, I have tried to make each entry reasonably self-contained and to strike a proper balance between economy and duplication.

Miscellaneous entries. These are of two kinds. First, entries that cover groups of works such as plays or poetry. Here I follow the same procedure as for individual works. Second, entries – of which there are only a few – that consider some background or associated matters useful for the understanding of Rousseau. These cover both ideas (for instance, the **Enlightenment**) and works (for instance, *The Encyclopaedia*).

Cross-references. When the reader looks up alternative words or names to the ones appearing in the Dictionary, he or she will find the usual kind of entry head cross-reference. For instance: ***Du Contrat Social*** *See* SOCIAL CONTRACT; or **Liberty** *See* FREEDOM. As explained, I have tried to keep cross-references in entries to a minimum. The Index supplies a much more comprehensive specification of relevant topics than does cross-referencing to entry heads.

Introductory sections. These comprise, first, a brief account of Rousseau's life and works; second, a chronological table; third, an attempt to evaluate Rousseau's overall achievement. The purpose of this essay is to provide a synoptic picture of the man and his work. It is, of course, no substitute for reading longer, continuous discussions of Rousseau's life and works, but it should help in providing some landmarks.

Bibliography. This has two parts, each subdivided; Part I deals with principal works by, Part II with works on, Rousseau. Full details are given on p. 250.

Index. Not every significant name, term, and so on appears as an entry head. In including such names and terms, the index supplements the entry heads; whatever topic, concept or work the reader wants to investigate, it is probably best always to look first in the Index. Where appropriate, a name or term appears in the Index in both English and French.

Rousseau's life and works

Rousseau's life has been as extensively studied and discussed as have his works. This is in part because some of his major works are about his life, such as his autobiography *The Confessions* and *The Reveries of the Solitary Walker*, or emerge from and connect very directly with events in his life, such as the *Letters Written from the Mountain*; and in part because his life is, in many ways, fascinating and strange in its own right. It is, therefore, particularly desirable to have some awareness of the principal episodes of that life, and what follows is a brief account of them. In addition, it is important for the understanding of Rousseau's thought to know in what order his principal works were written, and the Chronology (pp. 16–20) makes this information available in a succinct form.

Rousseau was born on 28 June 1712 in Geneva, the second son of Isaac Rousseau, a watchmaker, and Suzanne Bernard. Rousseau's brother, François, was born ten years before Jean-Jacques, but very little is known of him. Jean-Jacques was baptized on 4 July into the Calvinist faith of Geneva; two days later his mother died, aged forty. (Much has been made, by biographers and interpreters of Rousseau, of his motherless upbringing.) Rousseau's father, who was a full citizen of Geneva, was a reasonably well educated man with some literary interests. Rousseau records, in *The Confessions*, the reading he and his father did together, which included the works of Plutarch, his favourite author at a very early age. After the death of his wife, Isaac Rousseau's circumstances declined, and he and Jean-Jacques were obliged to move to a more impoverished quarter of the city, St Gervais. Whether François was with them is not recorded.

In October 1722, when Rousseau was ten, his father fled from Geneva after a fight, and settled at Nyon where he remarried four years later. The boy was put in the care of his maternal uncle, Gabriel Bernard, who sent him, together with his cousin Abraham, to live with the pastor J.-J. Lambercier and his sister Gabrielle at Bossey near Geneva (though now in France) where he was to proceed with his education. After a couple of years living in a state of perfect equality and happiness with Abraham, Rousseau and he returned to Geneva, where the differences in station and fortune between Abraham's comfortably-off family and Rousseau's near poverty were made apparent. In April 1725, Rousseau was apprenticed to an engraver, Abel Ducommun, with whom he lived. Rousseau was very unhappy at this time – by his account, Ducommun was a cruel and harsh man and Rousseau no very adept or assiduous apprentice, and there was great ill-feeling between them.

In March 1728, having worked in Ducommun's business for nearly three years, Rousseau returned to Geneva one Sunday from a trip into the countryside with friends to find that the city gates had just been closed. Although he had been locked out before, this occasion was to precipitate a decisive change in his life. He decided to leave Geneva, and after a day or two wandering he sought the help of a Catholic priest who sent him, with a letter of introduction, to see Françoise-Louise de la Tour, Baronne de Warens, at Annecy, as a potential Catholic convert, though the seriousness of Rousseau's religious concerns at this time is rather doubtful. Mme de Warens was the estranged wife of a Swiss landowner, herself a recent convert, and in receipt of various pensions granted to her to assist her in recruiting further converts to the faith. Rousseau's meeting with her was a fateful one and their lives were to become closely intertwined over the next few years. To him, she was his *maman*; to her, he was her *petit*.

In the first instance, it was determined that Rousseau should go to Turin to undergo instruction in the Catholic faith to ready him for admission to the Church. It is uncertain how seriously he took the matter; like as not, he was merely willing to do what was expected of him to gain some security and retain the interest in him that Mme de Warens and others had shown. He arrived in Turin sometime in April 1728, and abjured on the 23rd. (Rousseau exaggerates, in *The Confessions*, the resistance he put up to his admission to the Catholic Church.) No occupation was immediately provided for him by the Church authorities, however, and after some vicissitudes – including episodes of helpless love and bizarre exhibitionism – he eventually found a place as a footman in the house of the Comtesse de Vercellis. There he met the Abbé Gaime, whose ideas were to influence deeply his religious beliefs in later life. After the death of the Comtesse, in December 1728, took place the episode of the stolen ribbon, when Rousseau falsely accused another servant, Marion, of the theft. This is piercingly recounted by Rousseau in Book II of *The Confessions*, and so preyed on his mind that he returned to it again at the end of his life in *The Reveries of the Solitary Walker* (Fourth Walk). He soon found further work, as secretary to the Abbé Gouvon, but he was not very committed to his duties and was dismissed in the early summer of 1729.

After various adventures, Rousseau eventually made his way back to the home of Mme de Warens, where plans were laid for him to train for

5

the priesthood. He studied for a while under the Abbé Jean-Baptiste Gâtier at Annecy, who along with the Abbé Gaime had a formative influence on Rousseau's religious ideas. The figure of the Savoyard Vicar, whose *Creed* is set down in Book IV of *Émile*, appears to have been largely modelled on the Abbé Gâtier, though the beliefs ascribed to this Vicar are a compound of Rousseau's own views together with some traces of those of both abbés. Rousseau showed no aptitude for religious training, and conceived instead the desire to become a musician. His ever-indulgent *maman* arranged for him to enter a choir school, where he acquired the rudiments of musical knowledge and some training.

A very unsettled period of around eighteen months followed, punctuated by further adventures. Some of these are disreputable – his desertion of his music teacher Le Maître in Lyons when the latter suffered a fit; some delightful – the idyll in the cherry orchard with Mlle de Graffenried and Mlle Galley; some of mere youthful excess – his carousing with Venture de Villeneuve, an adventurer and aspirant musician. During this time, Rousseau made what little money he acquired by giving music lessons (not very well), and by copying music (no better). He even made a short trip to Paris, probably in June 1731, but the city had no allure for him at that time. In the autumn of that year he finally returned to Mme de Warens, now living at Chambéry, with whom he was to remain more or less continuously for the next ten years. He occupied himself with teaching music, organizing musical evenings, reading a great deal, and assisting Mme de Warens with her many and various projects.

When Rousseau became twenty-one in 1733, Mme de Warens decided to initiate him sexually, an event which appears to have afforded him more confusion and sadness than pleasure. The situation was complicated by the presence of one Claude Anet. While nominally Mme de Warens' steward – a task he carried out with responsibility – he was her lover as well, and although she does not appear to have been troubled by having two sexual partners living with her in the house, serious tensions were introduced by her making this alteration in Rousseau's position in her life. Anet died, in slightly mysterious circumstances, in March 1734, and Rousseau then took his place more completely, not only in his sexual role but also in the (not very competent) administration of Mme de Warens' household affairs.

The next two years or so of Rousseau's life appear to have been particularly happy. He continued reading avidly in many areas – in history, philosophy, musical theory, mathematics; and although he experienced some periods of acute ill-health, his relationship with Mme de Warens, particularly when they were living in the valley of Les Charmettes, gave him deep pleasure. His first publications date from around this

6

time; a song of his, 'Un papillon badin' ('The playful butterfly'), was published in the *Mercure de France* in 1737; and he also wrote a longish poem, *Le Verger de Madame la Baronne de Warens* ('Mme de Warens' Orchard'), in 1738. In fact, though, by that time his relations with his *maman* were becoming soured. A preferred lover and assistant, Jean-Samuel-Rodolphe Wintzenried, had come into her life, and although there were a few months when all three lived together, Rousseau's intimacy with Mme de Warens was rapidly becoming a thing of the past.

It was, therefore, with some eagerness that he took the opportunity to move to Lyons in April 1740, where he became tutor to the two sons of Jean Bonnot de Mably, a wealthy nobleman and the chief of police. (The philosopher Condillac was one of de Mably's brothers, and Jean d'Alembert – *philosophe* and collaborator with Diderot on his *Encyclopaedia* – was a natural cousin.) Another significant phase in Rousseau's life had begun.

He was not a very effective tutor, though neither were his pupils very receptive, and his appointment was amicably terminated after a year. From around this time date two short educational essays concerning the tuition of M. de Sainte-Marie, de Mably's elder son, and also a number of poems addressed to friends. Rousseau returned briefly to Les Charmettes, but all remnants of his former pleasure in the company of Mme de Warens had evaporated. Ill and depressed, he determined to go to Paris to achieve celebrity and to make his fortune. He set off in June 1742 at the age of thirty, taking with him a copy of his *Project for a New Musical Notation* and his play *Narcissus*. These, he hoped, would establish a foundation for the achievement of his new ambitions.

With letters of introduction supplied by the de Mably family, Rousseau secured the chance to present his *Project* to the Academy of Sciences in August 1742. It received some favourable attention, but was rejected, not being considered by the Academy to be of sufficient merit. Among those who heard Rousseau's presentation was the composer Rameau, and although their relationship was later to become acrimonious Rousseau was at that time willing to admit the justice of his critical observations. He did not at once give up on his ideas; he worked up his scheme into a publishable form and – with some added material – it appeared in 1743 under the title, *Dissertation on Modern Music*. He began work on other musical projects also, which were to bear fruit a year or two later.

Rousseau began to make friends among the rising intelligentsia of Paris, his most significant association being with Denis Diderot. But success did not come readily to him; and he accepted in June 1743 the post of secretary to the new French ambassador to Venice, the Comte de Montaigu, although this took him away from Paris. Rousseau's account of his service in Venice, as given in Book VII of *The Confessions*, is probably largely accurate. He started off on a bad footing with the ambassador, and although for once he seems to have performed his duties rather well the two soon fell out irrevocably. Widely recognized as being the victim of mistreatment, Rousseau resigned his post in August 1744 and returned to Paris.

Once re-established there, he gave himself wholly to work on music. He completed his opera–ballet *Les Muses Galantes*, which he had begun before leaving for Venice, and parts of the score of this were performed at the house of the patron Le Riche de la Pouplinière before an audience which included Rameau (again) and the Duc de Richelieu. Rameau, perhaps jealous of this intrusion into his own domain of influence, suggested that the only decent parts of the score were the results of plagiarism. Moves were made to have the work performed at Versailles, but nothing came of this. However, Rousseau was charged with making an adaptation of Rameau's and Voltaire's *Les Fêtes de Ramire*, and this did receive a performance at Versailles in December 1745. A significant change in Rousseau's personal life had taken place in this year. In the spring he had met Thérèse Levasseur, an illiterate laundry-maid and general servant at his lodgings, who was soon to become his mistress, the mother of his (to be abandoned) children, and eventually his wife and lifelong companion.

Despite having achieved some successes with his musical works, Rousseau was not establishing any really firm, or remunerative, position in Paris. In the spring of 1746 he accepted the post of secretary to the Dupin family, and became the close companion of Mme Dupin's stepson Franceuil. For a time, he was a more or less regular member of their household, and for family performance at their summer residence, the Château de Chenonceaux, he wrote at least one play, *L'Engagement Téméraire* ('The Rash Promise'), and some poems and songs and other pieces. His friendship with Diderot and with other members of the emerging *encyclopédiste* circle now consolidated. In 1748 he and Diderot planned to take turns in editing a periodical, *Le Persifleur* ('The Mocker'), but this never got beyond the draft of an opening advertisement written by Rousseau. By this time Diderot was deeply involved in preparations for the publication of the *Encyclopaedia*, and Rousseau was drawn into writing – in a great rush – a large number of entries on musical topics. A few years later he contributed one further extensive entry, on political economy (usually known as (*A Discourse on*) *Political Economy*, which finally appeared in volume V of the *Encyclopaedia* in 1755).

Diderot's advanced views frequently brought him into conflict with the civil authorities, and in July 1749 he was arrested for writing seditious works and imprisoned at Vincennes, just outside Paris. On one of his visits to see him there, in August 1749, took place what Rousseau saw as the single most decisive episode of his life. He read in the *Mercure de France* the announcement of a prize essay topic set by the Academy of Dijon, posing the question of whether the progress of the sciences and the arts had corrupted, or purified, morals. Rousseau was transfixed; such a rush of new visions and ideas assailed him that he felt faint, and was unable for a while to proceed on his journey. This 'illumination' fixed the shape of the rest of his life. He determined to write on the topic, and his essay *A Discourse on the Sciences and the Arts* (the *First Discourse*) was the result. He won the prize, awarded in July 1750, and the whole text was published soon after. Rousseau's argument – that the advancement of the sciences and the arts had indeed corrupted morals – attracted great attention; many essays were written in response to his, and Rousseau carefully replied to most of them. Public notice, even fame, had arrived at last.

For the next ten years Rousseau worked with great intensity, and all his really enduring work was produced during this time, as he endeavoured to express all that had been revealed to him in his 'illumination'. He did not at once proceed with more work on topics of moral and social significance, however. His musical ambitions had not altogether left him. In the spring of 1752 he went to stay at Passy with his friend François Mussard, a lover of Italian music – by which Rousseau too had been much impressed during his stay in Venice. While at Passy he was inspired to write the words and music for *Le Devin du Village*, completing the outline of both in six days. This, his most famous and only enduring musical work, was selected for performance before the King and Mme de Pompadour at Fontainebleau in October 1752. It was an enormous success, and Rousseau – had he remained at Fontainebleau – would certainly have received a pension from Louis. But, pleading illness (he was already suffering from a urinary complaint which was to trouble him more or less acutely for the rest of his life) and – in retrospect – republican sentiments, he returned to Paris without appearing before the King.

Le Devin was taken up by the Paris Opera, and on the back of its success his play *Narcissus* (which he had brought with him to Paris ten years before) was put on by the Comédie Française. Mme de Pompadour herself took the part of Colin in a further private performance of *Le Devin* at her summer villa in 1753. All appeared to be set for Rousseau to become a composer of celebrity and distinction. And his involvement in musical affairs expanded in other directions also. In the summer of 1753 a travelling Italian opera company, calling themselves Les Bouffons (the Buffoons), came to Paris to perform operas of the Italian school. They had visited the previous summer without attracting much notice, but this time their appearance provoked a highly agitated and protracted debate over the relative merits of French and Italian music. Great numbers of pam-

9

phlets, essays and letters were written for one side or the other, and Rousseau gave his weight to the Italian side, writing in 1753 his *Letter on French Music* in which he gave large-scale cultural, social and national dimensions to this originally musical quarrel. Among his specific targets was Rameau, the great master of French opera, and this attack rendered permanent the rift between the two men. Rameau engaged in bitter recrimination towards Rousseau for several years afterwards – long past the point when Rousseau had turned his attention to other matters.

First among these was his return to issues of moral and political concern. The Dijon Academy had announced a further prize essay in the autumn of 1753, inviting consideration of the origin and legitimacy of inequality between persons. Rousseau again took up the challenge, and *A Discourse on the Origin of Inequality* (the *Second Discourse*) was the result. There is one other significant work, bridging his musical and political concerns, which he began at this time. This is the *Essay on the Origin of Languages*, which he appears never to have completed to his satisfaction; it was not published in his lifetime.

In the *Second Discourse* Rousseau distances himself more emphatically than hitherto from the optimistic, enlightened and progressive attitudes of his encyclopaedist companions, who had managed to see the argument of the *First Discourse* as essentially waspish and provocative. In the *Second Discourse* Rousseau envisages modern society as not only incorporating, but fostering and demanding, deep and hateful inequalities between people, which lead them further and further into corruption and misery. His slowly deepening estrangement from Parisian society and from the attitudes of his colleagues shows itself also in his decision to go to Geneva in June 1754, to be readmitted to the Protestant Church and to reclaim his rights as a citizen. On his way there he wrote for his *Second Discourse* a long and passionate dedication to Geneva, presenting that city to itself as the paragon of all human communities.

The *Discourse* did not win the prize, but when it was published in August 1755 it aroused considerable interest. Among those who were scornful of Rousseau's views was Voltaire, who wrote, after Rousseau had sent him a copy: 'One starts wanting to walk on all fours after reading your book.' The rift between the two men was to deepen over the next few years. They did not see themselves in life, as they have come to be seen in death, as brothers in arms. It was in the November of that year that Rousseau's article on political economy appeared in the *Encyclopaedia*.

Rousseau appears to have now decided to turn his precepts into practice. Mme d'Épinay, whose salon Rousseau had attended, offered him the use of the Hermitage, a cottage that she had recently had built at Montmorency. In April 1756 he withdrew from Parisian society, and went to live, together with Thérèse and her mother, in relative seclusion in the country. The next five years spent at the Hermitage and at nearby Mont-Louis were the most creative of his life.

He continued work on the large project, 'Political Institutions', that he had first conceived in Venice. He finally abandoned this, but its most famous residue in his treatise, *The Social Contract*. He was also engaged in compiling extracts from the works of the Abbé de Saint-Pierre (the *Extrait du Projet de Paix Perpétuelle* (extract from the *Project for Perpetual Peace*) and the *Polysynodie*); and in July 1756 he wrote a long letter to Voltaire (on optimism, or providence) in reply to the latter's poem on the Lisbon earthquake, in which he had derided the idea that 'all is for the best'. Other works that Rousseau had in hand were a dictionary of music, principally based on the articles he had written for Diderot's *Encyclopaedia*; and a treatise on morality and experience, 'La Morale Sensitive, ou le Matérialisme du Sage', which came to nothing.

The work that preoccupied him above all during 1757–8 was, in fact, one he had not thought of when he first moved to the country. Walking in the woods around Montmorency, Rousseau became absorbed in a fantasy world peopled by his amorous dreams, and out of these dreams emerged the plan of his novel, *Julie, ou La Nouvelle Héloïse* – the letters of two lovers who live in a little village at the foot of the Alps. He seems to have been somewhat embarrassed at undertaking this work – an epistolary novel of passion and high sentiments – when, in the eyes of the world, he had put on the cloak of an austere moralist. But his involvement with it only deepened when the living incarnation of his imagined Julie entered his life, in the form of Sophie d'Houdetot, Mme d'Épinay's sister-in-law, who lived nearby. Rousseau fell helplessly in love with her, and the feelings and struggles that this gave rise to found expression in the novel. The heady mixture of eroticism and virtue which pervades the novel can also be seen in the *Lettres Morales* (*Moral Letters*) which he wrote for Sophie during the winter months of 1757–8.

Rousseau's relationships seldom endured, and by the end of 1757 he had fallen out with Mme d'Épinay. He moved away from the Hermitage to Mont-Louis, nearby. Not long afterwards his affair with Sophie terminated, but he acquired some new friends, the Luxembourgs, who were greatly to assist him over the next three or four years. Not only did they give him house room, but Mme de Luxembourg helped with getting *Émile* published. Completion of his novel was delayed by other diversions as well. In October 1757 d'Alembert contributed to volume VII of the *Encyclopaedia* an article on Geneva, in which he recommended establishing a theatre there. Rousseau was roused to the defence of the republican moral customs of his native city, which he thought would be undermined

11

by the presence of a theatre, and over the winter wrote his *Letter to M. d'Alembert on the Theatre*. (He may have seen the influence of Voltaire behind d'Alembert's article.) This essay appeared in September 1758.

La Nouvelle Héloïse was finally published in Paris in early 1761, to prodigious success. It went through at least seventy editions in French in the next forty years, and ten English editions were published before 1800. But this spectacular triumph was to be short-lived. Sometime in 1758 Rousseau had begun work on *Émile*, his greatest work, which by 1761 was virtually completed. *The Social Contract*, too, was in its final draft by this time, and these two manuscripts were in the hands of the printers. But troubled by delays in printing, and ill and depressed, Rousseau wrote in January 1762 four self-revelatory letters to Malesherbes – the official director of publications, or censor – who was an advocate of press freedom and had already shown a friendly interest in Rousseau's work. These *Letters to Malesherbes* were really the forerunners of the great autobiographical works that Rousseau was to write over the next decade and a half. They were not intended for publication (they appeared posthumously), but their content was known to many of Rousseau's friends – and to some of his enemies.

Finally, in the spring and early summer of 1762, both *Émile* and *The Social Contract* were published. Catastrophe now befell Rousseau. *The Creed of a Savoyard Vicar*, contained in *Émile*, was found to be intolerably offensive to orthodox religion. On 7 June 1762 *Émile* was condemned by the Faculty of Theology at the Sorbonne, and copies were burned. Warned of imminent arrest, Rousseau fled Montmorency on the 9th, taking refuge at Yverdon in Switzerland. But he could not stay there long: in Geneva as well, *Émile* was burned – with *The Social Contract* added for good measure. He was obliged to move on; he found safety at Môtiers in the principality of Neuchâtel, at that time subject to Frederick II of Prussia.

Rousseau cannot, at first, have been totally stunned by this furore, since during his journey from Paris he wrote a prose poem, *The Levite of Ephraim*, which he later declared to be his 'dearest' work (*The Confessions*, Book XI). Furthermore, he was in sufficient possession of his powers to write a forceful reply to the pastoral letter that the Archbishop of Paris, Christophe de Beaumont, had published in August 1762 condemning the *Creed*. Rousseau's *Letter to Christophe de Beaumont* was published in March 1763. One other event of 1762 was the death of Mme de Warens. She and Rousseau had so long been estranged by then, however, that he does not appear to have been much affected.

Although Rousseau enjoyed some calm and safety at Môtiers, the full tide of his troubles was only really beginning to rise. He was so disgusted by the treatment that his works had received in Geneva that in May 1763 he renounced the citizenship that he had so eagerly reclaimed nine years before. The Genevan attorney-general, Jean-Robert Tronchin, would not, however, let matters rest. He published his *Letters Written from the Country*, justifying the actions of the Genevan council. This provoked a lengthy, polemical attack from Rousseau: his *Letters Written from the Mountain* were published in December 1764, and although they pleased some of the more revolutionary elements in Geneva they exacerbated the ill-feelings of the authorities. Not all Rousseau's time at Môtiers was given over to work, however. He began to take an interest in botany, which was to stay with him for most of his life. And we also have a splendid record of the bumptious James Boswell's visit to him there in December 1764 (*Boswell on the Grand Tour: Germany and Switzerland, 1764*). More serious approaches were also made to him: one Matteo Buttafoco wrote, in August 1764, on behalf of Paoli, the leader of the Corsican rebels, to ask Rousseau to propose a new constitution for Corsica – soon, he hoped, to be liberated from Genoese rule. Rousseau never finished his *Project for a Constitution for Corsica*, which in any event would have been fruitless since the rebel cause was soon lost.

The brief peace that Rousseau found at Môtiers did not endure. In late December 1764 Voltaire published, anonymously, *The Sentiments of the Citizens*, a pamphlet in which he made public, among other things, the fact that Rousseau had abandoned his children by Thérèse Levasseur. Rousseau was driven into a frenzy by this exposure, and together with the increasing trouble he was having with the religious authorities it may have helped to cause the serious paranoiac disturbance that he was to suffer, with some remissions, over the next several years. Stones were thrown at his house in Môtiers in September 1765, and after a brief idyllic interlude on the island of St-Pierre in the Lake of Bienne, he eventually made his way back to Paris, from where he was to travel to a supposedly safe haven in England under the protection of David Hume. Hume was, at that time, an intimate of several of the most powerful figures in France, some of whom also took a friendly and generous interest in Rousseau. But this amity was not to last.

In January 1766, Rousseau left France in Hume's company. He went first to stay in London (at Chiswick), and then to Wootton in Derbyshire. Hume had arranged that Rousseau should receive a pension from George III, but at first he turned it down. This rejection, and a number of other episodes, caused a bitter conflict between the two men. Hume – whose behaviour throughout appears to have been wholly sensible – wrote an account of their quarrel, which had become a matter of public interest (*The Concise Account*, October 1766). Rousseau became increasingly disturbed, morbidly suspicious, seeing plots and ridicule all about him. Such

13

work as he did at this time was on the first part of *The Confessions*. Then, in early 1767, he and Thérèse suddenly left Wootton, and after a few weeks wandering returned in May to France.

Rousseau was permitted, subject to the condition that he never wrote for the public again, to stay near Paris. This he did for a while, under the protection of the Prince de Conti and other influential persons. His *Dictionary of Music* – presumably not regarded as a turbulent or seditious work – did, however, appear in late 1767 (he had been correcting the proofs intermittently over the preceding year or so). Rousseau did not remain long near Paris; two very unsettled years followed, during which he lived at Bourgoin and at Monquin near Grenoble. In August 1768, while at Bourgoin, he finally married Thérèse.

In March 1770 Rousseau decided to return – for the last time, it would transpire – to Paris. He proceeded via Lyons, where he was fêted. Both *Le Devin du Village* and his monodrama *Pygmalion* were performed there in his honour. By June, he was well settled once more in Paris. He held readings of extracts from *The Confessions* to groups of friends, but these were soon banned under pressure from Mme d'Épinay, who suspected that she would not be portrayed to her advantage in them. In the last eight years of his life Rousseau mainly worked on further extensive autobiographical writings, although he also maintained his interest in botany, writing some pedagogic letters on the subject.

Some of these autobiographical works show marked signs of continuing mental distress. *Rousseau Judge of Jean-Jacques: Dialogues*, written between 1771 and 1776, is one such; but, on the other hand, the *Reveries of the Solitary Walker*, left unfinished at his death in 1778, is mainly suffused with a steady calm of mind. In addition to the *Elementary Letters on Botany*, Rousseau undertook one last political work. Count Wielhorski had been sent to Paris in 1770 by the members of the Confederation of Bar, who opposed Russian domination in Poland, to collect ideas for the reconstruction of the Polish constitution. Among those he approached was Rousseau, whose *Considerations on the Government of Poland* is a substantial work containing many important ideas. Although completed in 1771 or 1772, it was not published in Rousseau's lifetime. During this period his affairs were the object of intense curiosity, and although he largely shunned company, his personal reputation stood very high. His musical reputation was also on the rise again: *Le Devin* was revived, and attracted the admiration of the composer Gluck, with whom he established a positive relationship.

By 1776 Rousseau had finished the manuscript of the *Dialogues*, and in the February – in who knows what state of mind – he attempted to place a copy of it on the high altar of Notre-Dame, only to find the gates to the altar barred. In great distress of mind, he drew up a broadsheet – *To All Frenchmen who Still Love Justice and Truth* – and in a semi-crazed state wandered the streets of Paris attempting to push it into the hands of passers-by. Later that year, returning from one of his more composed walks, he was knocked down by a large dog and badly injured. In an inexplicable way this accident seems to have purged his spirit, and he began work on the *Reveries*, in which he recounts this episode (in the Second Walk) as well as voicing many and various reflections on himself and the circumstances of his life.

In May 1778 Rousseau moved with Thérèse to Ermenonville, not far from central Paris. On 2 July he died there, after a brief illness. He was buried on the Île des Peupliers at Ermenonville, and his grave became a place of pilgrimage for Parisians. In October 1794 his remains were transferred to the Panthéon. Thérèse outlived him by twenty-two years.

The bulk of Rousseau's posthumous papers were entrusted to his longstanding Genevan friends P. Moultou and P. A. Du Peyrou. They put in hand a collected edition of his works, which included many of the items that Rousseau had written during the preceding ten years but that had not hitherto been published. His posthumous reputation has steadily grown. There is no doubt that his was a presiding presence during the French Revolution, and that he is now established as one of the great figures of Western civilization.

Chronology

Note: Rousseau's life can be divided very roughly into three parts. (1) The apprentice years (1712–49), in which most of his work is on music, and which ends with the 'illumination' on the way to Vincennes. (2) The years of maturity (1750–64). His greatest works date from this period: *Le Devin du Village*, the *Discourses*, *La Nouvelle Héloïse*, *Émile*, *The Social Contract*, and the *Letter to d'Alembert*. (3) The years of decline (1764–78), marked by increasing mental disturbance and great self-absorption. His masterpiece *The Confessions* comes from this period, but much work is prolix and uneven.

1712	28 June: born 6 July: mother dies
1722	Father flees Geneva Put in the charge of his uncle; lives at Bossey
1725	Apprenticed to engraver, Ducommun
1728	14 March: shut outside gates of Geneva; leaves city Meets Mme de Warens 23 April: abjures Protestantism, Turin Meets Abbé Gaime; steals ribbon
1729	Trains as musician; wanderings
1731	Works briefly as clerk in tax office
1733	Sexually initiated by Mme de Warens
1734	Claude Anet (Warens' lover/factotum) dies
1736	Lives at Les Charmettes with Mme de Warens
1737	Song, 'Un papillon badin', published

1738   Writes *Le Verger de Madame la Baronne de Warens* (published 1739)

1740   At Lyons, tutor to children of Jean Bonnot de Mably.
Writes *Projet pour l'Éducation de M. de Sainte-Marie*; poems; *Épître à M. Bordes*; opera, *La Découverte du Noveau Monde*

1741   Resigns tutorship

1742   Goes to Paris, taking *Project for a New Musical Notation*, and play *Narcissus*
22 August: presents *Project* to Academy of Sciences
Writes *Dissertation on Modern Music* (a version of the *Project*; published 1743)

1743   Sketches opera–ballet, *Les Muses Galantes*
July: leaves for Venice, as secretary to French ambassador
Begins work on 'Political Institutions' (never completed)

1744   6 August: leaves Venice

1745   Meets Thérèse Levasseur, who becomes his mistress
Finishes *Les Muses Galantes*; parts performed
Revises Rameau/Voltaire *Les Fêtes de Ramire*; performed at Versailles, 22 December

1746   Becomes secretary to Dupin family (until 1751)
Writes poem *L'Allée de Sylvie*
Thérèse bears their first child

1747   Summer: writes *L'Engagement Téméraire* for performance at Chenonceaux
Autumn: Thérèse pregnant again
Father dies
Diderot and d'Alembert plan *Encyclopaedia*

1748   *Le Persifleur* planned, but never completed
Writes articles on music for *Encyclopaedia*

1749   24 July: Diderot arrested
August: experiences 'illumination' when on way to visit Diderot at Vincennes

1750   July: *Discourse on the Sciences and the Arts* (the *First Discourse*) wins Dijon Academy prize
November: *First Discourse* published

1751   Replies to critics of *First Discourse*
June: first volume of *Encyclopaedia* published

1752   Spring: drafts opera, *Le Devin du Village*
18 October: *Le Devin* performed at Fontainebleau to great acclaim
December: *Narcissus* performed at Comédie Française

1753   *Le Devin* published; *Narcissus* published
November: *Letter on French Music* published; second Dijon Academy prize essay topic, on inequality, announced
Essay on the Origin of Languages begun about this time (never completed; published posthumously)

1754   Writes *Discourse on the Origin of Inequality* (the *Second Discourse*)
Returns to Geneva to be readmitted to Protestant Church and to reclaim citizenship
10 October: returns to Paris

1755   June: *Second Discourse* published
Article on political economy (future (*Discourse on*) *Political Economy*) published in vol. V of *Encyclopaedia*
Letter to M. Philopolis, critic of the *Second Discourse*

1756   Moves to Hermitage at Montmorency
Works on 'Political Institutions'; compiles extracts from works of Abbé de Saint-Pierre (*Projet de Paix Perpétuelle*, published 1761; rest published posthumously)
July/August: *Letter to Voltaire on Providence* (unauthorized publication 1759, Berlin)
Autumn: starts work on *Julie, ou La Nouvelle Héloïse*

1757   Meets Sophie d'Houdetot
Quarrels with Diderot
October: d'Alembert's article on Geneva appears in vol. VII of *Encyclopaedia*
December: leaves Hermitage

Winter: *Moral Letters* written for Sophie d'Houdetot (published posthumously)

1758   *Working on La Nouvelle Héloïse*; starts work on *Émile*
September: *Letter to M. d'Alembert on the Theatre* published
Finally breaks with Diderot

1760   *La Nouvelle Héloïse* completed; *Émile* and *The Social Contract* well in hand
Les Amours de Milord Édouard Bomston drafted

1761   January: *La Nouvelle Héloïse* published

1762   January: writes *Letters to Malesherbes* (published posthumously)
April: *The Social Contract* published
May: *Émile* published
June: *Émile* denounced and burned; flees Paris; *Le Lévite d'Éphraïm* written during flight
11 June: *Émile* and *The Social Contract* burned, Geneva
July: settles at Môtiers; Mme de Warens dies
August: Christophe de Beaumont, Archbishop of Paris, publishes decree against *Creed of a Savoyard Vicar*
Autumn/Winter: writes *Émile et Sophie, ou les Solitaires* (published posthumously)

1763   March: *Letter to Christophe de Beaumont* published
May: renounces Genevan citizenship
Autumn: J.-R. Tronchin's *Letters Written from the Country* published

1764   August: receives letter from Buttafoco concerning Corsica
Starts work on *Project for a Constitution for Corsica* (unfinished; published 1861)
December: *Letters Written from the Mountain* published; Boswell visits; Voltaire publishes (anonymously) *The Sentiments of the Citizens*

1765   Work on *Dictionary of Music* largely completed
Stones thrown at his house in Môtiers; leaves
Interlude on island of St-Pierre
December: arrives in Paris

1766	4 January: leaves for England with Hume Works on *The Confessions* at Wootton June/July: quarrels with Hume In great mental distress October: Hume's *Concise Account*
1767	May: returns to France; lives near Paris November: *Dictionary of Music* published Late in year: leaves Paris for Switzerland
1768	August: marries Thérèse in Bourgoin
1770	Returns to Paris Finishes *The Confessions* (published posthumously); gives readings from it to friends Drafts *Considerations on the Government of Poland* (illicit copies circulate 1772; published posthumously)
1772	Works on *Rousseau Judge of Jean-Jacques: Dialogues* and on botanical studies Writes *Elementary Letters on Botany* (published posthumously) Starts *Dictionary of Botanical Terms* (unfinished)
1774	Meets Gluck Works on last opera, *Daphnis et Chloé* (unfinished)
1776	Completes *Rousseau Judge of Jean-Jacques* (published posthumously) 24 February: attempts to place manuscript on high altar in Notre-Dame May: writes pamphlet *To All Frenchmen . . .* Autumn: knocked down by dog Begins work on *Reveries of the Solitary Walker* (unfinished; published posthumously)
1778	20 May: moves to Ermenonville 2 July: dies
1780–9	Moultou and Du Peyrou publish *Collected Works*, including many pieces from Rousseau's last ten years
1794	Body transferred to Panthéon

Rousseau's achievement

The range and power of Rousseau's achievement is formidable. There are major and enduring works in many genres. *The Social Contract* is one of the permanent masterpieces of political theory; *La Nouvelle Héloïse* is a best-selling novel of illicit passion and spiritual redemption; *Émile or On Education* constitutes a seminal contribution to educational theory and human psychology; *The Confessions*, an autobiography, all but inaugurated a new mode of self-expression; *Le Devin du Village*, an opera, paved the way for a radical break in the evolution of French music. Hardly less significant are several of Rousseau's shorter works. The *Discourse on the Origin of Inequality* contains a diagnosis of the roots of social and civil inequality of exceptional penetration; the *Letter on French Music* considers the human basis and social ramifications of musical expression; the *Reveries of the Solitary Walker* (surely, better, 'The reveries of one who walks alone') articulates feelings of individuality and personal destiny with unique delicacy and sensibility.

All of this is still not the half of his output – in terms of pages, at least. There are further social and political essays (the *Discourse on the Sciences and the Arts*; the *(Discourse on) Political Economy*; the *Letter to M. d'Alembert on the Theatre*; the *Essay on the Origin of Languages*; the political proposals for Corsica and Poland); other major works of self-defence and self-explanation (the *Letter to Christophe de Beaumont*; the *Letters Written from the Mountain*; *Rousseau Judge of Jean-Jacques: Dialogues*); additional musical works and works about music (*Pygmalion*, *Les Consolations des Misères de ma Vie*, the *Dictionary of Music*); poems, plays, voluminous correspondence (including many letters of substantial intellectual significance); miscellaneous pieces, like *The Levite of Ephraim*, the *Moral Letters*, the *Letters to Malesherbes* and the *Letters on Botany*. For one who said quite frequently that he regretted the day he ever took up his pen to write and that he rued the fame (or notoriety) it had brought him, it would seem that he had acquired an incurable vice.

It is easy to feel swamped by this almost overwhelming mass of work. Often people become first acquainted with Rousseau's ideas and presence from different works, and their senses of the centre of the man and his creative achievement can be quite disparate. Some first read *The Confessions* and know nothing of his theoretical works on political philosophy. Others – perhaps the majority – start with *The Social Contract* but have no idea that he wrote a novel. Some may first come across *Le Devin du Village* – still occasionally performed, and available on record. I know someone who for a long time assumed that the composer called Rousseau merely shared the same name with whoever wrote *The Social Contract*. Any assessment that one makes of Rousseau's overall achievement is, then, bound to reflect the manner in which one has come to know him, as well as one's individual sense of significance and value.

My own view is that it is Rousseau's work in social and political theory, with its underpinning in his views on psychological development, that should be seen as the basis for his position as a thinker of the first rank. The *Discourse on the Origin of Inequality*, *Émile* and *The Social Contract* comprise, in my estimation, the 'essential' Rousseau, and should be given priority in any attempt to understand and evaluate his ideas in a comprehensive way. I do not, of course, want to marginalize the other works, nor to insist that all that is of value in them is so because of its links with the central themes of these three works. But Rousseau would not have the same rightful claim on our attention if one placed, say, *La Nouvelle Héloïse* or *The Confessions* at the pinnacle of his achievement.

What, then, is there in these three works that can convince one that one is meeting an exceptional mind? At the cost of over-simplification, one might highlight the following points. First, Rousseau's precise and cutting diagnosis of the roots and nature of the inequalities of power and privilege and of the enjoyment of human dignity in modern society – and here 'modern' can adequately straddle both the society Rousseau knew and our own. There is in this a deep, but controlled, hatred of oppression and of the dispossession and dehumanization suffered by people in society. Rousseau's insight into the causes and ramifications of the craving for ascendancy and the relentless determination to negate others that shapes and pervades social relations and structures still retains a unique force and the power to shock. We might suppose that it was Marx who first drew the picture of capitalist society as a body of persons estranged from themselves and each other, delivered into servitude, cut off from their own nature and from the possibilities of happiness and self-realization. But, I would suggest, this vision was just as well, if not better, articulated by Rousseau – though not, of course, for Marxian reasons.

Second, the other side of the coin: Rousseau's paramount emphasis on liberty and equality as the inalienable titles that belong to each and every human being, the full enjoyment of which is his or her absolute right. So important is this to Rousseau that he argues for a form of civil authority in which every member of the community shall stand as an equal member of the sovereign body, such that the common laws regulating society have no legitimacy without the willing assent of every member. No other basis of law and authority, Rousseau contends, can escape degeneration into brutality and enslavement.

Third, he offers a penetrating and wholly original account of the psychological determinants of human development and association, together with an attempt to show how a person may be preserved from the pains and distortions of self-estrangement and from alienation from others. He endeavours to reveal a way of life that will enable the individual to remain in touch with his own capacities for full self-development and expression, in a fashion that will give rise to a life as creative and fulfilling for that individual as it is for others. In roughest outline, these three points summarize the primary concerns of the *Second Discourse*, *The Social Contract* and *Émile*.

If one wishes to label Rousseau a 'philosopher' – and this, together with the more broadly significant *philosophe*, was a title he consistently disowned – it is clear that he should not be considered primarily as a metaphysician, an epistemologist or a logician, but rather as a philosopher of man, society and politics.

Although it is, of course, ridiculous to trace large-scale shifts in ideas and changes in society to the work and influence of one person alone, it cannot be denied that Rousseau had a great deal to do with the gradual emergence of the moral and political impossibility of supposing that subordination is the natural lot of any man or woman – with the consequences of which, it might be added, we are still contending today. That alone makes him a significant shaping genius in the history of Western, indeed of world, thought. I would find it soul-destroying to write about a person and his works if I did not think that what he was and did mattered. But it is clear that many books and articles on Rousseau are exercises in denigration, scorn and even loathing. Why is this?

Few important thinkers attract uniformly high regard. But Rousseau has the capacity to divide opinion more extremely and violently than most. I have been drawing attention to his 'good' side. Others, however, insist that he was vindictive, a thinly veiled totalitarian monster, overbearing, intolerably righteous, self-deceiving, the apologist for all those who take their own delusions of righteousness as proof that they are the manifest bearers of God's will for humanity.

As many of these epithets suggest, the judgement is made not only of the creative personality embodied in the works, but of the man in his entirety. With Rousseau this happens not, I think, just because it is a natural, albeit inappropriate, tendency for criticism of the *oeuvre* to con-

23

taminate the author. Many of his writings are explicit works of autobiography and self-declaration, in which we are invited, not always very agreeably, to take sides, to announce ourselves for or against him, or as better or worse than he was. Many of the apparently more theoretical pieces, even, clearly reveal the author's presence. So it seems inevitable that we should form as firm an opinion about the man as about the work. He was, unquestionably, not always easy to like. Often self-righteous, at once cringing and combative, challenging and insistent, he maintained that it was right and truth that spoke through him and called for an answer.

It is essential, nevertheless, to try to keep judgement on the man and on his work apart. One might suppose, indeed, that with him dead for two hundred years this would not be so difficult. Yet there is clearly some way in which he 'gets to' people, irritates and provokes them. Of course, maintaining any such division will not suddenly vindicate the works. One may well still find in them ideas, tendencies or views that one cannot accept and that one wishes to combat. It is clear that in political philosophy, for instance, it is not only the fate of an idea that is at issue: for inextricably linked with any given idea may be possibilities for making sense of society and for taking significant action within it. So matters over and above the merely cerebral are in contention here. But, for all that, some of the condemnatory verdicts delivered on Rousseau do seem extravagant. Even if one were to agree with Nietzsche that 'every great philosophy' has been 'a kind of involuntary and unconscious memoir' (*Beyond Good and Evil*, para. 6), the issue remains of how interesting and valuable the content of that memoir is; we are not entitled to see it as mere neurotic outpourings.

Most prominent among those philosophers who were impressed by Rousseau's ideas is Kant. There is the famous story of Kant, who was renowned for the regularity of his life, deserting his normal pattern when he first came across *Émile*, so absorbed was he by the book. There are whole passages in Kant's essay *Perpetual Peace*, and in those parts of the *Metaphysic of Morals* which deal with political right, that are virtual transcriptions of passages in Rousseau. And it is widely argued that Kant's insistence that nothing can be a moral law unless it receives the rational assent of all is a reformulation of Rousseau's conception of the equality and freedom proper to human beings. Hegel, also, refers frequently to Rousseau, though often in disagreement (not always well founded). And, as mentioned before, it is possible to see some of Marx's fundamental conceptions regarding the relations between the individual and society as prefigured in Rousseau's work – although, like Hegel's, Marx's own view of Rousseau's ideas was largely critical. Rousseau appears to have been esteemed less by nineteenth-century English social and political theorists, but today he stands as one of the presiding figures whose ideas determine the very shape of the discipline. A modern work, John Rawls's *A Theory of Justice*, demonstrates the continuing force of Rousseau's ideas.

The practical impact of his social and political works is harder to assess. It is worth noting that, to begin with, *The Social Contract* was less well known and less well regarded than *Émile*. Hume, in a letter to a friend, said that Rousseau's belief that *The Social Contract* was better than *La Nouvelle Héloïse* was as absurd as Milton's belief that *Paradise Regained* was better than *Paradise Lost*. Whether and how Rousseau's works, or his 'presence', may have contributed to the French Revolution is a matter of perennial debate.

Other issues to which there can never be a definitive answer arise from some of his other works. *The Confessions* has been held to be the instigator and palmary instance of the Romantic celebration of individual genius. Goethe, in particular, is said to have been much impressed by this work. *La Nouvelle Héloïse*, a tremendous popular success, no doubt played some part in changing people's outlook on themselves and on morality. But influence is hard to assess. *Émile* certainly caused some people to change their child-rearing habits during Rousseau's lifetime, as we know from letters that he received; and it is possible to see the educational ideas of, for example, A. S. Neill of Summer Hill School in England as rooted in Rousseau's emphasis on placing minimal constraints on children. *Le Devin du Village*, and Rousseau's writings on music, certainly had a direct impact on Gluck, and helped to effect a change in French musical style and a shift in direction. But it is as much a matter of the audience being ready to hear as of there being someone with fresh things to say.

More subtle changes in 'sensibility' – even harder to assess – have also been traced to Rousseau's influence: matters such as the importance attached to love of countryside and of nature, the cultivation of simplicity of manners, the increasing emphasis on emotional self-expression and the enjoyment of 'feeling'. Such shifts tend to elude analysis. What is certain is that it is hard to be indifferent to Rousseau. Whether it is pleasure and admiration, or irritation and hatred, that he inspires, he retains the capacity to move. In this way, at the very least, he still speaks powerfully to all of us.

Abbreviations and references

C   *The Confessions* [18]

DI   *A Discourse on the Origin of Inequality* [2]

DPE   *(A Discourse on) Political Economy* [3]

DSA   *A Discourse on the Sciences and the Arts* [1]

E   *Émile, or On Education* [11]

GP   *Considerations on the Government of Poland* [19]

OC   *Jean-Jacques Rousseau: Oeuvres Complètes*, ed. B. Gagnebin and M. Raymond

PCC   *Project for a Constitution for Corsica* [16]

RJJ   *Rousseau Judge of Jean-Jacques: Dialogues* [20]

RSW   *The Reveries of the Solitary Walker* [21]

SC   *The Social Contract* [14]

Full details concerning these works and the translations used in the text are given in the Bibliography (Works by Rousseau, pp. 251–60).

References in the text give the book, chapter and page numbers (as appropriate) in the translation employed, followed by the volume and page number in *Jean-Jacques Rousseau: Oeuvres Complètes*. (This edition is not yet complete, so reference to it has not been possible in all cases.) References in the *Further reading* at the end of each entry give the author's name followed by a round-bracketed number; this number indicates where in Part II of the Bibliography, Works on Rousseau (pp. 261–74), the item appears (with publication details).

A

Abbé de Saint-Pierre *See* ÉCRITS SUR L'ABBÉ DE SAINT-PIERRE.

alienation (self-estrangement)   The notion of alienation finds explicit employment in the works of Hegel and Marx, from whose writings it is best known. They do not agree between themselves over what precisely the phenomena of alienation consist in nor about how they are caused, but there is sufficient similarity between what Rousseau considers and what is discussed by Hegel and Marx to say that Rousseau had also identified the phenomenon of 'alienated' man and society, even though he does not use this specific term, nor does what he says correspond directly to the ideas of these later writers.

Rousseau argues that in ordinary society – that is, society not reformed or refounded on the egalitarian principles enunciated in The SOCIAL CONTRACT – human beings come to be corrupted in a particular way. When they associate with each other, he maintains, they are apt to jockey for position, to seek domination over others, and to glory in the inferiority or subordination of those beneath them. This comes about, in Rousseau's view, because of the demands of a person's AMOUR-PROPRE.

In thus seeking invidious distinction for themselves, people become alienated from their own proper needs and nature, become estranged from themselves, in at least two ways. First, the objective of securing invidious superiority, Rousseau argues, works against a person's own true good. It is no part of human good to need to dominate or to require the abjection of others. Such a desire is an expression of aggression, which is as damaging to the aggressor as it is to the targets of his aggression. To live a life dominated by aggressive purposes is not simply to desert, but to thwart, cooperative and creative concerns which promise fulfilment in accordance with real human needs. So in giving himself over to the objective of domination a person sets himself at odds with his own true nature and good; this objective causes him to be, and to do, other than that which his intrinsic personal need requires. He becomes alienated from himself.

Second, in order to achieve an invidious precedence in the forum of

27

human affairs a person has to have, or has to put on a convincing show of having, attributes and accomplishments that are capable of winning or extracting esteem and deference from others. This requires that he play to the crowd, tailor his self-presentation to their proclivities. If an individual's persona has been dictated by the taste of his audience, he loses touch with the character and concerns that are properly his own – that is, those he would have were he not predominantly or exclusively concerned with the figure that he cuts in the eyes of others. According to Rousseau, in the quest for superiority an entire system of pseudo-values comes into existence, which serve only as markers of prestigious distinction in the competition for personal visibility. These he variously calls ARTIFICIAL, CAPRICE, fashion or factitious values. Once a person has become an artificial creation fashioned by the dictates of others, his sense of himself, of his own value and importance, is entirely in their hands. Another, alienated, self has replaced his own self.

Styles of dress, codes of manners, social stations, and in particular wealth are seen by Rousseau as principally valued as the badges of invidious superiority. In time, the whole structure of law, property ownership and social institutions will come to embody and consolidate the self-alienating mode of life. No alternative mode of action or achievement will appear to be possible for people. An alienated society will have come into existence.

It should be noted that Rousseau does not criticize all forms of superiority or ascendancy among people. He holds, for instance, that athletic prowess is worthy of esteem. But this is because it comprises a real distinction, a real excellence, and because its aim is not simply to provide a basis from which to despise or negate others as inferiors (though, of course, it can be twisted to that end). Even in a 'rectified' society there may be distinctions of rank and power, but these will exist only with the authorization of the whole social body, and will be held by persons who have served and continue to serve the real good of the other members of society.

If Rousseau's idea of alienation as the acquisition of a self other than, and in conflict with, a person's true or proper self is to be defensible, he must give a cogent account of the latter idea. If he does not, then there is nothing for an alienated self to be alienated from or to be alien to, and this conception must collapse. He does give such an account in his discussion of man's NATURAL GOODNESS and of the proper basis for cooperation in society. It is a very widespread – but, I would suggest, mistaken – view of Rousseau that he maintains that all forms of social existence are necessarily self-alienating. In fact, he holds that we can, in principle, hold a rank and standing with others in society which wholly accords with the real needs of our proper being.

There are two other aspects of Rousseau's thought to which a notion of alienation applies. First, in *The Social Contract* (I, ch. 6, 174; *OC* III, 360) he actually uses the term once: he says that as a condition for establishing a just and free society each person must 'alienate himself' completely to the whole body. The term as he uses it here signifies resigning or relinquishing all purely self-possessed rights or belongings to the command of another or others. One can see readily enough why the term 'alienate' should be used in this case – which Rousseau justifies – and in the others discussed (even though he sees an inherent corruption being involved in the cases discussed earlier). Why this resigning of right should take place is made clear in the argument of *The Social Contract*.

Second, at several points Rousseau makes a distinction between the private, self-interested concerns of people and those that they may take on by virtue of their occupying a certain position in society and acquiring purposes for the common good of all in that society. He sometimes makes this distinction in terms of a contrast between the *moi particulier* and the *moi commun*, between the self as a discrete, self-absorbed entity and the self as the bearer of attributes and dispositions drawn from that self's role in society. He often argues that if we are to have a just, prosperous and happy society the *moi commun* must dominate or displace the *moi particulier*: people must become at one with their place in society, absorbed by their social role. But this too may be seen as a form of alienation: for the separate, particularized identity of individuals is substituted a socially constructed identity. Certainly, Rousseau uses the term DENATURING to describe this process, but the issues here are complex. On the one hand, it is fairly clear that he sometimes sees the *moi particulier* that is to be displaced as already alienated (in the first sense). But, on the other, providing the *moi commun* involves identification with purposes that genuinely serve the good of others, it will also incorporate needs and desires proper to true self-expression. There is no decisive answer as to whether the assumption of a different self does or does not involve self-alienation of the damaging kind.

Sources: *DI*, especially Pt 2
       E, especially Bks II, IV
       RSW, Eighth Walk

Further reading: Bloom (163); Charvet, ch. 3 (23); Dent, ch. 2 (24); Horowitz (27);
       Laing (291); Shklar, ch. 3 (36); Reisman (343)

amour de soi (love of self)   A semi-theoretical notion which Rousseau deploys to explain and interpret the purposes and behaviour of all animate creatures, but particularly human beings. Its literal English translation, 'love of self', gives no real key to understanding the notion as he uses it.

He gives an explicit elucidation in *Émile* (IV, 212–13; *OC* IV, 491): 'The source of our passions, the origin and the principle of all the others, the only one born with man and which never leaves him so long as he lives is *amour de soi* – a primitive, innate passion, which is anterior to every other . . .' And in the *Discourse on the Origin of Inequality* he wrote (66 n. 2; *OC* III, 219 n. 15): '*Amour-propre* must not be confused with *amour de soi-même*: for they differ both in themselves and in their effects. *Amour de soi-même* is a natural feeling which leads every animal to look to its own preservation, and which, guided in man by reason and modified by compassion, creates humanity and virtue.'

From these and other passages we can draw the following points. First, Rousseau holds that all animate beings are innately so constituted as to be concerned to preserve their own lives and procure their own well-being (whatever that may consist in). In the lower animals this concern is not conscious, but arises, rather, from a pattern in instinctive desires and behaviour which tends to the conservation of a creature's life. A notion related to this one of Rousseau's is Spinoza's *conatus* – the endeavour in all beings to persist in their own nature. Spinoza, though, unlike Rousseau with his *amour de soi*, extended this idea to inanimate things.

Rousseau maintains that acting out of *amour de soi* is naturally good (*see* NATURAL GOODNESS). By this he means at least three things. First, that living creatures should strive to conserve themselves is not wrong or wicked – to believe so would be to damn the very existence of such creatures. Second, that *amour de soi* directs a creature to its own good and is therefore a naturally healthy, well ordered and benign disposition in the creature. Rousseau tends to say that the substance of the well-being that *amour de soi* directs any creature (including human beings) to seek comprises their basic health and complete physical functioning. (It will be explained later that *amour de soi* is not, however, in its essence so restricted in its objectives.) Third, Rousseau argues that the dispositions and behaviours which *amour de soi* directs are not, in their nature, cruel or malicious. Even if, as may happen especially in the animal kingdom, one creature's *amour de soi* brings it into conflict with another, this conflict is brief and serves no vindictive ends. In humans, such conflict is additionally apt to be tempered by COMPASSION; and, most importantly for Rousseau, *amour de soi* contains no desire to get the better of another, as a proof of personal superiority (*see* AMOUR-PROPRE).

Amour de soi is not confined exclusively to instinctual patterns of behaviour. This same general concern for individual well-being is manifest when conscious awareness, foresight and knowledge of the components of individual good come into play. Awareness of the need to provide for the future, or to check present impulses if they will be harmful, requires deliberate regulation of conduct. When this occurs, another capacity – one exclusive to humans, in Rousseau's view – comes into play: that of free will which, in the sense intended here, signifies just this ability to act, or to refrain from acting, on the basis of advised judgement regarding future good or harm (*see* FREEDOM).

Also exclusive to humans is a plasticity and adaptability of behaviour, the capacity to learn from experience. Humans are not confined to rigid routines, but can learn how to manipulate their environment and adjust their behaviour so as to increase their advantage. The capacity to do this Rousseau calls PERFECTIBILITY. This, and free will, are, he says, innate to humans.

When *amour de soi* works in conjunction with free will and perfectibility, so that a person is consciously regulating and adapting his behaviour with knowledge of future results, then we see the familiar pattern of someone acting in their own self-interest. For Rousseau it is important, however, that any concern to profit at the expense of others be excluded from the personal interest that *amour de soi* is directed towards. It is because Rousseau emphasizes this that it is easy to think that *amour de soi* concerns the good of persons only as wholly isolated from each other. (This, as will be suggested below, is, however, not essential.) Rousseau does sometimes condemn the excessive foresight that causes a person always to live tomorrow, never today. But in general he regards this developed form of *amour de soi* as unequivocally good.

There is a further aspect of *amour de soi* which Rousseau alludes to in the *Discourse on the Origin of Inequality* (66 n. 2; *OC* III, 219 n. 15). This involves having a sense of one's value and merit as a competent and successful agent in one's own affairs. His thought here appears to be that human beings reflect not only on their purposes and their environment but also on themselves and on their attributes and accomplishments. It is part of our well-being to be able to think that there is something creditable about us; that we are, in our way, good and competent creatures. *Amour de soi* will cause us to form this opinion of ourselves, so that we may carry with us a happy consciousness of our personal effectiveness. It is crucial to Rousseau's overall argument that we should be quite clear that this sort of self-esteem in no way derives from a sense that we have got the better of others, have gained ascendancy over them, or regard ourselves as creditable for having forced negation on them. Competition for precedence

31

plays no part in this self-possessed and self-contained sense of personal value.

It is Rousseau's view that, as a person's awareness of himself and his situation grows, it will lead him to a realization that he is a creature loved by God and blessed with signal powers, a creature who has the capacity for virtuous action at the prompting of CONSCIENCE (*see* CREED OF A SAVOYARD VICAR). With this much enlarged sense of his character and place in the ordered universe, the individual will be directed by *amour de soi* to strive after a good conscience and to live and act in ways that accord with the designs of his Creator. *Amour de soi* is virtually transcended at this point:

> It was simple to rise from the study of nature to the quest for its Author.
> Once we have gotten there what new holds we have given ourselves over our pupil . . . It is only then that he finds his true interest in being good . . . He does this not only for the love of order, to which each of us always prefers *amour de soi*, but for the love of the Author of his being – a love which is confounded with that same *amour de soi* – and, finally, for the enjoyment of that durable happiness which the repose of a good conscience and the contemplation of this Supreme Being promise him . . . (*E* IV, 314; *OC* IV, 636)

According to one extremely pervasive, and fairly persuasive, interpretation of Rousseau's ideas (referred to earlier), *amour de soi* is confined to the need and good of a person as a separate being unassociated with others, and is thus largely restricted to securing physical well-being. This interpretation arises because it is held that, in Rousseau's view, when humans associate with each other (in any but the most casual ways) *amour de soi* is displaced by a different kind of concern for oneself – namely *amour-propre* – a concern which is, moreover, antithetical to *amour de soi*. I suggest that this assessment of Rousseau's ideas is deeply mistaken.

If this were indeed his view, it would be doubtful whether the life procured at the direction of *amour de soi* were in any real sense human. Language – in fact, all arts and skills that require cooperation – depend on society. But if social contact leads at once to the displacement of *amour de soi*, then that alone can procure for us a life scarcely different from the animals. Although these conclusions are sometimes attributed to Rousseau, this is not his position. He holds that it is inevitable that humans shall associate with each other in all sorts of permanent ways, and that although too often this association harms them, it is not bound to. A proper part of our personal good in human association is our acquiring from others recognition and honour as persons whose existence and interests count as significant. We value this not only for the benefits it brings, but because it constitutes an element of our human dignity and worth. *Amour de soi* directs us to acquire this position for ourselves, as a person among persons, as the human and moral equal of all. The concerns of *amour de soi* thus extend to our moral being as a right-possessing member of society, and are not confined to our physical being alone as a separate entity (*see* MORALITY). To desire and to claim this social recognition for ourselves does not require that anyone else be dispossessed or negated: indeed, Rousseau argues that it requires our granting like recognition to others. In this way he can hold that *amour de soi* operates in human social relations, while remaining beneficial to its possessor and to those with whom he has dealings. This interpretation of Rousseau's ideas on this point is not widely accepted.

Sources: *DI*
    E, Bks I–IV

Further reading: Charvet chs 2–3 (23); Dent, ch. 3 (24); Dent (82); MacAdam (93); Masters, ch. 3 (69); Shklar, ch. 2 (36)

amour-propre (self-love)   The notion of *amour-propre*, which Rousseau uses in a semi-technical way, is one of the most important in the whole of his social and political theorizing. A sound grasp of its significance is essential if his views on a great many matters are to be understood. First, the familiar and widely accepted account of the term.

According to this, Rousseau holds that as soon as a human being forms any kind of settled relationship or association with another this brings out in him a desire, which readily becomes dominant and all-consuming, to establish himself as superior over that other, to acquire overbearing power, to enforce subjection and ignominy on the other, in whose debasement he finds pleasure and proof of his own importance and value. Human relationships are thus, through and through, disfigured by a craving for domination and prestige, which demands and enforces deference and subordination.

Since everyone alike has this same desire, relentless competition and conflict pervade all human association. Deception, aggression and malice are the predominant notes of human intercourse. ARTIFICIAL or CAPRICE values – those whose significance is only to divide people into the superior and the inferior – replace all real values, i.e. those that produce real growth and fruitfulness. People become alienated (*see* ALIENATION) from themselves as they take on the guises necessary to procure and retain their invidious precedence. Their own sense of personal worth and success, of the value of their lives, depends on their occupying a high position in society. It is from the opinion that others have of them that they borrow their sense of their own reality. Offices, ranks, allocations of goods – all are structured to sustain the pattern of superiority and inferiority, of the individual ascending while doing down others.

Amour-propre comes to displace AMOUR DE SOI, substituting for the intact self-possessed good with which the latter is concerned the delusive good which consists in procuring invidious personal dominance over others. According to this account, Rousseau is apt to see *amour-propre* as, above all else, the source of personal corruption and suffering and social evil. When he says, as he often does, that man is by nature good but corrupted by society, it is the fact that social contact brings out *amour-propre*, and reinforces and extends its influence, that he has in mind.

Since social contact inevitably draws out *amour-propre*, and since *amour-propre* is unrelievedly harmful and corrupting, Rousseau sees the prospects for humans to live rich and rewarding lives together in society as very slight indeed. Man is profoundly at odds with himself and with others; it is no longer possible to envisage the harmony of individual and group depicted, say, by Aristotle, who held that social life brought out the full realization of human potential. The best remedy given Rousseau's bleak vision of the predicament of modern man would be complete withdrawal from society, a 'return to nature'. But Rousseau holds – again, according to this interpretation – that there is no real prospect of this; only some slight mitigation of the evil is possible. Partial withdrawal into dispersed family units might provide some solution; abolition of the individual as a self-concerned entity and substitution of a self moulded to the needs of society might provide another (*see* DENATURING). Perhaps the worst evils of *amour-propre* can be tempered by reinforcing the collaborative and cooperative dispositions of COMPASSION. But *amour-propre* tends to extinguish these. And in none of these eventualities is any fully human or fully satisfactory life possible. Social man is a fractured, disabled and miserable being.

'*Amour-propre*' is sometimes translated as VANITY, pride, self-aggrandizement, all of which serve better than 'self-love' though that gives the most literal translation. But none quite captures the term's sense. The most significant aspect of its meaning has to do with seeing what is good and valuable in and for oneself in terms of others' lack of these things, in terms of others being of little or no account in comparison with oneself. *Amour-propre*, so understood, is an aggressive desire containing the need to control others and to obliterate them. In Rousseau's view, it is rooted in a child's imperiously wilful reaction to frustration by which he hopes to command other people and the world to his service.

Thus goes the familiar account of Rousseau's notion of *amour-propre*. It is undeniable that he does say all these things about the situation of man in society. But I would suggest that he does not think that they are the inevitable outcome of a person's entry into human association – because he does not see *amour-propre* as inevitably taking on an aggressive and controlling character. The above account describes what is characteristic of excessive or, as Rousseau puts it, 'petulant' *amour-propre*, but does not describe what is intrinsic to it. Whilst *amour-propre* is, indeed, necessarily brought out by human association, Rousseau proposes in The SOCIAL CONTRACT a form of human society that can be creative, beneficial and self-enlarging for all concerned.

Amour-propre, intrinsically, directs us to secure for ourselves recognition from others and a standing in society in which we are honoured as significant beings whose needs and desires have an absolute title to be taken into account on the same footing with anyone else's. To have such standing is inherently valuable, as recognition of our human and moral dignity. To enjoy it is one of our proper goods; in fact, *amour-propre* is simply the form that *amour de soi* (which directs us to the enjoyment of our proper good) takes when the personal good sought is one that we need in our dealings with others. It is the desire to have what is our own (*proprius*), what belongs to us, as equal members in our association with others.

Claiming such recognition as our due does not in any way involve denying the same due to others. Rousseau endeavours to show, indeed, that it is only if we grant it to others that we can receive it from them. There is, thus, no competition or striving for domination involved here – this only enters in when other people are perceived as threatening to deny or deprive one of honour or standing. It is in response to such a perceived threat that *amour-propre* takes on an excessive, deformed character, and in its own defence seeks to deprive others. In what is perhaps one of his deepest arguments, Rousseau shows that there is no real cause to see other people as necessarily presenting such a threat. Our aptness to do so is the projection of our own unrecognized anger, an expression of infantile grievance. It is both humanly possible, and very desirable, to perceive others as sources of care and support from whom one can readily expect recognition and to whom one can then equally readily grant it.

Although this alternative account of the nature and effects of *amour-propre* gives to Rousseau's work overall a much greater level of consistency and intelligibility, it is not generally accepted. It receives some confirmation from Kant, however, who writes here with Rousseau clearly in mind:

> The predisposition to humanity can be brought under the general title of a self-love which is physical and yet *compares* . . . that is to say, we judge ourselves happy or unhappy only by making comparison with others. Out of this self-love springs the inclination *to acquire worth in the opinion of others*. This is originally a desire merely for *equality*, to allow no one superiority above

oneself, bound up with a constant care lest others strive to attain such superiority; but from this arises gradually the unjustifiable craving to win it for oneself over others. Upon this twin stem of *jealousy* and *rivalry* may be grafted the very great vices of secret and open animosity against all whom we look upon as not belonging to us – vices, however, which really do not sprout from nature as their root; rather they are inclinations, aroused in us by the anxious endeavours of others to attain a hated superiority over us . . . the vices which are grafted upon this inclination might be termed their vices of *culture*, in highest degree of malignancy, as, for example, in *envy*, *ingratitude*, *spitefulness* etc. . . . they can be called the *diabolical vices*. (*Religion within the Limits of Reason Alone*, Bk I, section 1)

Sources: DI, especially Pt 2
    E, Bks I–IV
    RJJ Dialogues 1, 2
    RSW, Eighth Walk

Further reading: Bloom (163); Charvet, ch. 3 (23); Dent, ch. 2 (24); Horowitz (27); Kant (289); MacAdam (93); Masters, ch. 1 (69); Plattner (99); Shklar, chs 1–3 (36); Skillen (101)

artificial Rousseau often uses the term 'artificial' in an ordinary, colourless way to signify that which is the product of human work and contrivance, the product of artifice. He also, however, uses it with a more specific significance, to say or imply of something that it is in some way fraudulent or suspect, an improper deviation from, or replacement of, what is natural, fair and good.

The DISCOURSE ON THE ORIGIN OF INEQUALITY is structured around a contrast between natural and artificial inequalities. Here Rousseau means to imply, with regard to the latter, that not only are such inequalities the product of, and sustained by, human convention and work but that also these are inequalities that have no reasonable foundation and are unjustified and hurtful. Thus he maintains that all 'moral' relations between persons – that is, all relations, whether just or not, involving duties, obligations, responsibilities and titles regulating mutual conduct (*see* MORALITY) – are artificial in the ordinary, colourless sense, in that it requires human intent and activity to ensure that such relationships are properly maintained and conducted (even if one might believe that the basis for such relationships does not itself repose in anything man-made).

Such relations he often calls, non-committally, 'conventional'. However, there are some forms that such relations take which are, in Rousseau's view, also artificial in the specific, condemnatory, sense indicated. The relations in which some are established as lords and others as servants, some as honourable and others as ignominious, are artificial in this more specific sense. In such cases, a relationship is structured by claimed moral demands and moral responsibilities, but these are demands which merely mask overbearing power and control that have no licence or justification. The history of human society shows the gradual development of social and moral forms which serve to disguise – in manufactured dress, as it were – the realities of domination, force and terror which structure many social relationships and processes. That 'artificial' moral inequalities should gain currency and acceptance is an element in this development. (Here we may see an echo of Thrasymachus' argument about justice being in the interest of the stronger, in Plato's *Republic*, Bk I.) Rousseau does not call 'artificial' a human relationship governed by 'naked' force, although he would not, of course, think it any the more tolerable – except, perhaps, in that it shows its character on its face.

It is in connection with human inequality that Rousseau uses the term 'artificial' most incisively. But it occurs in related usages when he speaks of artificial values (*see* CAPRICE) and of an artificial self (*see* ALIENATION); in these cases it is the development of pseudo-values, or of a contrived persona, that is at issue. But in all instances it is the masking of the underlying strategies of domination and control that causes Rousseau to use the term 'artificial'. In the case of artificial values, the desire to achieve invidious superiority over others is given scope by introducing badges of personal distinction. In the case of the artificial self, this same desire involves acquiring, or putting on a show of possessing, those attributes or accomplishments that will yield a competitive edge, enabling a person to delight in the contemptible negligibility of others. In every case, these are the effects of disordered AMOUR-PROPRE, which shapes people, ideas and individual and social relationships.

One further context in which Rousseau poses the question of artificiality is in considering the position and duties of WOMEN (in Bk V of *Émile*). There he discusses whether some, at least, of their duties are nothing more than 'unjust man-made inequalities'; but he does not here imply that if something is 'man-made' or a 'human institution' it is automatically suspect (as his addition of the word 'unjust' displays).

It might be said that the two significances of 'artificial' – the one merely descriptive, the other condemnatory – correspond to two different ways of contrasting artifice with nature. In the first, neutral, sense, what is artificial goes beyond that which is a mere process or product of nature: human design and contrivance are involved. In this sense, even the best form of civil society that Rousseau attempts to depict in The SOCIAL CONTRACT is an artificial, or conventional, form of human association. In the second, critical, sense, what is artificial is in conflict with what is natural – that is, in conflict with what Rousseau conceives to be healthy,

37

intact, benign and good (*see* NATURAL GOODNESS). The aggressive designs which find covert expression in the erection of artificial inequalities put people, in Rousseau's view, in conflict with those dispositions and potentialities in themselves which accord with their natural opportunities for fruitful life. That is the reason for condemning such artificial arrangements.

Sources: *DI*
    E, Bks IV, V

Further reading: Charvet, ch. 3 (23); Horowitz, ch. 8 (27); Masters, ch. 4 (69)

arts *See* DISCOURSE ON THE SCIENCES AND THE ARTS.

authority Rousseau does not attribute any special *sense* to the notion of authority. He uses it to mean the rightful, legitimate title to command or require actions and forbearances from others. Correlative with authority is the obligation of obedience. It stands in contrast to mere superior force, which exacts only subjugated compliance (servitude). What is of significance is Rousseau's discussion of the *grounds* on which a person or body of persons are properly entitled to claim or to enjoy authority. Although he discusses in passing the authority of parents over children and of tutors over pupils, his principal concern throughout is with the grounds of sovereign authority in a state (*see* SOVEREIGN BODY), and with the authority of governors (*see* GOVERNMENT) and of the LAW. What he says about authority in the other cases is usually only in relation to these central concerns.

The sovereign authority in a state is, by definition, the ultimate source of the right to direct the conduct of the affairs of the state and to regulate the lives of its members. (There need not be, either in theory or in fact, any one specific person or body who is such an ultimate source; final authority may be spread amongst several bodies, though Rousseau thought this undesirable.) Such an authority is legitimate and acts rightfully, in Rousseau's view, only if it has a certain composition and conducts itself in a certain way. If it lacks this composition or fails to proceed appropriately it becomes invalid, and, if it does not cease to exist altogether, it survives only as a subjugating power. (Such a power may, and probably will, still *claim* to possess authority – that is, the right to command. But it does not actually *have* it.) The sovereign authority must be composed of all adult members of the society, who are to be regarded as the constitutive members of it and who will be subject to authoritative direction. No act or procedure has authority unless it receives the rationally advised consent of all these members.

Thus, crudely, one may say that for Rousseau the source of the authority of the sovereign in a state reposes in the authorizations given by all the constitutive members of that state. And all authoritative general rules (laws) in society, or authoritative bodies (such as magistrates), derive their authority from the sovereign body. Obligations of obedience to rules or persons are, thus, acquired through a form of voluntary consent on the part of those obligated, either directly in the case of consent to the fundamental rules of the civil association (society), or indirectly in the case of consent to the direction of a magistrate, whose existence and functions are established by decision of the sovereign body as fundamental to the operations of the civil body.

That authority is grounded in, comes from, 'the will of the people' is certainly the concept for which Rousseau is best known and which his writing (particularly in The SOCIAL CONTRACT) appears most clearly to present. Closer inspection of his argument suggests, however, that the matter is not quite so simple. In particular, Rousseau sometimes suggests that people may mistake their proper interests, or may not be able to see clearly where they lie, and so give their authorization to rules and procedures that are harmful to them, or that inflict on them mere subjugation. In this case Rousseau would say that these rules lack authority, even though authorization has been given to them. (It would be a mere verbal trick to say that in such cases consent does not amount to authorization.)

It then emerges that a body and its acts enjoy authority only if they meet certain, essentially moral, criteria in their composition and functioning. These criteria include the successful protection of the person and goods of each member of the society, and the guaranteed recognition of that member as fully participating in the society. It is only when a body in its composition and actions achieves these objectives that it has authority and functions authoritatively. And it is only because Rousseau believes that in a sovereign body consisting wholly of adults, functioning with the well advised consent of all of them, we are most likely to find these criteria met, that he espouses this as the proper embodiment of authority in the state. It is conceivable that some otherwise constituted and operating body might meet the criteria more fully, although then Rousseau would make other objections to it: in particular, that it neglects to give every citizen his proper dignity in having knowledge of civic virtue and the disposition to act on it for the public good. So even if, through failure to meet the appropriate criteria, 'the people' do not make properly authoritative decisions, it remains for Rousseau that the objective of making them bearers of properly possessed authority must be a paramount objective in any well ordered society.

39

That government and law possess authority only with the consent of the governed is something that is now almost universally accepted – though sometimes more in theory than in substance, and the ways in which such consent is held to be obtained are very various indeed. Authority claimed on the basis of divine right, hereditary succession and so on is no longer recognized as legitimate authority. To the extent to which Rousseau contributed to this shift in the understanding of the basis of sovereign authority, he may be credited with being one of the founding fathers of modern political thinking. This does not mean that his notion of the way in which the sovereign should be constituted and should act in order to carry authority has found favour. Very large states, with very mixed members, cannot assemble and function in the way he envisaged. (In his view, this does sometimes throw doubt on the authoritative status of the requirements imposed on the subjects of such states.)

One special case of the possession and exercise of authority, which is central to the issue of 'the people' avoiding mistakes in their deliberations, is that of the LEGISLATOR. This figure is intended by Rousseau to form the people's attitudes and expectations in such a way that their deliberations will more effectively meet the moral criteria noted above and will thus unequivocally possess authority. In order to achieve this objective, the directions of the legislator must themselves carry authority over those who are guided by him.

According to Rousseau, when a person is not a member of any association or civil society, he enjoys absolute authority to direct and dispose his own affairs as he sees fit. It is not intrinsic to some people to be subordinate to others, to lack the right to command their own affairs, to be obliged to wait on the direction of others or to be in any other way unfit to govern their own lives. It is from the original authority over themselves that all possess that, Rousseau thinks, any authority over other people must, in the end, derive.

Sources: *DI*
       DPE
       GP, chs 7–13
       SC, Bks I–III

Further reading: Dent, ch. 5 (24); Gildin (123); Leigh (127); Levine (128); Masters, chs 7, 8 (69); Noone (140); Shklar (146)

B

botanical writings [22] *See* BOTANY.

botany   As early as 1738, when he was still living, however uneasily by that time, with Mme de Warens, Rousseau records the delight he took in plants. Indeed, he must have learned a good deal about herbs and other plants used for medicinal purposes, since the preparation of herbal remedies was one of the activities of Mme de Warens herself and of Claude Anet, her factotum (though Rousseau was later, in *The Reveries of the Solitary Walker*, to decry attention paid to plants with a view merely to their medicinal uses).

During the next two decades, while Rousseau was preoccupied with his musical and theoretical works in Paris and elsewhere, this interest receded. When, forced to flee Paris in 1762, he returned to Switzerland and in the July settled at Môtiers in the principality of Neuchâtel, he resumed his botanical researches, deriving enormous pleasure from the many trips that he took into the hills and valleys in the company of friends. About this time he began to plan a botanical dictionary, the *Dictionnaire des Termes d'Usage en Botanique*, drafts of which survive. The work of Linnaeus made a great impression on him; he believed that the system of classification that Linnaeus introduced was essential to any adequate study of plants.

Rousseau's stay at Môtiers did not last long. The victim of public attack and condemnation by the religious authorities, he had to move on again in September 1765, stopping for a while at the island of St-Pierre in Lake Bienne where, he says, he spent some of the pleasantest days of his life, studying flora. Even during his troubled stay in England during 1766 he continued his botanizing, gathering ferns and mosses in the neighbourhood of Wootton. When he settled again in Paris in 1770, having taken up morning work as a music-copyist, in the afternoons he would walk out into the country collecting plants, cataloguing, drying and pressing them, and preparing herbaria for friends. Over the next couple of years he wrote eight letters on botany to Mme Étienne de Lessert, the daughter of a close friend, for the instruction of her child. In these *Elementary Letters on Botany*;

(*Lettres Élémentaires sur la Botanique*) he recommends the study of plants as a way of learning both how to see clearly, without preconceptions or assumptions, and how to classify, systematize and understand the miracles of nature in a spirit of humility. Rousseau thinks that such a study stills the anxieties of the greedy self, while appreciation of the beautiful gifts of nature calms and pleases the soul. In the First Letter he writes: 'I am convinced that at any stage the study of nature abates the taste for frivolous amusements, subdues the tumults of passion, and bestows upon the mind a salutary nourishment by filling it with a subject most worthy of its occupation.'

In the Seventh Letter, whilst warning that the importance of botany should not be exaggerated, he notes that 'it is a study of pure curiosity, one that has no real utility except what a thinking, sensitive human being can draw from observing nature and the marvels of the universe.' It should not be thought, though, that this is his way of denigrating botanical study. The purity, the very uselessness, of the interest is, for Rousseau, its highest recommendation, since wherever questions of use arise man disfigures nature either by exploiting it or by making it into something it is not – simply to gratify himself – instead of opening his mind to the wonder of the natural world.

By *c.* 1776 Rousseau had more or less given up his botanical expeditions and the preparation of plants, finding the effort too much. But the passion never left him: a year before his death he was seized again by the 'mania' for plants, though this time thinking more about the scientific aspects of botanical inquiry.

Neither the *Letters* nor the drafts for the dictionary were published in Rousseau's lifetime, but they were included in a collected edition of his works published in Geneva in 1782, and were first translated into English in 1785. In 1805 the painter P. J. Redouté came across them and prepared an exquisite edition (Rousseau's *Botanique*), with the most wonderful illustrations: it was an enormous public success, and remains one of Redouté's finest achievements.

Sources: *Dictionnaire des termes d'usage en Botanique* (*OC*, IV)
Lettres Élémentaires sur la Botanique à Madame de Lessert (*OC*, IV)
RSW, Seventh Walk

Further reading: Cantor (218); Scott (230)

C

caprice Caprice – the tendency to sudden and unpredictable changes in attitude and behaviour – is a common enough human phenomenon. But Rousseau sees in it the expression of a deeper and more important human concern. He additionally uses 'caprice' or 'capricious' as an adjective to qualify values or codes of honour.

In Bks I and II of ÉMILE, Rousseau is insistent that those who wish to bring up children to be well and happy must pay careful attention to the question of whether a child's cries, requests and actions reveal his attempts to make sense of his world and to act effectively in it as best he can, or whether they are all the expression of caprice. He believes that the wilfulness – in contrast with practically realistic efforts of will – with which the child attempts to command those about him and to make them his servants, compliant to his every imperious demand, is in fact a manifestation of caprice. The inclination to wilfulness is very strong in children (and in adults), he thinks, but it is invariably hurtful to them and to those about them if not eliminated.

A child's attempt to impose his domineering will is, Rousseau holds, the expression of fear and of rage at frustration, which then creates a fantasy world of thwarting or malign figures who terrorize the child and can only be controlled by efforts of domination and imperious self-assertion. A child is apt to see all human transaction as an issue of control, and will – without conscious design – find whatever means he can to gain and retain that control. Caprice is one manifestation of this. The anxious parent, concerned that his offspring is bored, miserable, dissatisfied, hurries hither and thither to placate and gratify him. The child thus becomes accustomed to a world that renders him service at a mere word. But, just as often, people and things are not so compliant: now the child thinks that what he is encountering is wilful refusal, a desire to do him down. He lacks any grasp of the real limits of his power, and true sense of how the world works or of how people can be brought to render aid reliably and consistently – by kindness and generosity rather than by command and scowls.

To grow up with these beliefs and feelings benefits the child no more than it benefits those who have dealings with him either now or later, when he is an adult. Rousseau thinks that a principal educative priority must be to prevent the consolidation of these patterns of response in the child. It is for this reason that he recommends that, as far as possible, a child be brought up in an environment where he is not, apparently, being controlled or directed by the will of others. He must seem to inhabit a world that is not shaped by others' intentions, but that proceeds 'of its own accord'. In this way, he will lose his proneness to think that when things are not as he would like, some thwarting or denying figure is responsible. There will be nothing to encourage this idea; the world around him will not pay this kind of attention to him. Perceiving this, he will turn instead, Rousseau believes, to acquiring the knowledge and learning the skills that he requires to make properly judged real changes in his situation which will improve it in the way he wants. The sulks of thwarted wilfulness and capricious waywardness will be replaced by effective, concrete action.

This element in Rousseau's educative programme has been seen as both unrealistic and perverted. To insulate a child from contact with other human wills is seen as impossible and as likely to inflict psychological disturbance on him. It is probable, indeed, that Rousseau's practical proposals lack judgement. But that should not conceal the real significance of the issue that he has identified and is attempting to resolve. It is indisputable that great harm is done to a person, and to those he comes in contact with, if he thinks that what human transaction is all about is the struggle for domination and control. We need not to dismiss Rousseau's concern with this matter, but to think of better ways in which this belief, and all the feelings and behaviour that go with it, can be expunged or prevented from forming in the first place.

It is in connection with this desire for domination and control – in its fully fledged form of excessive AMOUR-PROPRE – that Rousseau speaks of 'caprice values' and 'capricious codes of honour'. A caprice (ARTIFICIAL, fashion, factitious) value is, in fact, of no real value at all, although it parades as such. What it relates to in reality is some possession, attribute or accomplishment that is deemed to be estimable or distinguished because it provides a way of claiming prestigious ascendancy over others who, for lack of the relevant item, are identified as contemptible and worthless. Its sole purpose is to provide a way of making 'sheep' and 'goats', and then divide the former from the latter. The same applies to capricious codes of honour.

Just because such pseudo-values express and foster this determination to control others, to do them down, Rousseau places the same strictures on them as he does on that determination. He sees in all cases the work of aggression and hatred in distorting human relations and affairs; and he holds throughout his works that such dispositions are not and cannot be admirable or beneficial, either to their possessors or to those who are their objects.

See also EDUCATION.

Source: *E*, Bks I, II

Further reading: Bloom (163); Carr (165); Dent, ch. 2 (24)

citizen   Rousseau explains his notion of 'citizen', one of his key themes regarding the standing of persons as members of a civil society, at *SC* Bk I, ch. 6, 175. Of the formation of a civil society he says: 'it is called by its members *State* when passive, *Sovereign* when active, and *power* when compared with others like itself. Those who are associated in it take collectively the name of *people*, and severally are called *citizens*, as sharing in the sovereign authority, and *subjects*, as being under the laws of the State (*OC* III, 361–2).

There are four principal points to be noted regarding citizenship. First, to be a citizen is to possess a certain status or position in the state. It is to have certain rights and entitlements (as well as duties and responsibilities) conferred upon one by the positive laws of the state, towards one's secure enjoyment of which the whole force of the body politic is directed. Second, to citizenship proper, as Rousseau understands it, one particular title is central: that of participation in the formation or ratification of sovereign legislation (*see* SOVEREIGN BODY). An individual is not a citizen if he is the passive recipient of the legislative direction of others, even if those others are genuinely acting for his benefit. Still less does he enjoy citizenship if he is subjugated by force or inescapable power – that is servitude. Rather, a citizen is someone who stands on an equal footing and plays an equal role along with all other persons (citizens likewise) in formulating the common authoritative general rules by which all of them shall order their lives in the state (*see* AUTHORITY).

Third, acquiring the status of citizen introduces, Rousseau says, a 'moral change' in the persons and acts of hitherto merely 'naturally' connected individuals. In acting as a citizen a person is exercising not merely his native force and energy, but his rights and titles; and he has moral and civil justification for his actions, and will be protected, if necessary, in carrying them out. Such actions do not express desire alone: they embody rationally justified projects, with the weight of legitimate reason behind them. Fourth, Rousseau maintains that in any just and well ordered state the status of citizen is enjoyed precisely alike by every single member of the state; and it is the most important status anyone can enjoy. A person may occupy other positions in the state, but none of these entitles him to override the citizenly titles of another. Indeed, all these other positions are authorized by, and their occupants are answerable to, citizens in their capacity of members of the sovereign body. Thus, some are governors and some are governed, but those who occupy such positions of importance do so only by the decision of all acting in their capacity of citizen.

It is this absolute, and irrevocable, equality in membership of the highest station in society contained in Rousseau's notion of citizenship that made the titles *citoyen* and *citoyenne* such key terms in the rhetoric of the French Revolution. It was not so much that all ranks were removed as that all persons were members of the first rank, constitutive members of the sovereign body, subordinate to no one.

The French Revolution went through many perverse and malign episodes, and these have tainted the name of *citoyen*, so loudly shouted at that time. There can, anyway, be something covertly aggressive in the peremptory insistence on punctilious observance of all that is due to one as a citizen. Rousseau himself foresaw that liberty too easily won would readily breed insolence and become another form of tyranny. But there is nothing of this in his notion of citizenship. Since it is a title shared alike by all, it neither requires servitude nor licenses domination. It is only on the basis of this equality that the position of citizenship can truly be established. For if equality is removed, domination and subordination must take its place; and such a situation prevents reciprocal human and moral recognition between persons.

So although the name of citizen is open to abuse, the idea contained in it – that it is a proper part of human dignity that every member of a state has a guaranteed standing in it, denial of which is a fundamental moral wrong – remains a significant and influential one.

Sources: *DPE*
       E, Bk V
       SC, Bks I–III

Further reading: Gildin (123); Jimack (168); Mason (134); Masters, chs 2, 6 (69); Shklar, chs 1, 5 (36)

civilization In the first work of his maturity, the DISCOURSE ON THE SCIENCES AND THE ARTS, written in 1749–50 after the 'illumination' on his way to visit Diderot at Vincennes, Rousseau shows himself to be a critic of, even the enemy of, civilization. By civilization he understands, in a rather ill defined way, the growth of arts and letters; the introduction of refined manners and dress and elaborate social customs; the development of large cities as centres where many people enjoy leisure time, and hence the personal and social diversions which this both makes possible and demands. In his criticism of civilization he later attacks the growth of unthinking faith in the power of REASON, both in its technological employment and in its (supposed) scope for arranging the affairs of men; and questions the desirability of PROGRESS, which he sees as a matter of the increasing secularization of society and its organization on mercantile principles.

Rousseau is critical of all these aspects of modern life. He argues that the refinement of arts and letters is born of idleness, and serves not just as a diversion to fill empty time – which should be better employed – but also as a vehicle whereby people seek personal advancement and strive to show off their cleverness and wit to the detriment of others, often in the process destroying beliefs and customs central to their security and sense of meaning in life. Elaborate social customs, also, are designed to establish a basis for making invidious distinctions between people – as sophisticated, elegant and accomplished or lumpish, boorish and stupid. Such codes encourage affectation and the assumption of a way of life which estranges a person from what would be of real benefit to himself and to those around him (see ALIENATION).

Rousseau reserves some of his most stringent censure for life in large cities. These depend on the land for their maintenance, yet their populace despises the inhabitants of the country and does nothing but impoverish them. In cities, people are not intimately known to each other; many of their actions are concealed, and they hide behind masks. Conspicuous consumption (see LUXURY) and competition for prestigious ascendancy are the keynote of urban social life, leading people to corrupt themselves and to rejoice in the hurt they inflict on others. Sexual morality in cities is debauched, not only for reasons of ostentation but because social life is in general disorderly, and such behaviour does not impinge on settled relations – since there are none – and so does not attract the censure it deserves. Not least, those who live in cities are removed from the pure and simple delights of the country, where the peace of nature can refresh even the most jaded soul.

Recognizing, as part of the 'triumph' of civilization, a growing confidence in the limitless power and scope of reason, Rousseau holds that, on the contrary, there are many areas of life where reason is at best powerless and at worst destructive. People are not primarily motivated by rationally deduced convictions, he argues, but by passion and desire; it is idle, then, to try to govern and direct them by appeals to reason, however cogently presented. More specifically, religious conviction is principally a matter of faith, love and an intuitive feeling. Attempts to prove religious tenets by rational argument always fail, leading to endless conflict and concluding in a disabling scepticism and emptiness. And through a failure to direct people's sentiments and loyalties towards devoting their new scientific and technical powers to really beneficial ends, to the general good, the ingenious application of scientific advances to practical affairs has gone towards developing the luxury trade rather than improving basic amenities.

Towards the end of the *Second Discourse* (the DISCOURSE ON THE ORIGIN OF INEQUALITY), Rousseau pronounces a comprehensive indictment of 'civilized man':

> Civilized man ... is always moving, sweating, toiling ... and even seeks death to put himself in a position to live, or renounces life to acquire immortality. He pays court to men in power, whom he hates, and to the wealthy, whom he despises; he stops at nothing to have the honour of serving them ... proud of his slavery, he speaks with disdain of those who have not the honour of sharing it ... there are men who set a value on the opinion of the rest of the world; who can be made happy and satisfied with themselves rather on the testimony of other people than on their own ... always asking others what we are, and never daring to ask ourselves, in the midst of so much philosophy, humanity, and civilization, and of such sublime codes of morality, we have nothing to show for ourselves but a frivolous and deceitful appearance, honour without virtue, reason without wisdom, and pleasure without happiness. (*DI* 104; *OC* III, 192–3)

'Civilized' man is thus the virtual epitome of all that Rousseau sees as corrupt, malign and wasted.

It was when, having received a copy of the *Second Discourse*, Voltaire wrote to Rousseau thanking him for his essay against the human race, that he remarked that, having read it, he was half-moved to attempt walking on all fours again. Voltaire's famous comment displays one of the most common responses to Rousseau's criticisms of civilization: namely, that he is advocating a return to primitive nature, a retreat to the woods, and urging us to divest ourselves of all social habits and attributes so that we become once more like the animals. Despite Rousseau's frequent denials that he has any such thing in mind, this impression is still widespread (*see* NOBLE SAVAGE).

In fact, he thought that social life was inevitable for humans, and, indeed, essential to the development of full humanity; he had no doubt that it *could* be made creative and enlarging. His criticism was, rather, of those perverse developments in social life that produce quite the opposite

48

result. He is quite clear, even in the *First Discourse* (on the *Sciences and the Arts*) that there are those – he mentions Bacon, Descartes, Newton and Socrates among others – whose genius and discoveries have truly ennobled the human race and made more fruitful life possible for us. His complaint is against those who turn cultivated study to personal aggrandizement, and against societies in which such pseudo-learning is thought of as a distinguished achievement. There is nothing here of encouraging a return to acorn-gathering.

Other, more personal, criticisms were levelled against Rousseau for his attacks on civilization. When, soon after the completion of the *Second Discourse*, he left Paris to live in a cottage in the forest of Montmorency, several of his erstwhile companions, particularly Diderot and Grimm, viewed this as a gesture of personal affectation by which he was hoping to achieve that personal celebrity and distinction that he purported to despise. But by this time the differences between the basic attitudes of Rousseau and of these leading ENLIGHTENMENT figures were deepening. Rousseau had come to feel that they had a shallow and facile approach towards many issues, and he could no longer believe that his concerns would be recognized or understood by them.

Sources: *DI*
      DSA
      Émile et Sophie

Further reading: Horowitz, ch. 2 (27); Shklar, chs 1–2 (36)

comparison   Rousseau deploys the notion of comparison in two distinct ways in his writings, and it is important to maintain the distinction. In the first usage, making comparisons is seen as something that humans inevitably do, and that serves necessary and desirable purposes. In the other usage, he sees a concern with drawing comparisons as corrupt and damaging.

In assessments of Rousseau's arguments it is often supposed that all comparison-making is of this second kind. Commentators note that he also holds that drawing comparisons is inevitable, and so conclude that he thinks either that humans are condemned to corruption if they associate together and start making comparisons between themselves and others – as they are bound to do – or that the only way humans can preserve themselves intact is by withdrawing from society. This conclusion does not, however, follow, owing to a misconception about the significance of making comparisons. These commentators' determination to reach this particular conclusion is part of their overall concern to present Rousseau as maintaining the existence of a radical conflict between nature and society, between natural and social man; and he is then either praised or criticized for holding this view. In fact, he adopted no such simple position.

To return to the first notion of comparison: one of our purposes in gathering the relevant information that will enable us to act effectively in the world is to make accurate comparisons between ourselves and other things, and between those other things (objects, people, animals) themselves. Thus, it is essential if one is to move a heavy object that one compares one's strength against the weight to be shifted. It is useful to know, if one requires advice, that one person is more knowledgeable than another. What we are doing when we gather such information is simply equipping ourselves to live in a rightly understood world. It is inevitable that we should want such essential information.

In the DISCOURSE ON THE ORIGIN OF INEQUALITY (77–8; *OC* III, 165–6), having just introduced the above points, Rousseau moves to a further aspect which serves as a transition to the second sort of comparison that he considers. Humans note that they can outwit and outmanoeuvre the animals, even the largest and fiercest, and conclude that their species is 'of the highest order' – that it is 'the most advantageously organized of any' (*DI* 47; *OC* III, 135). This, he says, gives rise to 'the first emotion of pride', of pleasure and self-satisfaction at this generic excellence in power and ability. Here, the knowledge born of making comparisons is used not for practical purposes but as the basis for an estimate of one's worth. And it is this sort of comparison-seeking exercise that is central to the second type of comparison-making, the one that Rousseau censures.

Here, one draws comparisons in order to demonstrate to oneself that one is better, in some way or another, than other people. The basis for drawing such distinctions need not be real merit, but any personal difference that enables one person or group to compare themselves favourably with others, while at the same time enjoying others' chagrin. But a real merit can, equally, be turned to this purpose. For example, it is meritorious to help those in need. But this can be done in such a way as to make it clear that the real purpose of the act is ostentation, the desire to attract admiration for one's beneficence, making others, by comparison, appear mean and insignificant. Where CAPRICE pseudo-merits are concerned, the point is even more obvious. No personal merit is shown by wearing clothes bearing a particular label, or by attending some gala performance: all one is demonstrating is the desire to have comparisons drawn to one's own credit and to the detriment of others.

Finding, even inventing, such comparisons for such purposes is an expression of the obsession with superiority and with establishing the inferiority of others that comes from excessive AMOUR-PROPRE. Hatred and contempt for others is exhibited in these practices, and this is the reason why Rousseau is critical of them. But in order to avoid this perverse form of comparison-making there is no question of ceasing to make comparisons of any kind at all, or of removing oneself from situations where comparisons can be drawn – that is, by withdrawing from society. What matters, for Rousseau, is the purpose for which the comparison is drawn – and in some cases, the objective is entirely good and useful.

One final example should make the issues here quite clear. In *Émile*, Rousseau imagines the hero winning at running, thus revealing superiority. He maintains that it is wholly proper that Émile should think well of himself because of his achievement, but then goes on to explain carefully the exact character of this favourable self-estimate: 'He will not precisely say to himself, "I rejoice because they approve of me", but rather, "I rejoice because they approve of what I have done that is good. I rejoice that the people who honour me do themselves honour. So long as they judge so soundly, it will be a fine thing to obtain their esteem"' (*E* IV, 339; *OC* IV, 670–1). It is clear from this that Rousseau is not excluding comparison-making, nor the practice of basing self-approving judgements on such comparisons. What he is excluding is turning such comparisons to purposes of self-aggrandizement at the expense of others.

Sources: DI
      E, Bk IV

Further reading: Charvet, ch. 3 (23); Dent, ch. 3 (24); Veblen (301)

compassion (pity)   In the DISCOURSE ON THE ORIGIN OF INEQUALITY, Rousseau states that in addition to AMOUR DE SOI there is another 'principle prior to reason', which excites in us 'a natural repugnance at seeing any other sensible being, and particularly any of our own species, suffer pain or death' (*DI* 41; *OC* III, 126). It is from the 'combination and agreement' of these two principles, he goes on, that are derived 'all the rules of natural right' – which appear, though erroneously, to need a foundation in reason. He says little more in the *Discourse* about the basis, nature and functions of this repugnance, which is a disposition for compassion, or pity, but he states that this feeling has the potential to combat the evils brought on by excessive AMOUR-PROPRE. However, it is a disposition rather readily extinguished in civilized man (see *DI* 66–9; *OC* III, 153–7). He stresses, though, that compassion is a natural feeling and that, prior to the use of reason or force of law or the exercise of conscious virtue, it has the power to move us to acts of generosity, clemency and gentleness – all of which are pleasurable to us.

51

Rousseau returns to the topic in Bk IV of ÉMILE, where compassion emerges as the most fundamental factor on which he hopes to ground the possibility and actuality of creative, cooperative and humane relations between persons, on an individual and on a social scale. In compassion we find the basis for an alternative form of human relationship to that established by the combative, competitive and aggressive concerns which petulant *amour-propre* gives rise to. Through the influence of pity, people may come to feel benevolent concern for each other, and want to live together in mutual support. Human society could then be an aid and a blessing instead of the blight and source of suffering that, in Rousseau's estimation, it so often is.

To extend compassionate concern is a way of becoming aware of and sensitive to another's state of mind, and hence of being drawn into a relationship of mutual awareness and response; it is a very different way from that characterized by the desire for ascendancy over others which *amour-propre* brings with it. Compassionate concern enters the same territory as *amour-propre*: that is, it comprises a route by which humans engage with the most fraught and complex issue – that of finding a footing for themselves in the lives, feelings and concerns of other people. No issue is more decisive for the individual's life prospects. If it can be resolved satisfactorily, the prospects for a rewarding, constructive and happy life are immeasurably enhanced, both for the individual and for those he comes into contact with. It is through the settlement of pity, Rousseau believes, that this satisfactory resolution can be achieved.

Although, in Rousseau's view, the capacity for compassionate concern for the suffering of others is innate, this does not mean that this capacity will develop, or that the disposition for compassion will dominate a person's habitual attitudes and responses to others, without guidance and cultivation. Thus, he argues, it is important, if compassion is to become a habitual response, that a person first gain experience of others in situations where his own good is not at risk, where he is not likely to be taken advantage of, where he is not going to feel 'put down'. Only then will he feel the confidence and trust that he needs in order to heed and act on the promptings of pity, and not ignore or silence them for fear of some loss or exploitation.

According to Rousseau, in a compassionate response one 'identifies' with the suffering person who is the object of concern. His use of this term has led some critics to say that the feeling of pity abolishes the distinction between persons, and so does not establish any real relationship between distinct individuals – which Rousseau intends to be seen to be the case. This is a misunderstanding. What he means is that, moved by pity, one aids the sufferer with the same immediacy and spontaneity as one would seek to relieve *oneself* of pain. One's readiness to help is not mediated through thoughts of reciprocity or reward. In this sense only, one takes on another's pain as if it were one's own; there is no loss of awareness of the separateness of the other self. Indeed, Rousseau says that one reason why helping a person who is suffering is often not felt as an imposition is that his relative weakness gives us a quickened sense of our own strength and well-being, which we take pleasure in expressing. This would hardly make sense if any genuine amalgamation of self and other had occurred.

One further aspect of this elementary compassionate concern is of particular significance for Rousseau. In the first instance, the attention of the sufferer is absorbed in his own distress; he pays no special regard to, has no primary interest in, his helper. The helper is thus able to establish his presence in relation to the sufferer without any judgement or appraisal being made of him by the sufferer. In this way, the need to 'cut a figure' before the sufferer's appraising gaze is eliminated; the combative self-assertion of *amour-propre* lacks occasion.

Of course, matters do not conclude at this primary level. It is natural, Rousseau goes on, for the person who is aided to feel gratitude towards his helper. Providing the aid is given spontaneously, without any covert design to obligate or to enforce subservience – as often enough happens – there is room for an equally spontaneous and unconstrained expression of friendly gratitude. Now the helper is indeed being appraised by the other; an estimate is being made of his value and significance to that other. And the verdict will be that he is good and kind, that he is an aid and not a threat, a support and not an attacker. Thus, the compassionate person learns not only that he has the power to act effectively in regard to others, but that he has value and meaning for them and is the object of their favourable regard. The sufferer, too, learns that he is honoured and valued. As well as his pain being relieved, he himself was left free to respond to his helper in any way that seemed fit to him. His weakened state was in no way used as a means to humiliate or nullify him. Rather, he was restored as an intact person whose attitudes and responses were afforded weight and value.

Rousseau emphasizes that if this many-layered relationship of recipro-cal care and regard is to be sustained it is essential that roles be reversed from time to time. Circumstances will normally bring this about natu-rally, but if not, the role reversal must be contrived; otherwise, the helper's compassionate response will become muddied by, for instance, the idea that he is exempt from the common human lot of pain and weakness, or that the frailties of others reveal their inferiority. Such deluded beliefs will distance the helper from other people and make him insensitive to their needs – or, worse, will make him gloat over his own charmed position. On the other hand, one who is always helped and never allowed to give help may be apt to feel that he is powerless and that there is nothing in him to command the good opinion of others. Rousseau is never so naïve as to suppose that such patterns of reciprocal loving concern will flourish unimpeded. If anything, he is over-concerned about the distortions and deformations they may suffer.

If positions are reversed, then, and the gestures of help and the grateful responses can be made without impediment, a steady and enduring bond of mutual confidence and esteem will slowly be established. Each person will feel that he has real power to be constructive in his dealings with the other, and is valued and honoured for it; and each will feel that he is cherished and that his thankful response is valued by his carer. The need of each to mean something to and for another person – the need inherent in *amour-propre* in its non-distorted form, in fact – is met through such a relationship. So, in Rousseau's definitive argument, it is not that relations established through compassion displace those established through *amour-propre*: rather, the former provide the only effective way whereby the need for recognition and honour that *amour-propre* demands can be met. It is only when that need becomes excessive that feelings of pity will be an *alternative* to the inflamed passions of *amour-propre*. Only in a relationship between equals, where each values and esteems the other and each feels his own value and power, can real human recognition be found.

Rousseau develops his argument within a very restricted framework – namely, in terms of a relationship established between two individuals. However, such a relationship can readily apply on a broader scale – indeed, it can involve any persons or groups, providing there exists the potential for feeling a sense of common cause and common human predicament. In this way, he thinks, we find the root of the golden rule, 'Do unto others as you would have them do unto you' – not in rational principles devised by the intellect, but in sentiments emanating from the heart. In addition, such sentiments provide a basis for a commitment to JUSTICE: the desire that all shall receive their due as worthy bearers of dignity and recipients of honour.

The extensibility of these sentiments of loving regard is not, however, indefinite, in Rousseau's view; or, rather, the more widely they extend beyond friends and fellows, the more apt they are to be silenced or deflected by other, intrusive, factors. This is one reason why he thinks that, if we are to have a society in which there is real care and commitment to the well-being of all, by all, then that society should be small, and people should be able to feel their common destiny and share a sense of common inheritance. It is possible that Rousseau underestimated the human capacity to broaden the horizon of concern to incorporate the fate of those with whom we have nothing in common other than being human and feeling pain. On the other hand, we do not need to be cynical to appreciate that in many gestures of aid, particularly governmental, there is more than a fair degree of attention to national self-advantage, as well as a readiness to find reasons for applying the most stringent discrimination in distributing even the little that is given. And on a more intellectual plane, no one has yet been able to offer a cogent rational argument in favour of universal justice to all alike. For Rousseau to rest his case on the extensibility of sentiments may not, then, be so ill advised.

Rousseau discusses compassion and its allied phenomena with a firmness of purpose, a control of detail and a subtlety without sophistry that make his argument a *tour de force*. His insights into the subject are central to an understanding of his position on many questions regarding the individual, society and the state. Rousseau himself thought *Émile* was his most profound work: one reason for sharing that view is his treatment of this issue.

Sources: DI
    E, Bk IV

Further reading: Bloom (163); Charvet, ch. 3 (23); Dent, ch. 4 (24); Grimsley, chs 3–5 (26); Masters, ch. 3 (69); Orwin (274); Shklar, ch. 2 (36)

Confessions, The (written *c.* 1764–76; published 1782/1789) (*Les Confessions*) [18]   In late 1761 Rousseau's usual publisher, Marc-Michel Rey, urged him to write his autobiography. At first he did not warm to the idea, but none the less he made some rough notes about himself at this time and at intervals over the next two years. (Whether these fragments all date from this time is disputed; they have been collected together under the title, *Mon Portrait* (*OC* I).) Clearly, Rey's suggestion had touched a chord, and Rousseau began to assemble copies of letters and other items of information so that he could begin serious work on the project that was to become *The Confessions*.

It is difficult to know what his work pattern was. He would take up the manuscript, and then leave it for long periods; some parts went through several versions, others were scarcely revised at all. It would appear that he had made a serious start by late 1764, and he continued to work intermittently on Part 1 (which takes us up to 1741–2, when he went to Paris) during his stay in England, having more or less completed it by the time he had returned to France and was staying at Trye in the spring of 1767.

Part 2 (covering the years 1742–65) was begun at Monquin in 1769, and was completed by June 1770 when Rousseau had returned for the last time to Paris. He originally planned a third part, bringing the narrative up to 1770, but this was abandoned – no doubt partly because his readings to friends of the first two parts had been banned, under pressure from those who feared they would be harmed by Rousseau's story. Neither Part 1 (Bks I–VI) nor Part 2 (Bks VII–XII) was published in his lifetime; they appeared separately to begin with, in 1782 and 1789 respectively, the first complete edition of *The Confessions* as we now know it not appearing until 1796.

The question of the accuracy of Rousseau's narrative is often raised: as regards bare matters of fact, where these can be checked he is found to be by and large accurate; though on some points – for example, how long it was before he abjured Protestantism when he was in Turin (described in Bk II) – he gets it wrong, and probably for emotional reasons. Accuracy is hardly a relevant criterion, however, when it comes to examining his self-evaluations, interpretations of significance, judgements of others' motives. We may perceive the kind of sense that he was attempting to make of himself and his life. We may think that some of his interpretations are self-serving or self-deceiving. But all these matters require judgement, and we are not necessarily impartial enough or well enough placed to make a definitive assessment. Few people have attempted to do what Rousseau did with quite the same candour; and those few have scarcely succeeded as well as he.

The book opens with a proud and defiant declaration:

I have resolved on an enterprise which has no precedent, and which, once complete, will have no imitator. My purpose is to display to my kind a portrait in every way true to nature, and the man I shall portray is myself . . . I shall come forward with this work in my hand, to present myself before my Sovereign Judge . . . let the numberless legion of my fellow men gather round me, and hear my confessions. Let them groan at my depravities, and blush for my misdeeds. But let each one of them reveal his heart at the foot of Thy throne with equal sincerity, and may any man who dares, say 'I was a better man than he.' (Bk I, 17; *OC* I, 5)

Rousseau then proceeds to recount, often with tenderness, sometimes with wit, occasionally with alarming honesty, the main events of the first twenty-nine years of his life, until, leaving the scenes of his childhood behind him, he attempted to establish himself as a man of letters in Paris in 1741–2. He tells, for example, of how he and his father – the one motherless, the other deprived of his wife – would stay up until dawn, reading; and how his father, telling stories about Jean-Jacques' mother, would end in floods of tears. In passages of considerable beauty he evokes the delights of the country and the joys of boyhood friendship experienced when he was staying with his cousin at Bossey. But he also describes, with great directness, the erotic pleasure he got from Mlle Lambercier's beatings, which fixed his sexual proclivities for life. (She was the sister of the pastor with whom he and his cousin were living.) And in a passage of more sombre force he tells how he was falsely accused of breaking the teeth of a comb, and how his resentment of this unjust charge made him suspicious, furtive, deceitful. This seemingly trivial incident, more than any sexual precocity, constituted Rousseau's real loss of innocence. This same resentment, which he insists is not intrinsic to his nature but forced on him by the abuse he suffered from others, deepened during his apprenticeship to the engraver Ducommun, a position which Rousseau dramatically left when, finding the gates of Geneva closed against him, he walked away from the city in March 1728.

In Bk II, Rousseau prepares the reader, with conscious artistry, for his first meeting with Mme de Warens. Details of the hour, the setting, are all assembled to give this fateful occasion a proper dramatic impact. He tells of his time in Turin, not disguising the sodomitical practices of his fellow-converts, and of the various adventures he had while there. Within the same few months he is to be found prostrate before Mme Basile (with whom he lodged for a while) in mute adoration, but also exposing himself to unsuspecting women in the town. One of the most significant episodes of his moral history took place in Turin. When the Comtesse de Vercellis died, an inventory of her effects was taken. A ribbon was missing; Rousseau had taken it but, when asked, lied and accused another servant, Marion, of the theft. Why did he lie? Shame, embarrassment? Whether we accept his pleas in self-exculpation or not, it is impossible not to be moved by the intensity with which he evokes this episode, the feelings it aroused, and the agonized wranglings he had with himself over it (Bk II).

Several parts of the narrative are given over to Rousseau's accounts of his pleasure in idle walking, unpressured by time or business. His writing at such moments has genuine beauty, and he infuses the scenes he depicts with delight and sweetness. The same joy, and quick humour as well, pervade his description of the day of unalloyed pleasure spent picnicking in a cherry orchard and engaging in half-amorous play with Mlles Galley and de Graffenried (Bk IV). Much less full of unimpeded delight is his sexual initiation at the hands of Mme de Warens in 1733; the strange incestuous feelings this brought out are forcefully conveyed. Set against this is his one taste of untrammelled sexual delight, with Mme de Larnage (a vivacious fellow-passenger on one of Rousseau's journeys), while he was pretending – for the most ridiculous reasons – to be an Englishman, a 'Mr Dudding'. The reader shares Rousseau's remembered

57

pleasure at this episode, and perhaps also wishes that he had enjoyed better fortune in this regard.

One aspect of *The Confessions* over which commentators consistently accuse Rousseau of falsification is his discovery of the usurpation (as he saw it) of his place in Mme de Warens' household by Wintzenried (Bk VI). Clearly there is great bitterness and misery in his memories of this, and it likely that he modified some of his recollections to make the loss more tolerable and to retain some sense of personal purpose as he attempted to recover a viable life course for himself. Part 1 concludes with Rousseau leaving Mme de Warens finally almost jauntily, to make his way in the great social whirlpool of Paris.

Although some of Part 1 was being revised and rewritten during periods when Rousseau was suffering great mental distress and paranoiac delusions, this is scarcely noticeable in the text, which is marked by an extraordinary clarity and an ease and simplicity of expression. Part 2, on the other hand, was never properly revised, so that the writing is clumsier and more prolix. In many asides he speaks of the threats and darkness that surround him, and – often exclaiming over his trusting innocence of days gone by – he tends to see sinister and devious plots underlying past dealings with those he regarded as his friends. Much of this Part is given over to analysis and explanation of schemes and ploys he sees as directed against him, and the lightness of touch so striking in Part 1 is largely absent.

For the rest of Part 2, the narrative follows Rousseau's affairs over the years 1742–65. We hear of his attempts to establish himself as a composer and music theorist; of his triumph with his opera *Le Devin du Village*, and his declining a pension from the King – 'I was freeing myself from the dependence it would have imposed upon me' (Bk VIII). He describes his time in Venice as secretary to the French ambassador where, despite many, for once, real provocations, he appears to have behaved in a level-headed fashion; and Bk VIII includes a report of another disastrous sexual encounter.

In his account of his stay at the Hermitage in 1756–7 (Bk IX) he evokes the intense dreams and feelings which preceded his writing of *La Nouvelle Héloïse*. But many of his recollections are shot through with doubts and suspicions. It is particularly his passion for Sophie d'Houdetot that he sees as fateful – 'As it was the first and only love in all my life, and as through its consequences it will ever remain a terrible and indelible memory to me, may I be forgiven for describing it in some detail' (Bk IX, 408; *OC* I, 438–9). He was convinced that gossip and scandal about his liaison were being put about, and it was no coincidence that his friendships with Mme d'Épinay, Diderot and Grimm suffered irreversible damage at this time.

When real disasters overtook Rousseau, such as those that followed the publication of *Émile* and *The Social Contract*, he recounts them in a straightforward enough fashion. As is often the way with those suffering from morbid suspicions, a genuine difficulty serves to return him to the real world, and for a while he recovers a stable sense of himself and his situation. But this clarity of mind did not endure. Bk XII starts with the words:

> 1762.   Here begins the work of darkness in which I have been entombed for eight years past, without ever having been able, try as I might, to pierce its hideous obscurity. In the abyss of evil in which I am sunk I feel the weight of blows struck at me; I perceive the immediate instrument; but I can neither see the hand which directs it nor the means by which it works. (Bk XII, 544; *OC* I, 589)

Yet there are still moments of repose and delight: he takes obvious pleasure, for instance, in the few days he spent botanizing and idling on the island of St-Pierre in Lake Bienne, just before he went to England with Hume in 1766, where he was to suffer some of his darkest days of mental disturbance. Part 2 concludes as he sets out to be enmeshed in these toils of intrigue, as he saw them. (What these were is outlined in the section 'Rousseau's life and works' at the start of this Dictionary.)

As a self-portrait, as the story of a life, as a narrative of events and feelings, *The Confessions* is a deeply arresting work – indeed, it is generally regarded as a masterpiece. Perhaps its most singular aspect is its powerful evocation of the drama of individual existence. Rousseau is often credited with being one of the instigators of Romanticism, but this term is of such diffuse significance that it is difficult to evaluate such a view. Although he tells us of the main public events of his life, it is not his standing as a figure in the history of affairs that he treats as paramount, but the meaning and value of those events as episodes in his emotional and moral destiny. Aside from those passages of obsessive self-concern where Rousseau writes with a troubled mind, *The Confessions* is neither tediously self-absorbed nor the depiction of a case-history. Rather, we sense here the extraordinary force of the presence of another living being; we witness the celebration of the miracle of existence.

Further reading: Ellis (172); France (173); Grimsley (176); Hartle (178); Williams (184)

conscience Nowhere in his writings does Rousseau give a full and systematic account of the nature and functions of conscience, although there is no doubt that he considered it a very important element in man's moral and spiritual make-up. (He makes most of his significant points concerning conscience in THE CREED OF A SAVOYARD VICAR in Bk IV of *Émile*).

Rousseau does not see conscience as the exclusive source of moral understanding and moral motivation in human beings. He thinks that the sentiments of COMPASSION, for example, can direct us towards generosity, clemency and justice without recourse to the guidance of conscience (see *E* IV, 235; *OC* IV, 522–3); interestingly, these sentiments probably have the same root in our nature as conscience has in Rousseau's view. He gives a loose definition of conscience in the middle of the Vicar's creed: 'There is in the depths of souls . . . an innate principle of justice and virtue according to which, in spite of our own maxims, we judge our actions and those of others as good or bad. It is to this principle that I give the name *conscience*' (*E* IV, 289; *OC* IV, 598).

First, Rousseau tries to prove that there is in all of us the capacity to admire and to rejoice in acts of justice, of kindness and of moral beauty, even when we ourselves have nothing to gain from them and are not involved with any of the parties to them. Except when the intrusion of personal interest masks or silences these feelings, there is no man who is not moved by such acts, or outraged by cruelty and iniquity. This same capacity for disinterested esteem for justice and good is found in all ages and places. It cannot, therefore, be simply the product of experience; it must be an innate capacity, even if it requires experience and maturity to awaken it.

Rousseau then asks what the presence of this capacity reveals about us, and on what basis it functions. Conscience is to the soul, he says, what instinct is to the body: it is man's true guide. How is this?

It is an element of Rousseau's faith – not so much something known and rationally demonstrable as deeply felt and believed in – that God by his power, goodness and love has ordered man and the universe providentially. It is true that man enjoys FREEDOM to choose good or evil; but if he chooses good, he can be assured that the good he desires to do will be in accord with the good order that God has created in him and in his relations with his world, and that he will not be the loser by doing that good. It is, then, Rousseau's view that the 'voice' of conscience is an expression, an awareness, of the demands of this proper inner order of man, which constitutes his true need and good and directs him to act well in accord with God's overall providential design for all human beings.

The voice of conscience is not a direct, personal revelation of the will of God to any one individual. Rather, it is the echo in everyone's soul of the harmony that exists in the depths of the human personality and that, if listened to, will inspire man to proceed with God's loving work by his own actions.

> The good man orders himself in relation to the whole, and the wicked one orders the whole in relation to himself. The latter makes himself the centre of all things; the former measures himself and keeps to the circumference. Then he is ordered in relation to the common centre, which is God, and in relation to all the concentric circles, which are the creatures. (*E* IV, 292; *OC* IV, 602)

Rousseau does not underestimate the difficulties in being certain that what one is hearing are the directions of one's intact being, following God's good design for all. The clamour of the passions, the urgent demands of the senses, the sophistical ingenuities of reason, can drown this 'still, small voice', or can, perhaps, be mistaken for it. But he remains convinced that the directions of conscience are accessible if one will open oneself with sincerity and humility to the promptings of one's soul. It may not be so easy for us to share his confidence about this, not only because we may doubt that there is a God but because we may also doubt that awareness of His providential purpose for us is achievable in this way.

Rousseau expresses thus his own confidence: 'I have only to consult myself about what I want to do. Everything I sense to be good is good; everything I sense to be bad is bad' (*E* IV, 286; *OC* IV, 594). A rash thing to say, perhaps, but it takes a peculiar perversity to read this – as has in fact been done – as Rousseau's claiming that he is the creator and arbiter of good and evil in his own person and thus above obedience to any moral law. What in fact he is saying is that, in the most essential sense, he does not belong to himself; the character of his proper destiny and duty is printed in his very constitution – all that remains for him to do is to recognize this and freely to elect to follow its dictates.

It is now possible to see how it comes about that sentiments engendered by compassion and the promptings of conscience have, in the end, a common root for Rousseau: in both cases, it is our own constitution directing us to follow our own nature and good that is being expressed. In the case of conscience, it is the requirements of our whole nature as an element in God's design that is becoming manifest, whereas in the case of compassion it is only one part of the whole. But both derive from the good order which makes for harmony between the good proper to each individual, each individual's good acts, and promoting the good of others.

Rousseau's conviction that this harmony makes the best sense of moral action finds its most impassioned expression in this declamation:

> Conscience, conscience! Divine instinct, immortal and celestial voice, certain guide of being that is ignorant and limited but intelligent and free; infallible judge of good and bad which makes man like unto God; it is you who make the excellence of his nature and the morality of his actions. Without you I sense nothing in me that raises me above the beasts, other than the sad privilege of leading myself astray from error to error with the aid of an understanding without rule and a reason without principle. (*E* IV, 290; *OC* IV, 600–1)

He speaks virtually the same words in his MORAL LETTERS to Sophie d'Houdetot (Fifth Letter), which also discusses the nature and role of conscience.

At one point in the *Creed* Rousseau says: 'If the divinity does not exist, it is only the wicked man who reasons, and the good man is nothing but a fool' (*E* IV, 292; *OC* IV, 602). In this more secular age, this is perhaps our fear – from which Rousseau's account of the significance of conscience may not, in the end, save us.

Sources: *E*, Bk IV
       Moral Letters

Further reading: Blum (21); Dent, ch. 7 (24); Grimsley (187); Horowitz, ch. 6 (27); Masters, ch. 2 (69)

Considerations on the Government of Poland (*Considérations sur le Gouvernement de Pologne*) (written 1770–1; published 1782) [19] Working from information about contemporary conditions, social structures and political procedures supplied to him by Count Wielhorski, Rousseau proposes, in this work, many ways of conserving, strengthening and enriching the social and political integrity of Poland. His suggestions cover such matters as education, the social classes, the composition and procedures of the legislative and administrative bodies, the army, and the position of the King.

Since 1764 Poland had been ruled by a king elected under Russian pressure, and it now appeared that it was destined to be absorbed by Russia. In 1768, however, a group of powerful landowners began to resist Russian domination and established a confederation, the Confederation of Bar, of which Wielhorski was a representative. The influence of the Confederation steadily increased. In 1769 it called members from all parts of Poland to an assembly, which commissioned Wielhorski to approach

Rousseau, among others in France, for proposals for amending the Polish constitution in such a way that Poland would be able to retain its integrity and independence against foreign annexation. Rousseau's suggestions were not taken up, so we cannot know if they would have been effective. The Confederation did not survive, and by 1795 Poland had ceased to exist as a single nation, having been divided between Russia, Prussia and others – a fate it was to suffer again on subsequent occasions.

Many have seen Rousseau's essay as another attempt (*see* CORSICA) to play the role of LEGISLATOR. It is clear, though, that this was not his concern. In fact, it is the customs, tastes, habits and prejudices (in Burke's sense) of the Polish people that give them a sense of themselves as a single, distinctive people who aspire to sustain a common identity and national independence. Rousseau attaches key importance to idiosyncratic customs and tastes; the governing idea which pervades his argument is the need to extend and intensify these so that they reach into the hearts of all Poles and make love of their country and loyalty to the maintenance of their nation their most precious concern. His remarks sometimes verge on the rhapsodic:

> Every true republican has drunk in love of country, that is to say love of law and liberty, along with his mother's milk. This love is his whole existence; he sees nothing but the fatherland, he lives for it alone; when he is solitary, he is nothing; when he has ceased to have a fatherland, he no longer exists; and if he is not dead, he is worse than dead. (*GP*, ch. 4, 'Education'; *OC* III, 966)

Rousseau emphasizes – or, as some will see it, alarmingly overemphasizes – public loyalty and love of the 'fatherland' for three reasons. First, without these a country is vulnerable to foreign influence and invasion, leading to the people's dispossession and oppression by others who have no concern for their distinctive way of life. Second, without these sentiments people will place their private concerns, or their own and those of just a few others, above the concerns of the rest in their society, towards whom they will be indifferent or whom they will exploit. In such a situation, the people belong to one common society only in name. If love of country is not a foremost concern, then it will be the fate of many – possibly all, in the case of foreign invasion – to be effectively enslaved, disinherited, deracinated.

These considerations lead to the third, more positive, strand in Rousseau's thinking. He claims that love of country is a necessary condition for the maintenance and enjoyment of common liberty and of equitable law for all alike. And only if all alike feel a dominant concern for their homeland will they not merely tolerate, but positively want, social and constitutional institutions which will guarantee that the needs and the good of all persons, seen as their fellows in common cause, will be respected and honoured. For any one Pole to be dispossessed or harmed will be a hurt to all, since that person's well-being is a shared concern. Where a sense of common identity is not all-powerful, the fate of such a person may become separated from the fate of the rest, and he is then no longer regarded as a real, constitutive member of the society.

It is these ideas that structure the whole of Rousseau's discussion. His suggested amendments to educational practices, to systems of honours, to membership of legislative and administrative bodies and so on, are made with these points in view. He proposes, for instance, that payments for public service be minimized, since money foments private interest and creates a society in which anything or anyone is merely an object available for purchase. Instead, he says, people should be recompensed with produce, and by work done on their behalf. The corvée should take the place of taxes.

Rousseau recognizes that in a society such as Poland with a long-established and deeply rooted social hierarchy, where the present system sanctifies oppression, it will take more than a moment to introduce laws that will secure equal liberty and protection for all. Not only will the noble classes object to the achievement of citizen status by the serfs, but the serfs themselves – brutalized over centuries – will find in the removal of familiar patterns of authority and control only the occasion for anarchic destruction. Law alone, without the appropriate sentiments to support it, can achieve nothing. Rousseau recommends only a very gradual process of manumission, accompanied by intensive education to prepare the serfs for their new role of maintainers of the 'law of liberty'.

He never compromises his view that there remains a 'law of nature, that holy and imprescriptible law, which speaks to the heart and reason of man', which does not allow legislative authority to be restricted, 'nor does it allow laws to be binding on anyone who has not voted for them in person'. However,

> liberty is a food easy to eat, but hard to digest; it takes very strong stomachs to stand it . . . To free the common people of Poland would be a great and worthy enterprise, but bold, perilous, and not to be attempted lightly . . . But whatever happens, remember that your serfs are men like you, that they have in themselves the capacity to become all that you are. (*GP*, ch. 6; *OC* III, 947; *see* AUTHORITY)

For the Poles, Rousseau sees the country's great size and the wide dispersal of the people as two of the greatest difficulties in the way of establishing a powerful national identity and love of country. These factors make it hard for any idea of common destiny and loyalty to unite them. To resolve the difficulty, he advocates the principle of federation, as being developed at the time by the members of the Confederation of Bar. Federation will enable people to retain a strong and palpable sense of common life in their localities, while coordinating their objectives for common protection under a central constitution: 'This federative form of action, although it may have arisen by accident, strikes me as a political masterpiece' (*GP*, ch. 9, 218; *OC* III, 998). He recognizes the pressures towards break-up that are present in any confederative association, but believes that it can be made to work without either turning into a centralized dictatorship or disintegrating.

Although Rousseau believes that, for a law to be ultimately legitimate, all who live under it must agree to it, he recognizes that this is not feasible in Poland. Legislative progress is made very difficult there in many areas of public policy by the fact that a single member of the legislative body can exercise the right of veto – and this frequently happens. So, having examined how laws are actually passed in Poland (ch. 9), he proposes some amendments which at first appear contrary to the spirit of his declared principles: he proposes, *inter alia*, restricting the right of veto.

Though it may surprise, this proposal may not be at all inconsistent with Rousseau's view. He makes a rough distinction (also to be found in THE SOCIAL CONTRACT) between 'fundamental laws' which define the very terms of association which establish the body politic; 'ordinary' acts of legislation, concerning the prosperity and good conduct of the state; and 'mere acts of administration'. In regard to the first, unanimity is required, so a single dissenting voice would be sufficient to prevent a law being passed. However, no person should dissent for capricious or self-interested reasons. Indeed, he who dissents must show grave cause before a court of distinguished citizens, who will either condemn him to death for paralysing the public will of the nation, or compensate him with public honours for life. Although the means are ruthless, the point is cogent enough: Rousseau is trying to ensure that those who dissent do so wholly on the basis of concern for the common weal; and that it is their public or social concerns, not some hope of individual advantage, that make them draw back. For it is the terms and conditions that will establish the same social standing for all that are at stake.

As far as ordinary legislative acts are concerned, majorities of three quarters or two thirds may be called for, depending on the gravity of the issue. Only in respect of the least serious issues does a bare majority suffice. It may be objected that Rousseau does not establish a procedure for determining the gravity of issues. He might well reply that, if no consensus can be achieved on such a simple point, then the possibility of ever undertaking legislation of any degree of gravity is so slight as to make the prospects for the survival of the state – or of its creation – negligible.

Attentive as he is here to the exigences of practical statecraft, at the same time Rousseau is considering the practicalities of obtaining the assent of the people in such a way as to achieve the highest possible level of willing concurrence. Some of his ideas may well be impractical or misconceived; but he reveals in this essay the sense inherent in, and the potential for the feasible application of, his more abstract political theorizing.

Further reading: Barnard (151); Cohler (152); Dent, ch. 6 (24); Masters, ch. 8 (69)

contract Rousseau employs the idea of contract in two contexts. The first, less significant, occurs at Émile's first encounter with the idea of contractual exchange as a basis for regulating and coordinating human activity. In the episode of the uprooted beans, recounted in Bk II of ÉMILE, he introduces the primitive basis for ownership (the right of the first occupant by labour): the gardener Robert has the right through his work to use a corner of the garden. To this Rousseau adds a 'clear, distinct, simple' idea of exchange, whereby Émile can have and retain some property and goods on condition that the same is permitted to Robert. A simple contract is thus established between them. Rousseau presents this as a robust and effective basis – which functions in the light of clear interest and realistic recognition of the practical necessities of the situation – whereby cooperation and accommodation between persons can be achieved. He is insistent that contractual duties should not be seen as impositions: if so, the attempt to evade them will only encourage cheating and trickery. Rather, they should be seen as the obvious terms whereby several persons, each with his own proper interests, can reach a sensible, and profitable, accommodation with each other.

Rousseau then generalizes on the basis of this 'lesson' to argue that material exchange is a fundamental component in and ground for all human association, and should be understood as one of the basic elements of any society. No one, he claims, can or should expect to receive goods and services from others gratis, let alone as if were his title. Everyone should equip himself, if he can, with skills and resources to make himself useful and valuable to others, at least at the level of having some 'product' he can offer in exchange for others:

> The ideas of social relations are formed little by little in a child's mind, even before he can really be an active member of society. Émile sees that, in order

to have instruments for his use, he must in addition have instruments for the use of other men with which he can obtain in exchange the things which are necessary to him and are in their power. (*E* III, 193; *OC* IV, 467)

Ultimately, Rousseau says, 'A man and a citizen, whoever he may be, has no property to put into society other than himself' (*E* III, 195; *OC* IV, 469). This is the ineluctable context of our dealings with others, and exchange is a fundamental form that such dealings take.

It does not follow from this that contractual relations are the sole form of intercourse between persons in society: obviously, such is not the character of loving relations or familial ties. But we need to consider whether the bond of union of several persons together in one *civil* body is contractual in character. This leads to the second context in which Rousseau employs the notion of contract: namely, in the interpretation of the basic character of the tie which binds people together as common subjects of a body of laws.

The very fact that the title of Rousseau's most famous work of political theory is The Social Contract should suggest to us that he saw the human union embodied in one civil order as basically contractual in character. Thus, the basic terms of the social contract (or compact) whereby civil association is instituted come to this: 'Each of us puts his person and all his power in common under the supreme direction of the general will, and, in our corporate capacity, we receive each member as an indivisible part of the whole' (*SC* I, ch. 6, 175; *OC* III, 361). This he calls an 'act of association'.

There are clear echoes here of the more explicit and detailed accounts of mutual promises and undertakings lying, supposedly, at the root of civil institution and obligation given by Hobbes and Locke (in *Leviathan* and in the *Second Treatise on Civil Government*, respectively). This lends colour to Marx's criticism of Rousseau that, despite having claimed not to have 'transferred to the state of nature ideas which were acquired in society' (*DI* 45; *OC* III, 132), he none the less utilizes the framework of ideas that is proper not to man as such but to bourgeois man only (Marx, *Introduction to a Critique of Political Economy*). But Rousseau's lack of explicit detail is unlikely to be accidental; nor did he really see the bond of union between persons as members of a single civil association as contractual in character.

Two points appear to be central to the idea of a civil contract. First, that obligation is generated through a voluntary act like promising (or by giving adequate signs that such an act has been or will be carried out). And, second, that prior to the contract each contractee has certain property and rights which he will trade (in part or whole) in order to better secure his possession (in an altered form) of these and, possibly, additional advantages. In both these respects, contracting posits a relation between persons whereby each is independent of the other and undertakes to accommodate and cooperate with that other only for personal advantage, understood in terms of advancing his good still as an independent person, albeit one who needs to negotiate with the other.

It is clear, however, that Rousseau does not envisage this as a character proper to persons united in civil society. In his view, personal advantage, understood in terms of the advancement of one's good as a separate unconnected person, is and must be transcended in some major respects if a just and worthwhile community is to result. People must, in his view, come to see themselves (not exclusively, but dominantly) as sustaining members of the common polity, as CITIZENS, not as private individuals whose foremost concerns lie aside from or in conflict with the common weal. The ability and disposition to share the promotion and maintenance of a common valuable life is a precondition of, and is further sustained by, the formation of a civil association (see especially *SC* II, ch. 7, concerning the LEGISLATOR).

Rousseau consistently holds that if people in society retain a dominant sense that their own advantage lies apart from the maintenance of law and equity for all, they will, at the very least, constantly resent what they see as nothing but demands imposed on them for the sake of others they care nothing for but cannot do without. And that will, he thinks, soon lead to the perversion of law for private or factional advantage, or to the evasion of law, or to the dissolution of the civil association. The very willingness to observe the terms of a mutual promise – which no power or law can alone enforce – expresses a willingness to honour and respect those to whom one has promised. And this shows at least a minimal willingness to acknowledge the human significance of the other person, and to incorporate this as material to one's own concerns. Rousseau most fully expresses these points in a chapter of *The Social Contract* omitted from the final version, normally known as 'The general society of the human race' (see, especially, pp. 158–9; *OC* III, 284–5); (A DISCOURSE ON) POLITICAL ECONOMY also goes into these issues in greater depth.

If, then, we see contractual relations in this way, we cannot say that Rousseau maintains that the basis for a just, humane society is contractual. It is perhaps possible to say that the 'act of association' is, in Hegel's terms regarding marriage, 'a contract to transcend the standpoint of contract' (Hegel, *Philosophy of Right*, section 163), but this may be straining words to no good purpose. Although it may appear paradoxical to say so, *The Social Contract* does not really contain any contractual theory. All that Rousseau uses of the idea of contract is the notion that membership of a civil association should be seen as voluntary; no one is tied to member-ship and obedience to the association for reasons that have nothing to do with the furtherance of one's good. But to say that every person should have good reason for membership and obedience is not to say that the association and its terms were instituted by a contract made for those reasons, and that it exists through the maintenance of contractual rela-tions between its members. Rather than supposing that he was some kind of 'social contract' theorist, we should note Rousseau's vision of the good state in the following: 'There can be no patriotism without liberty, no liberty without virtue, no virtue without citizens; create citizens, and you have everything you need; without them, you will have nothing but debased slaves, from the rulers of the state downwards' (*DPE* 135; *OC* III, 259).

Sources: *DI*, especially Pt 2
      DPE
      E, Bk III
      SC Bks I–II

Further reading: Crocker (117); Gildin (123); Levine (128); Masters, chs 6, 7 (69); Noone (140); Rosenfeld (145)

convention   Chapter 5 of Bk I of The Social Contract is entitled: 'That we must always go back to a First Convention'. At this early point in his argument Rousseau is principally considering, and attacking, accounts of the origins of civil association – the basis of political authority and obligation – that he disagrees with. He has disposed, he believes, of patriarchal models of authority (ch. 2), and of might as the basis of right (ch. 3), and he is about to develop his own positive account of these matters (ch. 6). In ch. 5, which forms a transition between these phases of his argument, Rousseau is concerned to identify the fundamental level at which civil obligation, as opposed to mere subjugation or enslavement, originates. He argues, first, that even were he wrong to deny that superior strength or conquest establishes a right to obedience, the only right that could establish would be over subdued individuals as individuals, not that of a ruler over a people.

For there to be 'a people' – an association, not a mere aggregation, of persons – to be ruled over, or to be self-ruling, there must be 'an act' by which scattered individuals become 'one people' who may give itself to a king or conqueror, or be the subjects of self-rule. A people is a body which can engage in public deliberation by which what is decided is, in some way, a rule or command for all alike. Tom, Dick and Harry may command the same thing, or be commanded to do the same thing. But unless there is some way in which the decisions or actions of Tom, Dick and Harry are integrated and combined, these commands are not the commands of a body, or over a body, of persons. And if such integration or combination exists, then, if appropriate, what any one of them commands, or is commanded to do, may be the voice of all of them or apply alike to all of them.

This formation of a body or group, of a people as a collective entity having an integrity in virtue of the establishment of rules or practices common to all, must, Rousseau insists, depend on agreement and institution, on convention. Merely calling two persons, say, 'the terrible twins' does not make them a collective entity. Nor can either one of them act for 'the terrible twins' by his own decision alone. For any act to be attributable to that source, some form of ordered integration of the designs and desires of each must have been achieved. Rousseau does not, of course, consider by what convention such a collective unit as 'the terrible twins' might be instituted; rather, his concern is with how a civil association, making one corporate body politic, may be established (*see* CONTRACT).

In ch. 5 of *The Social Contract* Rousseau asks why there should be any obligation on a minority to accede to the decision of a majority: 'The law of majority voting is itself something established by convention, and presupposes unanimity, on one occasion at least' (that is, unanimity in assenting, each one of us, to the law of majority voting). We are so used to the idea of the right established by a majority vote that we are apt to overlook his crucial point here. But consider the following case. Walking along, I pass three people trying to change the wheel of a car. Seeing me, they say: 'By a majority of three to one it has been decided that you should help us.' I may have reason to help them out of kindness; but this 'majority vote' is, if not wholly spurious, certainly not such as to create any obligation on me. And this is because I am not a member, with them, of the same body. It is that membership which demands a convention to establish it, after which, perhaps, I may incur obligations in virtue of majority decisions.

Rousseau's insistence on this being a matter of convention is both critical and constructive. From the critical viewpoint, it is an affirmation of his fundamental belief that no one is tied, by nature or birth, to obedience and obligation to another, but enjoys, as his basic right, self-sovereignty, answerability to no one and duty to no one (except to his parents – a bond which ceases as soon as need of them ceases, but which, if continued, is also maintained by a convention (*SC*, ch. 2)). From the constructive point of view, Rousseau believes that if we understand why each person has reason to enter into a conventional union with others as together making up one body politic, we shall understand the proper basis and constitution for such bodies and so have an answer to the central questions of political theory and practice regarding AUTHORITY and obedience (*see* SOVEREIGN BODY).

See also ARTIFICIAL.

Sources: *E*, Bk V
      SC, Bk I

Further reading: Masters ch. 6 (69)

corporate will   In any state, including the best kind of state – which Rousseau aims to depict in The SOCIAL CONTRACT – there will be groups of persons who, because of their position in the state, have common needs and interests that are distinct, on the one hand, from the interests which everyone has as a member of the state (as a CITIZEN), and on the other hand, from the interests each has as a wholly individual, separate being (as a particular person). These common interests are general in regard to the group – he is talking of magistrates, members of the government (*SC* III, ch. 2, 213; *OC* III, 400–1) – but particular in relation to the whole state, while still being distinct from what he calls the 'private' will of a person, which tends 'only to his personal advantage'. This general interest of the group is the object of its common will, and that common will is called a 'corporate will' (the will of magistrates as a corporate body).

    The idea of a corporate (or 'factional') will, once introduced, need not be confined to bodies established in a state, but can be extended to more informal groups united by their profession, such as farmers; or to groups with a shared interest, such as bird-watchers, environmentalists or cricket fans. Although there are marginal complexities in the idea, its central significance is plain enough. In virtue of their like position, profession or concern there may be certain things that will, for each one of them alike, promote the good of these persons. These things will be to their common advantage, and so it will be in their common interest to obtain them. This interest is common not because it so happens that there is one thing that each, as a private, individual person, will profit more or less equally by – though that can happen, and it is a perfectly proper instance of a 'common interest'. Rather, it is that *as* a magistrate, a cricket fan, or whatever, there are certain things that will be advantageous to anyone who is considered simply in his role of magistrate or cricket fan. The commonness of the interest derives not from the convergence of the concerns of private persons, but from the convergence of private persons who share common roles from which role-specific advantages are to be gained.

    Thus it is to the advantage of a magistrate, charged with administering

71

the law, to be able to do so quickly and easily, and to enjoy the power and resources necessary to do this. The corporate will of magistrates will, then, tend towards an increase of power, for example.

It is perhaps necessary to issue the familiar warning that we are not supposing anything to exist here other than individual persons who (have reason to) will this or that. There is no abstract entity – the corporation or corporate body – that has a will and interests. Individuals have interests and schemes as private individuals, and in their roles, personae and characters; a corporate will is just the will a person has as a public person, desiring or acting as one of a kind. Since, considered only in their role of one of a kind, persons will have more or less identical interests (depending on how tightly defined that 'kind' is), then the corporate will of, say, magistrates or environmentalists is just the same as what any individual magistrate or any ordinary person *qua* environmentalist wills – that is, rationally seeks as being to his advantage.

A person's private will and corporate will are distinct but not necessarily conflicting. If it is supposed, however, that they are indeed in conflict, confusion can arise. If I strongly identify with the objectives of the office of magistracy, then some of my own objectives will be those of a magistrate. We may say either that my private interest now includes the corporate interest; or that I have ceased to function as, to value continuing to act merely as, a purely private person. Conflict can often occur between role-acquired wills, such as in the common instance of clashes between the needs of family and work. In such cases, it is necessary to determine the priority or priorities – especially in the case of the GENERAL WILL. Resolution of such conflict may be a matter of enlarging private interest to include public goals, or of ceasing to be, or ceasing exclusively to attach paramount importance to being, a purely private person.

According to Rousseau, as a corporate body in the state, magistrates exist to serve essential purposes, on the authorization of the SOVEREIGN BODY. Properly ordered, their existence does not threaten the stability or welfare of the state. However, Rousseau was acutely aware that such bodies, with their special interests which remain particular relative to the general good of the whole community, may try to advance their sectional interests, in unauthorized ways, at the expense of that general good. Enjoying the power necessary for the discharge of their tasks, magistrates will tend to try to increase that power, either by (fraudulently) extending the role of magistracy, or by (fraudulently) using that same power to influence other affairs. The urge to do this is a further manifestation of AMOUR-PROPRE, albeit at one remove – it is the glory of being a magistrate that is being exalted at others' expense, or else it is an extension of the greed and ambition that every private person is apt never to lose, and thus to bring to any public position he may occupy. In this way will exist in society not only competition for invidious advancement between individual persons, but also competition between groups and factions, as well as the oppression of private individuals by factions. Such competition jeopardizes social harmony, and impedes yet further the achievement of any common good.

It was Rousseau's preference that the number, power and influence of such intermediate bodies standing between the general will of the whole community and the private will of one individual should be as small as possible while remaining compatible with the necessary governmental tasks being carried out. We are infinitely more suspicious than Rousseau was that the 'general will' will never in fact be general, but only a mask disguising some dominant, but partial, interest. To leave the private person unprotected in the face of that would be to court tyranny and servitude – a danger of which Rousseau is well aware:

> It is . . . essential, if the general will is to be able to make itself known, that there should be no partial society in the state and that each citizen should express only his own opinion . . . But if there are partial societies, it is best to have as many as possible and to prevent them from being unequal, as was done by Solon, Numa and Servius. These precautions are the only ones that can guarantee that the general will shall be always enlightened, and that the people shall in no way deceive itself. (*SC* II, ch. 3, 185; *OC* III, 372)

Some versions of 'market democracy' follow the Solonic pattern, though it may be that insufficient attention is paid to the rule preventing inequality between the sections, and to the question of who shall have the custody of the rules by which competing claims are mediated.

Even if we do not agree with all his statements on the nature and desirability of factions, sections, and the like, Rousseau's notion of a corporate will provides a useful tool of social and political analysis.

See also PARTICULAR WILL; WILL OF ALL.

Sources: *DPE*
       SC, Bk III and *passim*

Further reading: Masters, ch. 7 (69); Noone (140); Shklar, ch. 5 (36)

correspondence Rousseau was a voluminous letter-writer during most of his mature years, and a great number of his letters have survived. They cover a wide spectrum. First, there are works of substantial philosophical, political or apologetic significance which, as a purely stylistic device,

Rousseau cast in the form of letters, but with publication in mind. Such 'letters' include the LETTER TO CHRISTOPHE DE BEAUMONT (published in 1763), written to the Archbishop of Paris in reply to his condemnation of *Émile*, and the LETTERS WRITTEN FROM THE MOUNTAIN (published in 1764), composed in general response to the condemnation of that work and of *The Social Contract* by the Genevan authorities, and in specific response to J.-R. Tronchin, the city's attorney-general. We might also include in this category some of Rousseau's early poems, presented as 'epistles', such as the *Épître à M. Parisot* of 1741–2 (*see* POETRY AND MISCELLANEOUS PROSE).

Second, there are letters in which Rousseau makes major declarations about his ideas or himself: although these were not intended for publication, it is clear that he was making a form of public statement in them. Many such letters circulated in manuscript copies made with or without their recipients' knowledge, and some were published in Rousseau's lifetime without his permission. In this category fall the LETTERS TO MALESHERBES (written in 1762); the LETTER TO VOLTAIRE ON PROVIDENCE (written in 1756); and his *Elementary Letters on Botany* (written from 1771 onwards; *see* BOTANY).

One can identify a third category of letters, which would include the MORAL LETTERS written to Sophie d'Houdetot in 1757–8 and the 'Lettre à Franquières' of 1769, where Rousseau is writing in response to some specific problem or issue between himself and the recipient and is moved to explain some of his ideas or attitudes at length. Virtually all editions of his works include some of these letters as an essential part of his intellectual output, even though he probably did not view them in this light himself.

For the rest, Rousseau's correspondence covers the whole range of concerns that touched his life. There are many letters to his publishers; letters to admirers (some importunate), to friends, to children; letters of news, of condolence, of idle chatter. The 31st August 1757 is sometimes known as the day of the five letters. Rousseau's relations with Mme d'Épinay were at crisis point, and in one twenty-four-hour period letters of hurt, complaint, plea and reconciliation flew back and forth between them, as he suffered one of his seizures of anxiety and suspicion (*C* IX, 419–21; *OC* I, 450–3).

One gathers, in many respects, a more rounded and faithful impression of Rousseau's life and personality from these unguarded writings than one does from those carefully crafted works of self-disclosure to which he devoted so much of his last fifteen years. He drew extensively on his letters in preparing *The Confessions*, and one may sometimes gain a more accurate picture of his situation and state of mind from these than one does from that work itself.

In his pamphlet, *A Concise Account of the Controversy between Hume and Rousseau* (the *Exposé Succinct*, published first in French in 1766 and then in English the following year), Hume sets out quite plainly the supposed grievances that Rousseau has against him. And in the course of doing so he reproduces a number of Rousseau's letters, including one of the most piteous documents, many pages long, of Rousseau's mental disturbance. It includes the unforgettable remark – expressing, surely, the nadir of the paranoid state – that there was 'certain appearance of things on the whole' which was not to his liking. There can be no doubt that Hume was innocent of all the charges that Rousseau made against him that he had been mocked and humiliated. Rousseau's predisposition to paranoia can only have been exacerbated by the fact that he was a stranger in a foreign land, with no knowledge of the language, surrounded by urbane and sophisticated men, and an object of the mockery of some – of Horace Walpole, for one, who forged a letter to him purporting to come from the King of Prussia. Finally, it may be noted that Rousseau's immensely successful novel, JULIE, OU LA NOUVELLE HÉLOÏSE (published in 1761), is cast in the form of letters between the protagonists.

Two substantial editions of his letters have been produced, one edited by T. Dufour and P.-P. Plan, the other by R. A. Leigh – which is one of the greatest achievements of modern scholarship.

Sources: Dufour and Plan (eds), *Correspondance Générale*
Hendel, *Citizen of Geneva*
Hume, *Concise Account* (336)
Leigh (ed.), *Correspondance Complète*

Corsica, Project for a Constitution for (written 1764–5; published 1861) (*Projet de Constitution pour la Corse*) [16]   At the end of Bk 2, ch. 10, of *The Social Contract*, concluding his discussion of the kind of people who would be ready and equipped to receive good laws, Rousseau says: 'There is still in Europe one country capable of being given laws – Corsica. The valour and persistency with which that brave people has regained and defended its liberty well deserve that some wise man should teach it how to preserve what it has won' (*SC* II, ch. 10, 203; *OC* III, 391).

In 1734–5 the people of Corsica had rebelled against their exploitative Genoese rulers. The first rebellion was suppressed in 1748, but four years later fighting resumed under the leadership of Pasquale Paoli. It appeared, for a while, that the rebels had some chance of success. The conflict was protracted, and it was not until 1764 that Rousseau was contacted by a representative of Paoli, Matteo Buttafoco, with a view to preparing a new system of legislation and government for Corsica. Although Rousseau was interested in the task, he was beset by other demands and by personal troubles; the work was never finished, and the fragment that we have, left among his unpublished papers at his death, did not appear in print until 1861.

Rousseau's *Project for a Constitution for Corsica* is not as interesting or as well executed as his comparable essay on Poland (*see* CONSIDERATIONS ON THE GOVERNMENT OF POLAND). The principal concern of this surviving fragment is with the economic arrangements that Rousseau advocates for Corsica, although these ideas are subordinated throughout to the political and social objectives that he thinks Corsica should be trying to achieve.

Rousseau considers Corsica to be in severe economic disarray, with much of its social structure in ruins largely because of the many years of war. He thinks, however, that, unlike those who have experienced the allure of more abundant prosperity, the Corsicans will be able to turn their misfortune to advantage. Their experience of straitened circumstances will make them more willing to adopt an economic and productive system of a basic, non-luxury-orientated kind – which will be for their overall good. Agriculture will be given pride of place, and the role of farmer will be the most honoured and valued in society. This will have three desirable results. First, it will make Corsica materially independent of other nations, so that it will not become subject to the controls and demands that dependence on external trade imposes. Second, it will reduce reliance on money, which only foments private interests. Instead, people will use the barter system, so that the products of the different parts of the island can be widely distributed and everyone has access to the full range available.

Third, Rousseau thinks that a largely rural population, such as Corsica's, relatively evenly distributed, will provide the best basis on which to achieve a perfect equality for all – which should be the fundamental principle of the constitution. Democratic government would also be suitable, since it would be clear and direct in its functions, and would be cheap to maintain and administered by persons well known for their probity and ability.

The disordered social structure can also be put to constructive use, in Rousseau's view, in that the substantial disappearance of the Corsican nobility brought about by the Genoese means that wide differences in ranks will not now stand in the way of civil equality. Such odium as might attach to the abolition of ranks can be laid at the door of the Genoese, and the new legislation will capitalize on these circumstances, making the dignification of all a mark of the overthrow of the oppressor.

Rousseau discusses here, though less cogently than in his essay on Poland, the need to cultivate national character and customs and to inspire people with an overriding loyalty to their country and their fellow-citizens. He comments interestingly on vanity and pride as sources of people's inspiration, but says little about how these are to be turned to constructive purposes in establishing a democratic Corsica. Public service should be the basis for awarding distinctions of merit, but he gives little direction about how such a system may be brought about, or about how people can be made to accept it.

It is hard to guess how Rousseau might have developed the argument of the *Project*. It can perhaps most usefully be regarded as an adjunct to his more inspired essay on Poland.

Source: *Project for a Constitution for Corsica* [16]

Further reading: Cohler (152); Shklar, ch. 1 (36)

Creed of a Savoyard Vicar, The (1762) (*La Profession de Foi du Vicaire Savoyard*) [12] In Bk IV of ÉMILE Rousseau includes a long and more or less self-contained essay that he calls 'The creed [profession of faith] of a Savoyard Vicar'. Here he gives his fullest statement on the nature and basis of religious belief and sentiment; his account of the nature of God; a discussion of God's relations with His creatures; and an explanation of the connections between religious belief and morality. He is very critical of the significance ascribed to miracles and to revelation in religion, and of the intolerance amongst different religious denominations. This discussion is the most important for understanding Rousseau's religious ideas as they relate to personal conviction (*see* RELIGION (CIVIL)).

His pretext for including the *Creed* at this point in the book is the need to introduce Émile to ideas of religion, and to give an account of the kind of religious belief and allegiance that would be proper to his education in accordance with the requirements appropriate to the cultivation and preservation of intact nature. Rousseau had been considering these issues independently of the rest of *Émile*, and that work would hardly have been affected, except in the specific religious dimension that the *Creed* brings to it, if it had been published separately (as it has been subsequently).

The ideas presented find voice in an imagined vicar from Savoy, engaging in earnest conversation with the young Rousseau who enters the book at this point. But the rhetorical distance achieved is only slight, and there is no doubt that the vicar's views are Rousseau's own. None the less, it is said that aspects of the figure of the vicar and some of his ideas are drawn from two people that he encountered earlier in his life, the Abbé Gaime (whom he knew in Turin) and the Abbé Gâtier (with whom he studied briefly on his return to Annecy in 1729–30; see THE CONFESSIONS, Bk III, 116–19; *OC* 117–20). It is to the latter that Rousseau attributes, erroneously, the sexual indiscretion that he has his vicar commit, and that was responsible for the loss of office which provoked in him the intense meditations set down in the *Creed*.

It was this section of *Émile* that was principally responsible for the censure that fell on the book and for the misfortunes that Rousseau suffered as a result. Particular exception was taken to his criticism of the authority of miracles, and his denunciation of the cruel intolerance of the various Churches, particularly the Catholic Church. Although Rousseau sometimes later implied that his remarks were exclusively directed against the Catholic Church, it is clear that his concerns were general. (He hardly ever qualified or retracted his views – which must have taken considerable courage.)

To begin with, in the *Creed*, Rousseau is very critical of the contribution that philosophy can make to religious understanding. Philosophy deals with great abstractions which produce no illumination, but only confusion and dismay. Philosophers themselves are more concerned to achieve celebrity for their views than with uncovering the truth. We should, Rousseau says, confine ourselves only to what we need to know for our essential interests, and test all ideas against our simplest feelings, eschewing all speculation and grandiose theory.

Proceeding from this simple conviction, we discover that there are passive and active elements in the world: material objects are passive; intelligence and understanding are active. From this we can infer that matter is not capable of spontaneous motion, and so there must be a will which moves the universe and animates nature. This is the first article of faith. We see, in addition, that everything exhibits lawful order, harmony and interrelatedness. This shows that this will is intelligent. This is the second article of faith. Via these two articles alone, we arrive at a sense of the presence of God in the world: 'This Being which wills and is powerful; this Being active in itself; this Being, whatever it may be, which moves the universe and orders all things, I call *God*. I join to this name the ideas of intelligence, power, and will which I have brought together, and that of goodness which is their necessary consequence' (*E* IV, 227; *OC* IV, 581). We know, and need to know, no more of God's essence. These points are felt with overwhelming force, and they are sufficient to take a stand on.

In this harmonious order we find that man stands in the first rank. Not only does he occupy a position in the order of creation, but he knows the order and proportion of all things. In man we sense two principles: the soul and the body. Because of our soul, we love justice, moral beauty; because of our body, we are ensnared by the senses and by passion. But we enjoy free will too; if we commit moral evil it is our own responsibility. It is by abusing our faculties that we become unhappy; God has so made us that if we use our freedom to live justly and keep faith with our proper nature we shall be happy. It is true that in the world we often enough find that the wicked prosper. But this gives us reason to think that the soul is immortal, or that it survives for so long as God's justice requires to see that the good receive what they justly deserve.

The vicar then considers what rules of conduct should emerge from these articles and beliefs. He gives an account of CONSCIENCE as the power for sensing whether or not something is suitable to our nature – a nature that we know to be good and healthy because of God's provident work in ordering us and all things in harmony. In each of us there is a principle of virtue and justice which, duly heeded, will lead to a life beneficial to us and to all.

At one point in the earnest declaration of the *Creed* the listening Rousseau interjects that what he has heard seems to be very like that form of 'natural religion' that is reviled as atheism or irreligion. The vicar responds to this by launching into a criticism of religious creeds that go beyond what he has just declared. He insists that the true worship of God comes from the heart, and that true worship does not require particular ceremonies or practices as conditions of salvation. To demand that it should imposes the need to find extraordinary proof that only one form of worship is correct, and that those who do not follow it are damned. These extraordinary proofs – miracles, sacred words, special revelation – lack credibility: when we look closely, all we find is the authority that men claim for them. In attempting to vindicate that authority, trickery, sophistry and all the deceptions of control are used:

> See, then, what your alleged supernatural proofs, your miracles and prophe-
> cies come down to; a belief in all this on the faith of others, and a subjection
> of the authority of God, speaking to my reason, to the authority of men. If
> the eternal truths which my mind conceives could be impaired, there would
> no longer be any kind of certainty for me, and far from being sure that you
> speak to me on behalf of God, I would not even be sure he exists. (*E* IV, 301;
> *OC* IV, 617)

Furthermore, the insistence on a privileged revelation confined to a few makes men cruel, intolerant, and vicious. How can the Father of all be supposed to confine himself to a single people and proscribe all the rest?

There follows an extensive discussion of the prejudice, the unfairness and the suppression of argument that has gone into the defence of the Catholic Church and the attacks on such groups as the Jews. It is not in the books of men, the vicar declares, but in the book of nature – which is open and accessible to all alike – that we shall 'learn to serve and to worship its divine Author'. The vicar does not condemn the New Testament, which depicts a morality of love, compassion, patience and care – the essential message of the love of God that no sectarianism can displace. 'The sum of the law is to love God above everything and one's neighbour as oneself . . . no religion is exempt from these duties of morality . . . nothing is truly essential other than these duties' (*E* IV, 312; *OC* IV, 632). It is this humane morality and the worship of the heart, grounded in natural religion, that the vicar seeks to express. He does not claim to instruct, wanting only to share candidly his convictions.

Rousseau is extremely careful here to avoid dogmatism and resounding epistemological claims. For all that, one can well understand why his attack in these pages on the credentials of the Catholic hierarchy – indeed, on any religion claiming privileged status – produced a furore. In the long run, however, it has been the kind of view expressed by Rousseau, particularly on matters of religious toleration and on the problematic status of religious claims, that has prevailed, at least among the Churches of the Western world. The influence of the *Creed* itself is harder to determine. Certainly, Kant's moral argument for the existence of God and the immortality of the soul shows clear traces of Rousseau's ideas. But in the overall development of religious thought Rousseau's presentations of the 'first cause' and 'design' arguments have probably had little impact alongside those of their more famous expositors.

Sources: *E*, Bk IV
   Letter to Christophe de Beaumont
   Letters Written from the Mountain
   Moral Letters

Further reading: Dent, ch. 7 (24); Dickstein (185); Grimsley, ch. 6 (26); Grimsley (187); de Man (188); Masters, ch. 2 (69)

D

democracy   To understand Rousseau's views on democracy, it is essential to distinguish between democratic forms of sovereignty and democratic forms of GOVERNMENT, as he does. Moreover, the precise significance to be attached to the term 'democracy' – in some sense 'rule by the common people' – is not clear. But rather than trying to determine whether or not Rousseau was precisely a 'democrat', let us see what he says about 'rule by the common people'.

In the kind of state that Rousseau describes in The SOCIAL CONTRACT, every member shall be an 'indivisible' part of the SOVEREIGN BODY. If any one person is divided off from the rest, he is under no obligation of obedience to the sovereign will, or to the LAW, but is merely forced to comply. Although it is not exactly clear what being an indivisible part of the sovereign body involves, there would appear to be two primary factors. First, the person and goods of every member should be protected and sustained by the work of all. Second – and in this context more important – each member should have an assured right of participation in the sovereign deliberations and determinations by which the fundamental laws of the state are established. But Rousseau does not see it as following from this that unanimous consent is required to make an act one of sovereign authority. For he allows that persons may rightly be forced to obey the law which they have not assented to; by this, he says, they will be 'forced to be free' (see AUTHORITY; FREEDOM; GENERAL WILL). This, though, is a notoriously contentious issue in the understanding of Rousseau. It would be safe to say that he thinks that, ideally, unanimous, well advised agreement should be forthcoming: that would be the palmary way of legitimizing the authorization of law in the state.

Thus, the fundamental laws for any state require, for their legitimacy, the authorization of all members of that state. It is in their standing as CITIZENS that the members are empowered and entitled to give that authorization without which they are forced into servitude. In so far as a person's standing as a citizen is to be guaranteed in this way, certain matters must be exempted from determination by majority decisions.

There could, for instance, be majority decisions that certain minorities be deprived of civil standing; but such decisions violate the conditions of their own legitimacy. The protection of civil status is a precondition for the authority of majority decisions, and cannot therefore be the subject of such decisions (*see* CONVENTION).

The issue is complicated by the fact that Rousseau also holds that however carefully they undertake their deliberations, people may be unable to agree terms and conditions for their association which do secure a proper civil position for all alike. This may happen not through some party's corrupt intent to pervert the course of law-making (*see* CORPORATE WILL), but rather because of people's ignorance or lack of the appropriate concerns. In such a case, the guidance of a LEGISLATOR is required; and although, in the end, the people assume self-sovereignty, the original introduction of laws appropriate to them did not rest with them.

On matters of government, Rousseau takes a very different stand. In his analysis, government is a secondary or derived function of the state, licensed by the sovereign authority, charged with the administration of law and with the determination of those everyday practical issues concerning the good of the community that do not infringe upon matters of fundamental law. Rousseau holds that there is no one form of government appropriate to all places, times and peoples, though there are general principles concerning such issues as population dispersion, the nature of the land and economic development, which permit considered judgements to be made in particular instances.

In Bk II of *The Social Contract* he makes clear that 'democratic government' is not necessarily the best form of government for every community:

> He who makes the law knows better than anyone else how it should be executed and interpreted. It seems then impossible to have a better constitution than that in which the executive and legislative powers are united; but . . . It is not good for him who makes the laws to execute them, or for the body of the people to turn its attention away from a general standpoint and devote it to particular objects . . . the abuse of the laws by the government is a less evil than the corruption of the legislator, which is the inevitable sequel to private points of view. (*SC* III, ch. 4, 216; *OC* III, 404)

His thought here is that particular people or groups are necessarily singled in for the execution of the laws, and it will be very hard, if not impossible, for such people or groups not to seek private advantage from this function. And if the distinction between legislation and execution is muddied, it is likely that the impartiality necessary to legitimate legislation will be lost. It is clear that Rousseau is thinking here of a participative democratic government involving all citizens in acts of administration. He mounts numerous other objections to such an arrangement: there is insufficient time for people to assemble; they cannot be assembled in one place; business will have to be kept very simple, and so on. For these reasons, and more, Rousseau writes: 'were there a people of gods, their government would be democratic. So perfect a government is not for men.' Monarchy, aristocracy, or mixed forms may be much better governmental arrangements than democracy – though these, too, are fraught with difficulties.

It may be suggested that some of these difficulties will also attend the formation and actions of a sovereign body, as described by Rousseau. In fact, his view would be that, provided the primary task of the sovereign body – that is, the formulation and authorization of fundamental law – has been well done in the first place, it does not need to constantly reassemble in order to review and reassess. But the distinctions that Rousseau is making between sovereign and executive functions do not map very exactly on to the actual structure and operations of any existing state; and wherever we find supposedly democratic procedures, these are all representative in character (*see* REPRESENTATION), though theoretically taking place against a background of fundamental civil standing. However, establishing that civil empowerment is not the result of the kind of sovereign action that Rousseau envisages, but the work of a few; it might be said that those few do, in effect, function as legislators, in Rousseau's sense, and so speak for the whole people even when the whole people have no opportunity to speak for themselves.

Whether or not Rousseau should be regarded as a democrat, what is clear is that his account of the role of the will of the whole body of the common people in the functions of the state is a complex one.

Source: SC, Bks I–III

Further reading: Cohen (115); Crocker (117); Jones (124); Levine (128); Noone (140); Ritter (144); Talmon (74); Weirich (148)

denaturing

> Civil man is only a fractional unity dependent on the denominator; his value is determined by his relation to the whole, which is the social body. Good social institutions are those which best know how to denature man, to take his absolute existence from him in order to give him a relative one and transport the *I* into the common unity, with the result that each individual believes himself no longer one but a part of the unity and no longer feels himself except within the whole. A citizen of Rome was neither Caius nor Lucius; he was a Roman (*E* I, 39–40; *OC* IV, 249)

In this passage from ÉMILE and in the (DISCOURSE ON) POLITICAL ECO-
NOMY and in The SOCIAL CONTRACT (see, especially, Bk II, ch. 7),
Rousseau expresses an idea that many critics have seen both as central to
his social and political theory and as one of his most suspect.

To make sense of Rousseau's thought here we need to suppose a society,
or state, in which there are clearly defined social roles to which are
attached responsibilities and commitments requiring the holder of those
responsibilities and commitments to undertake certain tasks for the
maintenance and good of the whole society. Individuals are brought up
(perhaps from birth) with a view to taking on these roles, and with little or
no idea that they might have purposes, wishes or rights apart from those
that attach to them as role-holders. They become wholly absorbed by, and
identified with, their social roles, and have no sense of themselves and no
basis for self-esteem or personal action outside the criteria or possibilities
delineated by their roles. When this identification is perfected, they have
lost any idea of themselves as private, independent, selves; they conceive
of themselves as being 'servants of the state', 'citizens' – as 'Romans', in
Rousseau's instance. Their self-image derives from their position in the
whole body. It is by this that they are 'denatured'; they have lost, or have
never acquired, their 'natural' being as creatures who live and act entirely
for themselves.

Since Rousseau believes that to achieve denaturing is proper to 'good
social institutions', it seems reasonable to attribute to him the view that
any well functioning and effective society will be organized in this way.
This alarms most of his critics, who value the independence and autonomy of individual persons and see it as being diminished or abolished by
the process of denaturing. Indeed, in *The Social Contract* he appears to
subscribe to that view precisely:

> He who dares to undertake the making of a people's institutions ought to
> feel himself capable, so to speak, of changing human nature, of transforming
> each individual, who is by himself a complete and solitary whole, into part
> of a greater whole from which he in a manner receives his life and being . . .
> He must, in a word, take away from man his own resources and give him
> instead new ones alien to him. (*SC* II, ch. 7, 194; *OC* III, 381)

As always with Rousseau, matters are more complicated, not because
he is equivocal or undecided, but because he does not see matters in terms
of stark polarities – such as the denatured human 'ant' as against the
independent, self-contained individual. It is true that, seeing men's relations with current society in the way that he does, he thinks that this
choice – between their being good for themselves and being good for

others – has to be made (and in his day, he believes, the former is almost always preferred). But it is not true that he thinks this is inevitable. What he hopes to show in ÉMILE is that the 'double object' of being for ourselves and being for others can be attained, and in a way that does not leave the individual 'always floating between his inclinations and his duties', neither man or citizen. Indeed, it would be surprising if Rousseau did not think such an objective attainable, since, if he did not, his concerns in *The Social Contract* would be scarcely intelligible – which is precisely what some critics have said about this work, and others.

What, then, differentiates Rousseau's notion of citizenship (*see* CITIZEN) in *The Social Contract* from the conception of Roman citizenship which, he says, does involve denaturing man? Most obviously, it is that although Rousseau thinks it essential that everyone should identify himself with his role as citizen, and regard his duties and responsibilities in that role as paramount, being a citizen does not absorb all a person's time, being and action; in fact, his role as citizen is intended to secure for him the protection of his person and goods, rather than to divest him of them and make him just a cog in a social machine.

When Rousseau stresses the need to transform each individual into a part of a greater whole, it is in order that people shall overcome their preoccupation with the narrow, self-absorbed, private concerns that set them in conflict and competition with others. For so long as this remains their conception of personal interest, no proper social association can be established, let alone endure, on stable and just terms. People must come not just to see but to feel that the good of others and their own are intimately bound together, so that it can never appear really desirable to them to profit or advance themselves at the expense of others. If they achieve this state of mind, they will no longer see themselves as wholly set apart from, or in conflict with, others; they will, to a degree, have taken on the good and need of others as part of their own enlarged sense of personal good (*see* CONTRACT). This is perfectly familiar in family or friendship relations, and Rousseau thinks that such relations should be extended – albeit in a watered-down form – to the whole of the social body; but he is not suggesting the abolition of the individual self. In seeing the bond amongst people in society as an extended friendship relation, he is here, as so often, principally following the lead of Plato in his *Republic*. Indeed, he refers to the *Republic* when he presents the idea of denaturing in *Émile*: 'When one wishes to refer to the land of chimeras, mention is made of Plato's institutions. If Lycurgus had set his down in writing I would find them far more chimerical. Plato only purified the heart of man; Lycurgus denatured it' (I, 40; *OC* IV, 250; see also *E* V, 362–3; *OC* IV, 699–700).

There is no suggestion in Rousseau's writings that, in the best state,

85

people háve wholly lost their particular existence and acquired instead a *moi commun*, a self whose characteristics are derived wholly from their place in the community. In extending his social and civil relations to the community at large and thereby nurturing a wish to maintain the life and integrity of his society, the individual takes on the concerns of others. But the fact that his entire existence is no longer concentrated on himself alone does not mean that he has become denatured; it is part of our own good to want, to need, to care for others, and to share their concerns.

Sources: *DPE*
    E, Bk I
    SC, Bk II

Further reading: Horowitz, ch. 8 (27); Shklar, chs 1, 5 (36)

dependence   Rousseau distinguishes between two types of dependence, one of which is inevitable and benign, the other unnecessary and destructive (compare his thoughts on COMPARISON, in this respect). It is essential to make the distinction, for if all dependence is thought to be exclusively of the latter type, it will appear that he believes that only by withdrawal from social contact altogether can a person have any chance of preserving himself intact and well; and it will then seem to follow that Rousseau's attempts to establish a satisfactory form for human community, as described in The SOCIAL CONTRACT, are either vitiated from the start, or comprise only a very uneasy and unstable compromise between the corruption induced by social association and dependence and the intact independence of the separate individual.

First, the inevitable and benign type of dependence. Human beings are not, in Rousseau's view, self-sufficient. They need other people in many ways, for many reasons: for material provision and security; for emotional relations, friendship and love; for reasons of their own self-development and self-realization. Although at one point (*E* IV, 221; *OC* IV, 503) he implies that 'insufficiency' is an 'infirmity', he goes on to say: 'I do not conceive how someone who needs nothing can love anything. I do not conceive how someone who loves nothing can be happy'. And this is surely true.

Rousseau would be the first to agree that our various needs in regard to others open the door to the possibility of all sorts of deformation and corruption in our dealings. We may, for example, resent our need of another person, and attempt to control him. We may fear that our need of him invites his control of us. In these ways these necessary types of dependency are turned into unnecessary and perverse types. We must ensure, then, that our material reliance on others, for example, rather than turning into exploitation and servitude, remains what it is – an opportunity for collaborative effort towards mutual reward and satisfaction (*see* COMPASSION). Again, when in love, a person is extremely dependent on the favour and good opinion of the loved one – another situation which makes possible all sorts of domination by either party. It requires much care to ensure that love issues in a relationship of mutual respect and cherishing regard: when it does, the 'whole value of life' is to be found in this 'felicity' (*E* V, 419; *OC* IV, 782). It would be absurd to suggest that dependence of this kind should be eliminated from human experience.

However, the fact that we need others provides the occasion for the second type of dependency to arise. Speaking of children, Rousseau describes precisely the transition from the benign to the destructive:

> Nature provides for [the weakness of children] by the attachment of fathers and mothers; but this attachment can have its excess, its defect, its abuses . . . In giving [the child] more needs than he has, they do not relieve his weakness; they increase it. They increase it still more by exacting from him what nature did not exact. They do so by subjecting to their will the bit of strength which he has for serving his own, by changing into slavery on one side or the other the reciprocal dependence in which his weakness keeps him and their attachment keeps them . . . It is necessary that he be dependent and not that he obey. It is necessary that he ask and not that he command. (*E* II, 84–5; *OC* IV, 310–11)

What Rousseau is saying here is that either one-way or mutual need can become the occasion for establishing relations of control. In particular, such relations provide a forum in which the demands of AMOUR-PROPRE can readily take on an imperious and aggressive form. The requirement of *amour-propre* that we find a footing for ourselves with others is already a form of dependence, a need that others recognize and honour us as significant beings. But where there is also weakness and vulnerability in a relationship, the expression of this need can easily become distorted, so that only controlling others and forcing servitude on them will appear to satisfy the need for recognition and standing.

Writ large, the relations of dominance and subjugation that *amour-propre* can demand will come to pervade the whole of society, so that even the master can become dependent on his slaves for proof of the real substance of his being. Thus Rousseau writes: '[Émile] pities those miserable Kings, slaves of all that obey them . . . He would pity even the enemy who would do him harm, for he would see his misery in his wickedness. He would say to himself, "In giving himself the need to hurt me, this man has made his fate dependent on mine" ' (*E* IV, 244; *OC* IV, 536).

This form of dependence, where self-worth and personal meaning are measured in terms of the servitude and nullity of others, Rousseau roundly condemns. But it is not necessary that human dependence take on this character. It is therefore not necessary that, in order to avoid it, we have no need of others – if, indeed, we could survive in such a situation anyway. The occasion for mutual care, for collaboration and for extending ourselves that we can, and should, find in our need of each other is not a limitation, but an opportunity for growth.

Source: *E*, Bks I, II

Further reading: Charvet, ch. 3 (23); Levin (91); Winch (102)

Devin du Village, Le (*'The Village Soothsayer'*) *See* MUSICAL COMPOSITION.

Dialogues *See* ROUSSEAU JUDGE OF Jean-JACQUES.

Discourse on the Origin of Inequality (1755) (*Un Discours sur l'Origine de l'Inégalité*) [2]   Together with the (DISCOURSE ON) POLITICAL ECONOMY and THE SOCIAL CONTRACT, the *Discourse on the Origin of Inequality* constitutes Rousseau's principal statement of his social and political ideas.

The *Second Discourse*, as it is often called, was written, as was the *First Discourse* (the DISCOURSE ON THE SCIENCES AND THE ARTS), in response to a prize essay question set by the Academy of Dijon. When the question – 'What is the origin of inequality among men, and is it authorized by natural law?' – was published in 1753, Rousseau fell to work on it at once, finding the topic highly congenial to his newly won insights into the structure of society and the position of men and their prospects for happiness within it (*see* EQUALITY). In June 1754, when the main text was completed, Rousseau went to Geneva to reclaim his rights as a citizen (having relinquished Catholicism). While there, he wrote a long dedicatory note to Geneva for the *Second Discourse*. His essay did not win the prize, but when it was published in June 1755 it created a considerable stir, and served to consolidate Rousseau's reputation as one of the most original political thinkers and social critics. Although the work attracted much written comment, he did not – as he did in the case of the *First Discourse* – reply (with one exception, the *Lettre à M. Philopolis*).

The dedicatory note in the *Second Discourse* is a eulogy to the city of his birth: he acclaims it as a city-state in which a man may enjoy the most perfect benefits of a just, humane and prosperous society; here, liberty, order, peace and felicity are combined in an almost miraculous way, and it is with honour and gratitude that he feels entitled to reclaim his birthright and once more call himself a citizen. This highly idealized portrait was not true to the facts, nor did his good opinion of Geneva long survive after copies of *Émile* and *The Social Contract* were burned there in 1762. In 1763, after the action taken against him by the authorities, Rousseau renounced his citizenship, but he probably always remained hurt and dismayed by the turn that events had taken. At some level, his love of the city was genuine; put less charitably, he had a genuine need to make Geneva an object of love in his own eyes and to claim honoured membership of this idealized object.

In the preface, which comes next, Rousseau opens the argument proper by announcing that his task will involve stripping away all the accretions and modifications that man has acquired through living in society, in order to find what is original in his nature:

> Like the statue of Glaucus, which was so disfigured by time, seas and tempests . . . the human soul, altered in society by a thousand causes perpetually recurring . . . has, so to speak, changed in appearance, so as to be hardly recognizable. Instead of a being acting constantly from fixed and invariable principles . . . we find only the frightful contrast of passion mistaking itself for reason, and of understanding grown delirious. (*DI* 38; *OC* III, 122)

Although he does not underestimate the difficulty of uncovering the natural man in the 'attempt to determine the law originally prescribed to him, or that which is best adapted to his constitution' (*DI* 41; *OC* III, 125), he believes that we find in man 'two principles prior to reason, one of them deeply interesting us in our own welfare and preservation, and the other exciting a natural repugnance at seeing any other sensible being, and particularly any of our own species, suffer pain or death' (*DI* 41; *OC* III, 125). These 'principles' are AMOUR DE SOI and pity (COMPASSION), and it is from these innate impulses – not maxims based in reason – that the duties of man towards himself and others are derived. But what we actually find in society is 'the violence of the powerful and the oppression of the weak. The mind is shocked at the cruelty of the one, or is induced to lament the blindness of the other' (*DI* 42; *OC* III, 127).

These prefatory remarks set the terms for the whole essay – the contrast between natural man and artificial or social man, and between the compassion and gentleness proper to the former and the cruelty and malice shown by the latter. How, Rousseau asks, has the former been displaced or smothered? In particular, how does human inequality stand in relation to that law best adapted to the original constitution of man? Rousseau distinguishes two kinds of inequality: natural or physical, consisting in a 'difference of age, health, bodily strength, and the qualities of the mind or of the soul'; and moral or political (also, ARTIFICIAL or conventional), consisting in 'the different privileges which some men enjoy to the prejudice of others; such as that of being more rich, more honoured, more powerful, or even in a position to exact obedience' (*DI* 44; *OC* III, 131). His question then becomes: how have such conventional inequalities come to be established, and are they legitimate and justified?

In Part 1, Rousseau gives an account of what he takes to be the character, dispositions and capacities that are original in man, and of his natural environment. Natural man, in the first instance, is motivated only by a concern for his own preservation, without much foresight or con- scious awareness of himself. Not inclined to be combative, natural man is apt to be fearful of the strange or unknown. He keeps to what is familiar and safe, and after providing for his immediate wants concerns himself with little else and spends much of his time asleep. Although he has some capacity to regulate the immediate impulse of appetite (*see* FREEDOM), to learn new skills, and to adapt his behaviour towards utilizing his environ- ment more successfully (*see* PERFECTIBILITY), there is little occasion at first for him to use these powers. 'His soul, which nothing disturbs, is wholly wrapped up in the feeling of its present existence, without any idea of the future, however near at hand; while his projects, as limited as his views, hardly extend to the close of day' (*DI* 56; *OC* III, 144).

Reflecting further on the gap between primitive man, absorbed and guided by his sensations and scarcely different from the animals, and civilized man, who has knowledge and uses concepts, Rousseau discusses briefly (*DI* 58–63; *OC* III, 146–51) the development of language (*see* ORIGIN OF LANGUAGES). Returning to his primary thesis, he stresses the separateness and independence of original man in his natural setting. In so far as there is any contact between humans at all, it is fleeting and inconsequential; none of the passions and needs which bind people together have entered the soul of primitive man. There might be some violence in these encounters, but there is also natural compassion:

> In a word, each man, regarding his fellows almost as he regarded animals of different species, might seize the prey of a weaker or yield up his own to a stronger, and yet consider these acts of violence as mere natural occur- rences, without the slightest emotion of insolence or despite, or any other feeling than the joy or grief of success or failure. (*DI* 66n.; *OC* III, 219 n. 15)

Any differences of natural strength or mind would scarcely enter into account in a situation like this: it must have taken radical changes in human circumstances to make them significant, and even more to make these natural differences come to be replaced by artificial inequalities. What were these changes?

In Part 2 Rousseau turns to the history of man's downfall, by which he loses his primitive integrity and simplicity and becomes estranged from himself and cruel towards others (*see* ALIENATION). Inclement circumstances and the increase in numbers inevitably caused people to associate together and to acquire arts and skills dictated by anticipation of future need. Gradually, these associations became more settled and enduring, and from this phenomenon emerges the transformation of man. He traces two specific situations which cause people to rely on, to need, others in new ways. First, sexual feeling: this is no longer an impulse that directs a brief coupling, but a jealous, exclusive claim that sets people in competition for favour. Second, shared amusements, which leisure makes possible, such as singing and dancing. 'Each one began to consider the rest, and to wish to be considered in turn; thus a value came to be attached to public esteem . . . this was the first step towards inequality, and at the same time towards vice. From these first distinctions arose on the one side vanity and contempt and on the other shame and envy' (*DI* 81; *OC* III, 169–70). Everyone put in his claim to consideration; 'every intended injury became an affront . . . the party injured was certain to find in it contempt for his person.' These are the first germs of AMOUR-PROPRE, which now comes to dominate the relations of men.

Further material changes extended the influence of these alterations in humans' perception of themselves and others. Metallurgy and agriculture, Rousseau says, widened man's powers and needs; ownership and property began to be important. Possession was not merely a matter of equipping oneself better to meet natural need: it became the expression of power, superiority and distinction by which men could all the better command that deference they had come to require. 'Insatiable ambition, the thirst of raising their respective fortunes, not so much from real want as from the desire to surpass others, inspired all men with a vile propensity to injure one another, and with a secret jealousy' (*DI* 87; *OC* III, 175). Before long, conflict, exploitation and competition made social coexistence unbearable.

Rousseau then envisages a 'trick' having been played by the rich and powerful on the destitute and weak. Emphasizing the harmfulness of disorder, the rich proposed establishing the apparatus of government, law and sanction in order to stabilize the situation and to guarantee everyone some protection. Of course, the effect was to give new powers to the rich and to impose new chains on the poor. 'Such was, or may well have been, the origin of society and law . . . which irretrievably destroyed natural liberty, eternally fixed the law of property and inequality, converted clever usurpation into unalterable right, and, for the advantage of a few ambitious individuals, subjected all mankind to perpetual labour, slavery, and wretchedness' (*DI* 89; *OC* III, 178). From this basis, Rousseau then criticizes virtually all forms of established rule and government as nothing but the codification of power, riches and domination. So far from having any legitimate claim to obedience, they are no more than tyrannies in which a few profit from the abjection and oppression of the many.

It would be a mistake, however, to believe that these few really gain by the arrangements (as the many evidently do not). The few – rich, noble, powerful and honoured – suffer from an 'unremitting rage' to distinguish themselves, which means that they live only 'on the testimony of other people', and prize what they enjoy 'only in so far as other people are destitute of it' (*DI* 104, 101; *OC* III, 193, 189) (*see* CIVILIZATION). In the end, the rich man no longer belongs to himself; he has become wholly dependent for the consciousness of his own existence on the judgement of others. Rousseau regards it as largely otiose even to consider whether these inequalities of wealth, station and power are authorized by 'natural law', but he concludes: 'It is plainly contrary to the law of nature, however defined, that children should command old men, fools wise men, and that the privileged few should gorge themselves with superfluities, while the starving multitude are in want of the bare necessities of life' (*DI* 105; *OC* III, 194).

There are few indictments of society as forceful as the *Second Discourse*: it demonstrates the full scope and penetration of Rousseau's analysis. As an indicator of his social and political views overall, however, it is in certain respects misleading. His argument relies on a rather stark and absolute contrast between natural man – isolated, self-possessed, innocent – on the one hand, and civilized man – social, self-estranged, lost to others' control, perverted, malign – on the other. Impressed, perhaps, by the power and sweep of the argument, readers are apt to see all of his related works as functioning on the same basis. This is sometimes the object of admiration: Rousseau, it is said, diagnosed the malaise of man in society with unparalleled power. But, more often, it is the object of criticism: not only did Rousseau exaggerate beyond reason, he also fell into incoherence. For, if this is how he analyses the situation, there can be no harmonious and constructive integration of men in society. Yet this is precisely what Rousseau describes, in particular, in *The Social Contract*: here men do indeed find ways of interacting which are creative and self-enlarging, rather than destructive and debilitating. The *Second Discourse* should not be taken as definitive on these points: it is likely that Rousseau ceased to consider that the contrasts he drew in it were absolute and unbridgeable.

Further reading: Allers (78); Crocker (81); Hamilton (85); Havens (89); Lovejoy (92); MacAdam (93); Meek (96); Plattner (99); Wokler (105)

(*Discourse on*) *Political Economy* (1755) (*Un Discours sur l'Économie Politique*) [3]   Sometimes known as the 'third discourse' (following the *Discourse on the Sciences and the Arts* (1750) and the *Discourse on the Origin of Inequality* (1755), this work appeared first as an article in volume V of Diderot's and d'Alembert's *Encyclopaedia*, published in November 1755. In 1758 it appeared as a separate 'discourse', and although it is not a discourse in the sense that the other two are, it is by that name that it is known nowadays.

Rousseau probably began work on the article in 1754, and in some ways it represents an interim statement of some of the ideas that he was working on for his projected 'Institutions Politiques' ('Political Institutions'), the final upshot of which was *The Social Contract*. Although they are treated less fully than in this later work, much play is made in this *Discourse* of the GENERAL WILL and of the need to instil VIRTUE in citizens. On the other hand, much greater attention is given to property, the raising of taxes and public expenditure and the like, than is to be found in *The Social Contract*.

In spite of containing some of Rousseau's most trenchant statements, this *Discourse* tends to receive less attention than his other major political writings. He begins by distinguishing paternal government and authority from civil government and authority. The former depends on natural relationships and inclinations; the latter, in contrast, can only be founded on CONVENTION, since in the state all the members are naturally equal and their chief magistrate has no natural interest in the happiness of the individuals who compose the state. Rousseau insists that a clear distinction needs to be made between authority and government in the state. All authority is derived from the general will, 'which tends always to the preservation and welfare of the whole and of every part, and is the source of the laws [and] constitutes . . . the rule of what is just and unjust' (*DPE* 121; *OC* III, 245–6). Government, or magistracy, is a derived office: 'the Magistrates belong to the people' (*DPE* 123; *OC* III, 247), and in all their functions the governors must observe the general will or the laws.

> How can it be that all should obey, yet nobody take upon him to command, and that all should serve, and yet have no masters, but be the more free, as, in apparent subjection, each loses no part of his liberty but what might be hurtful to another? These wonders are the work of law. It is to law alone that men owe justice and liberty. It is this salutary organ of will which establishes, in civil right, the natural equality between men . . . It is with this voice alone that political rulers should speak when they command. (*DPE* 124; *OC* III, 248)

It follows, therefore, that not only must rulers act in accordance with the law, but also that their first duty is to secure observance of the law. Thus, citizens need to be educated in such a way as to love their country and its laws, so that their own dispositions will make them accept the yoke of public duty: 'Make men, therefore, if you would command men; if you would have them obedient to the laws, make them love the laws, and then they will need only to know what is their duty to do it' (*DPE* 127; *OC* III, 251–2). A 'reign of virtue', which brings particular wills into conformity with the general will, is necessary if there is to be a just and prosperous state. Also, such virtue will be essential if the general will is to be clearly and accurately established in the first instance, and if authority is not to be usurped by a 'partial society' or faction. Patriotic loyalty is the sentiment that will bind citizens together in common cause; one's country provides the only proper and effective focus for those attachments which transcend narrow self-interest but which are too feeble to extend to all mankind indiscriminately (*see* NATIONALISM).

It is when discussing the failure to instil a sense of patriotism in the citizens that Rousseau rises to his most eloquent in his denunciation of the abuses of government:

> Do we wish men to be virtuous? Then let us begin by making them love their country; but how can they love it, if their country be nothing more to them than to strangers, and afford them nothing but what it can refuse nobody? ... It must not be imagined that a man can break or lose an arm, without the pain being conveyed to his head; nor is it any more credible that the general will should consent that any one member of the state, whoever he might be, should wound or destroy another, than it is that the fingers of a man in his senses should wilfully scratch his eyes out. The security of individuals is so intimately connected with the public confederation that ... [the latter] would in point of right be dissolved, if in the state a single citizen who might have been relieved were allowed to perish, or if one were wrongfully confined in prison. (*DPE* 131; *OC* III, 255–6)

Such remarks should put paid to the common criticism that, for Rousseau, the rights and interests of individuals are sacrificed to the common good of the state. And, indeed, he goes on to comment that the saying 'It is good that one should perish for all' is 'one of the most execrable rules tyranny ever invented, the greatest falsehood that can be advanced'.

Most of the rest of the *Discourse* is given over to such issues as taxation and other ways of raising revenue. Rousseau is anxious that the fiscal burdens of government be kept as light as possible consistent with achieving its proper ends; and that these burdens be as equitable as possible, and be seen to be so – otherwise, differences between rich and poor will be exaggerated and, in effect, the fundamental convention will be dissolved by the enforced indigence of the poor and dispossessed.

In this *Discourse* Rousseau articulates many of the central themes of his political thought – at times with a clarity and force not always present in his more abstract and analytical discussions.

Further reading: Peled (97); Shklar, ch. 5 (36)

Discourse on the Sciences and the Arts (1750) (*Un Discours sur les Sciences et les Arts*) [1] This, the *First Discourse*, was Rousseau's first substantial essay on social and political themes and his first major work of maturity. Rousseau recounts, in THE CONFESSIONS and in his LETTERS TO MALESHERBES, that in August 1749 he was on his way to visit Diderot, at that time imprisoned at Vincennes for sedition, when he saw announced in the *Mercure de France* a prize essay topic set by the Academy of Dijon: 'Has the restoration of the arts and sciences had a purifying effect upon morals?' He was at once seized with so many ideas, and visions so intense, that for a while he could not continue his journey. Within half an hour his future destiny, both as a writer and as a man, was marked out. In his 'illumination' he seems to have seen into the very heart of human misery; to have understood that its causes lie in the corruption that social life inflicts on man, while recognizing the injustices and sufferings that produces. Most of Rousseau's major work was pre-figured in that extraordinary moment.

The *First Discourse* was the immediate product of his new fervour, as well as being his answer – a resounding 'No' – to the Academy's question; he was awarded the prize. Published in July 1750, the essay attracted great attention and afforded Rousseau considerable celebrity. Many replies to the *Discourse* appeared, to several of which he responded, sometimes explaining or amplifying his argument (collected in *OC* III, and including the *Lettre à M. l'Abbé Raynal*, *Réponse à Stanislas*, *Lettre à M. Grimm* and *Dernière Réponse à Bordes*). (The preface that Rousseau wrote to his play *Narcissus* (*see* THEATRE) is also relevant here; it provides a defence of the fact that he wrote for the theatre in spite of having deliberately made a name for himself as a critic of refined arts such as play-writing).

In the Part 1 of the *First Discourse* Rousseau seeks to show that the arts and sciences have often flourished in societies that are in a state of moral decay and enfeeblement; and that, conversely, where there is moral vigour and honour in society there is often little learning. Indeed, wise men have seen this connection before him:

Socrates had begun in Athens, and the elder Cato proceeded at Rome, to inveigh against those seductive and subtle Greeks, who corrupted the virtue and destroyed the courage of their fellow-citizens: culture, however, prevailed. Rome was filled with philosophers and orators, military discipline was neglected, agriculture was held in contempt, men formed sects, and forgot their country. To the sacred names of liberty, disinterestedness, and obedience to law, succeeded those of Epicurus, Zeno and Arcesilaus (*DSA* 11; *OC* III, 14).

Thus, what he sees as the substance of moral vigour are loyalty to one's country, courage in its defence, application to useful callings; and in his later writing he has more subtle and penetrating things to say on these subjects.

To find, as Rousseau claims to have done, a conjunction of moral vigour with indifference to higher learning, and of moral decline with esteem of learning, is not yet to show any real causal connection between these phenomena. But in Part 2 he sets out to establish this, and to determine the nature of that connection, the key to which he sees as idleness. In 'advanced' societies, some people are relieved of the need always to be working in order to sustain themselves and their fellows, and it is out of their idleness that emerges an interest in speculation and the refinement of learning. As mere diversions such occupations are useless, even hurtful, since they divert people from doing anything beneficial for others. But there is more to it than that. Not having enough real work to occupy them, people become obsessed with the need to show off, to display accomplishments and merits that will impress others. So inquiry and learning are pursued not for the sake of truth, benefit and edification, but for celebrity and applause. 'The question is no longer whether a man is honest, but whether he is clever. We do not ask whether a book is useful, but whether it is well written. Rewards are lavished on wit and ingenuity, while virtue is left unhonoured. There are a thousand prizes for fine discourses, and none for good actions' (*DSA* 22; *OC* III, 25). Although Rousseau does not call it that here, he is in fact outlining the nature of AMOUR-PROPRE and its effects on people's activities and relationships. In this *First Discourse* he says little about how and why the 'rage of singularity' comes to be so large a concern in people's lives. His thoughts on *amour-propre* were to deepen later; but already here we see him broaching issues of social and political theory that are fundamental to all his work.

Rousseau does not wish to dismiss works of real genius, such as those of Bacon, Descartes and Newton. Such persons, he insists, had, however, no need of the elaborate institutions of learning, were not fired by a desire for reputation in place of concern for truth; nor are they suitable models for emulation by third-rate people who would do better for themselves and for

96

others if they followed some useful trade, rather than letting themselves be seduced into aspiring after fashionable accomplishments that they can never master and that are anyway meaningless except as attributes of self-display.

> As for us, ordinary men, on whom Heaven has not been pleased to bestow such great talents . . . let us remain in our obscurity. Let us not covet a reputation we should never attain, and which, in the present state of things, would never make up to us for the trouble it would have cost us . . . why should we build our happiness on the opinions of others, when we can find it in our own hearts . . . we have no occasion for greater knowledge than this. (*DSA* 26; *OC* III, 30)

Although written with some flair, this essay, his first piece of serious work, is not among Rousseau's best. It is important, though, for the introduction of notions and motifs that were to become some of his most characteristic themes. The celebration of 'republican virtue', love of country, service to one's fellows; the hatred of luxury, ostentation and self-display; men's desire to achieve reputation and invidious distinction, and the perversion of activities to serve this sort of objective – are all notions that Rousseau was to continue to work on and that would figure prominently in his later, more profound, works.

It should not be thought that Rousseau favours reducing people to a state of ignorance and stupidity. The kinds of human virtue that he praises require a proper understanding of human relations and of the needs of society. What he is hostile to is the elaboration of learned inquiry into a refined art which serves only to satisfy the vanity of its practitioners. He may not have been wholly wrong to see this as the fate that can overtake academic work.

Further reading: Benda (79); Gourevitch (84); Hamilton (86); Havens (88); Mason (95); Veblen (301)

domination Domination, as Rousseau understands it, is an expression of an aggressive desire to control others, who are perceived as in some way threatening to one's integrity and to one's recognition as a human being. He believes that relations of domination and servitude, of overt or covert kinds, are endemic in society and entrenched in established social and legal structures. Dominance is sought after as an end in itself. In a dominant relationship, the desire to achieve significance in the eyes of others by controlling and subjecting them finds satisfying expression. Rousseau believes that to be led by the desire for dominance is hurtful to the dominant person as well as to his 'victims'. It may, then, be wondered

97

why this desire and its effects are as pervasive and powerful as he supposes them to be.

Many critics contend that Rousseau saw the emergence of the urge towards domination as the inevitable concomitant of persons establishing relations with each other: 'The first glance [Émile] casts on his fellows leads him to compare himself with them. And the first sentiment aroused in him by this comparison is the desire to be in the first position' (*E* IV, 235; *OC* IV, 523). Translating Émile's sentiment to the larger stage – all desire this first position, but only one can occupy it. Competition for dominance is therefore the apparently inevitable outcome. But what, in the first place, is Rousseau's evidence for this view? Second, how is this claim compatible with his insistence that man is 'naturally good' (*see* NATURAL GOODNESS)? For if any human contact brings out competition and aggression, surely people already possess these tendencies. Third, how can Rousseau, while holding this view, believe that any just and worthwhile human society can ever be established – as, in The SOCIAL CONTRACT, he clearly thinks it can be?

Rousseau has, in fact, an effective response to these questions. In the first two books of ÉMILE he explains how the frustrations that every child is bound to suffer are apt to provoke an outraged response in which the child perceives himself as being thwarted by others' spite, instead of realizing that this is just the inevitable lot of humans. Led on by his misperception, he sees himself faced with the need to evade or to get the better of these opponents. His conviction of the truth of this representation may be strengthened, Rousseau holds, if parents constantly impose demands on the child and require his obedience. This readily becomes a pattern in the child's expectations of and dealings with the world around him:

> A child cries at birth; the first part of his childhood is spent crying. At one time we bustle about . . . at another we threaten him. Either we do what pleases him, or we exact from him what pleases us. Either we submit to his whims, or we submit him to ours. No middle ground; he must give orders or receive them. Thus his first ideas are those of domination and servitude. Before knowing how to speak, he commands; before being able to act, he obeys. (*E* I, 48; *OC* IV, 261)

Rousseau gives a precise and detailed account of the genesis and character of this sort of relationship. That a child should respond with rage to frustration and disappointment is, in itself, neither good nor bad: it is simply characteristic of the human affective make-up. If it signifies anything, it is the child's very proper desire to lay hold on life and to claim what he needs for his existence. What can be damaging is the (often unwitting) encouragement and consolidation of this response as the primary mode of encountering and contending with the world. For it will then become habitual to the child (and to the adult that the child will become) to see all human transaction as a matter of command and service, domination and obedience. And that is both intrinsically misconceived (and hurtful) as well as ineffective – people will not tolerate being ordered around. This consolidation is the work of the adults who surround the child; there is no implication that the child is predisposed to be wicked.

In the light of this explanation, it becomes clear why the desire to dominate so pervades human relations and institutions. The very intense and primitive predicament out of which it grows will, if not successfully resolved, leave a residue in most people's character. The desires, the very presence, of others will be seen as an obstacle, an imposition, a thwarting intrusion, and it will seem that the only way to contain and control them is by domination. But it is clearly not necessary, and indeed rarely appropriate, to perceive human encounter in these terms. People can and do trust, cherish and sustain each other, and in so doing creatively enhance their own lives as well as others'. It is through the sentiment of COMPASSION, Rousseau thinks, that we can learn this better way of living and of being with others.

Thus the 'first position' that Émile seeks for himself need not be one that he occupies exclusively at the expense of others. It requires only that he be not, himself, forced into an inferior position or into subjugation, but rather that he occupy, along with those with whom he stands in mutual regard and respect, the highest rank in society – that of a human being with moral dignity – and that he be honoured as such. This 'first rank' – meaning not 'top dog' status but the most estimable rank in society – is that which in civil society all members occupy as citizens (*see* CITIZEN).

See also ALIENATION; AMOUR-PROPRE; CIVILIZATION.

Sources: *DI*, especially Pt 2
    E, Bks I, II, IV

Further reading: Charvet, ch. 3 (23); Dent, ch. 2 (24); Fromm (333); Harding (334); Kontos (261); Veblen (301)

Du Contrat Social   *See* SOCIAL CONTRACT.

E

Écrits sur l'Abbé de Saint-Pierre (written 1756–8; published 1761–82) (*'Writings on the Abbé de Saint-Pierre'*) [4] When, in April 1756, Rousseau left Paris and went to live at the Hermitage in Montmorency, the cottage provided for him by Mme d'Épinay, he stood at the threshold of the most creative period of his life. One of his projects was to select extracts from the voluminous works, both published and unpublished, of the Abbé de Saint-Pierre, who had written extensively on society, government, morality and other topics. It was at the suggestion of Mme Dupin, whose secretary he had been during the 1740s and whose salon the Abbé had frequently attended, that Rousseau had undertaken this work.

He made slow progress. Aside from a few miscellaneous fragments, all that issued from his labour were two short pieces, the *Extrait du Projet de Paix Perpétuelle* (*Project for Perpetual Peace*) and the *Polysynodie*, derived from the Abbé's published works, to which Rousseau attached his own commentaries (the *Jugements*). The *Project* was published in March 1761, but the *Polysynodie* and the *Jugements* did not appear until after his death, in the collected edition of his works published by Moultou and Du Peyrou from 1782. One other unpublished piece which originates with these are some thoughts on WAR.

These pieces, of only limited interest, do not form part of Rousseau's major social and political writings. The extracts from the *Project*, which show Rousseau's hand as much as the Abbé's, concern the objective of establishing a confederated Europe, united by common interests in peace and stability and ruled by a central assembly while retaining local customs. In his *Jugement* Rousseau declares the Abbé's project a noble and laudable one, but criticizes him for neglecting to consider sufficiently the ambition of princes and their desire to increase their power. The Abbé is too optimistic and too simplistic in supposing that states, any more than individuals, will be effectively directed, where their long-term interests are concerned, by rational foresight. The desire for glory, fame and prestige is too strong to be checked by rational considerations of the desirability of peace and stability. Although it may seem that Europe is now moving towards a realization of the Abbé's vision, Rousseau was surely right to suppose that his ideas were not applicable at the time.

The *Polysynodie* concerns an attempt to moderate and regulate the absolute powers of rulers by dispersing the several functions of government among different councils, so that there shall be no concentration of power in the hands of a single person or body. Although Rousseau is sympathetic to this objective, he is not convinced that the Abbé's proposals have a serious chance of working. For the councils will have their own sectional interests, which they may advance in a way no less damaging to the welfare of the whole community than often occurs in, say, the case of a monarchy. The Abbé is, again, over-confident, in Rousseau's view, in his assumption that human beings can be governed by precepts of reason; unless there is a general commitment to public virtue and loyalty, no form of government, however carefully balanced, will be free from abuse.

Although the *Polysynodie* could, conceivably, have given Rousseau scope for deeper reflection, it is clear that he was not fully committed to it; his attention may well have been absorbed with the development of his own ideas on similar subjects – *The Social Contract*, for example, emerged from the same period.

Further reading: Carter (219); Perkins (226); Waltz (231)

education   In 1740, principally through the good offices of Mme de Warens, Rousseau was offered the post of tutor to the two sons of Jean Bonnet de Mably, a nobleman and chief of police in Lyons. By all accounts, Rousseau was not very successful at tutoring: he lacked the necessary patience and the capacity to win the confidence of his (admittedly difficult) charges (see *The Confessions*, Bk VI). By mutual agreement he gave up the job after a year, returning for a short while to stay (unhappily) with Mme de Warens before going to Paris in 1742.

From his time in the de Mably household survive, however, two short pieces that he wrote about education. They are slight works, and substantially the same in content, although the longer *Mémoire Présenté à M. de Mably* contains a passage about Rousseau's own feelings and ambitions which the *Projet pour l'Éducation de M. de Sainte-Marie* ('Project for the Education of M. de Sainte-Marie') lacks. In them Rousseau maintains that education should aim not just to instil learning, but to form the heart, judgement and spirit. The acquisition of good habits and dispositions must come before abstract knowledge. A child is generally better taught through fables and stories than through abstruse reasonings. He must be led by his interest, not constrained by dry and dutiful lessons which arouse dislike and resistance. He should be taught in such a way as to enable him to be happy; and this, Rousseau says, is better done by learning to moderate rather than indulging the passions.

We do not know what, if anything, de Mably did with these two versions of essentially the same essay. Not published in Rousseau's lifetime, they first appeared in 1782 (and in a later version in 1884).

Rousseau's claim to be an educational theorist of the first rank derives not from these early works but from the major work of his maturity, ÉMILE (subtitled: *On Education*). It is not clear why he chose to write such an extensive work on the subject (he later said that it was more of a metaphysical treatise on human goodness than an educational treatise). Although he appears to have had no such project in mind when he first moved to Montmorency in 1756, it was there that he conceived and wrote *Émile*. It has been suggested that it was when several of his distinguished women friends asked him for advice and guidance that he determined to try to formulate his views more systematically. But though this may have been the occasion, the work is driven by larger concerns, and comprises a discussion central to the understanding of his mature thought.

The keynote of the educational approach that Rousseau favours is the idea of 'negative education'. By this he means refraining from controlling, directing, admonishing or cramming the child at every turn. Instead, we should realize that there is a naturally healthy and ordered course in the development of a child's body, understanding and feelings, and it is the educator's role to respect the integrity of this development, to give space and opportunity for it to take place in its due way and time, and to adjust the child's lessons so that they engage in an immediate and straightforward way with his current level of interest and abilities. In this way, the child is scarcely aware that he is under instruction. He thinks that it is all fun, and that he is being helped to do what his nascent powers and inclinations would have him do anyway.

There comes a time when, although it would be good for such instruction to continue, it can no longer be carried out in this simple way. In late adolescence and early adulthood, the teacher–pupil relation needs to be re-established on a voluntary footing. But by that time the major (negative) educational aims will already have been achieved. So it is best to concentrate on describing what these comprise.

In an early, incomplete, draft of *Émile* (the MS Favre), Rousseau divides the developmental stages of man into four: the age of nature (up to 12 years); the age of reason (intelligence) (12–15); the age of energy, force of life (15–20); the age of wisdom (20–25). Although he did not adhere to quite such a schematic pattern in the final work, it serves as a useful framework.

In the age of nature, the child's primary feature is his extreme weakness and vulnerability. He is born helpless, into a world not understood, and is dependent for all his needs and for his very survival on the help of those around him. Essential to good education in this period are two things, in Rousseau's view. First, the proper handling of a child's rage and of his attempts at imperious control, which are the obverse of his impotence and fear. He must be preserved from believing that command and obedience, domination and subservience, are the terms on which human beings deal with each other, and on which the world is brought to heel. Second, he must not be constrained physically (as long as his safety is ensured) nor by threats or demands. For he will see in this only attempts to thwart him, which will provoke resentment and induce in him combativeness, evasion and pretence. A child is naturally inclined to move, to act; he must be given liberty to live, breathe, feel his own energy freely, and find out for himself, by dealing with the material world, the scope and limits of his powers. Gradually he will acquire first-hand experience of how the world works, and learn how it may be used to advantage by working *with* it rather than trying to bend it to his command. The predictable, orderly environment that Rousseau insists upon will aid a child's progress in this, as well as quieting his fears and the constellation of other feelings – particularly his conviction that the world is maliciously intent on thwarting him.

At about the age of twelve, a child will have acquired a basic physical competence and ability to cope effectively with his immediate environment. Then comes a period when there is some free mental energy, so to speak, not given over to the resolution of practical issues alone. This is the time to extend his understanding beyond what is immediate and local, so that he learns some general truths and laws about the heavens and the earth. This is not best done, Rousseau holds, by book learning and passive instruction. Rather, the good educator contrives occasions where from the exigencies of a practical predicament some wider lesson may be learned or applied, to immediate benefit. Thus, by pretending to be lost on a walk, the teacher can cause the pupil to learn about landmarks, bearings and the significance of the angle and length of shadows. In this way, he is introduced to cartography, geometry, arithmetic and general sciences. But the issue here is not that he learn many facts and theories. Rather than relying on abstract learning, the pupil will acquire skills of general application, enabling him to sift, evaluate and make sense of what is going on around him.

The onset of the age of 'force' – of vivid, electric feeling and passionate energy – takes place around fifteen or sixteen. (The actual ages that Rousseau cites do not matter: it is the articulation of the different phases of development that is significant.) Now adolescent, the child feels the

103

onset of passion, an all-absorbing interest in those around him, especially in how they regard him, whether they love him or not. This Rousseau calls the child's 'second birth'; first he is born for the species, second for his sex. These pubertal changes have, for Rousseau, a specifically sexual origin which makes the issues of love and sex of obsessive concern.

This uprush of intense feeling for others poses great problems for the educator. Rousseau argues first of all that the flood of sexual interest should be checked: it is better that the adolescent first come to terms with others as friends, companions and fellow-humans than as sexual partners in erotic intimacy. The educator's purpose must be to enable him to find a footing with others in which he feels confident, secure, respected and capable of effectively holding his own without either excessive aggression or excessive servility. Nature provides the educator with passions, specifically COMPASSION, which is also present in the adolescent at this time and which the educator can use to further this more creative development in his relationships.

The scheme outlined in the MS Favre peters out at this point, but from the finished work we see how Rousseau thinks education, which will now involve a large component of self-education, should continue into the 'age of wisdom'. The pupil, now a young adult, learns about law, society and government, and also courts and wins a marriage partner. He has finally become a fully equipped, self-possessed and self-determining member of adult society and a citizen of a state; through his own virtue and conduct the welfare of society is now sustained. It is in regard to these matters that Émile and his tutor must renegotiate the basis of their relationship: Jean-Jacques can continue as Émile's guardian and guide only with the latter's permission. In these last stages of education the tutor uses a more theoretical approach – when dealing with law and government, for instance – but real experience is still emphasized. Émile is encouraged to travel so that he does not merely know about, but understands, other situations, other polities; and, as during his courtship, when Émile is about to destroy himself through uncontrollable passion, his tutor will sometimes stage-manage affairs or intervene.

All these educational proposals – often intriguing, often amusing, in their detail – are designed to serve Rousseau's dominant purpose: to enable a human being to grow up whole, intact, in possession of his own creative powers and possibilities, that he will use for his own and for others' benefit. And, given that he is so critical of the deformations and sufferings that society ordinarily inflicts on people, Rousseau is obliged to show what a whole person, true to nature, brought up according to the principles that he outlines in Émile, would be like. The educational programme is, throughout, subservient to this larger purpose.

It is generally held that Rousseau's ideas have been influential, and largely for good. That children should enjoy the liberty to experience their own powers; that instruction should be geared to their level and engage with their interests; that different tasks are appropriate to different ages; that skills and competences are of more value and endure longer than rote-learned knowledge – all of these would now be considered common sense. Rousseau would not have been happy, though, with the tendency of some child-centred education to allow the child to think that he may do whatever his whim directs, since to believe that his CAPRICE was law would be inimical to successful growth.

Sources: E, especially Bks I–III; MS Favre
    Projet pour l'Éducation de M. de Sainte-Marie

Further reading: Carr (165); Dent (166); Jimack (169); Meyer (171)

Émile or On Education (1762) (*Émile, ou de l'Éducation*) [11] Rousseau began *Émile*, his greatest work, probably in early 1759 when he was living at Mont-Louis near Montmorency. It has been suggested that it was his concern to advise some of his distinguished women friends about the upbringing of their children that induced him to formulate his ideas on education in book form. But, despite its subtitle, *Émile* is not exclusively, or even mainly, concerned with child-rearing techniques and objectives. For Rousseau took the issue of child-rearing and placed it in the context of life viewed in the long term; his concern was with the means whereby a person might come to live the best life for himself both as an independent being and as a being living with others in society and in the state. It is these issues which are paramount in *Émile* (for Rousseau's educational 'programme', *see* EDUCATION).

His progress was rapid, and the work was more or less ready for publication by July 1761. (An earlier draft, the MS Favre, about one third of the final version, survives.) The Maréchale de Luxembourg, with whom Rousseau had formed a close friendship at the time, appears to have thought his usual publisher, Marc-Michel Rey, unsuitable for the task, and for reasons of censorship she made arrangements for the work to be printed under the name of a Dutch publisher, Néaulme (though most of the printing was done in Paris). Rousseau became troubled by the slowness of the printing, and harboured morbid suspicions that the work was being sabotaged by the Jesuits. The Director of Publications, Malesherbes, surprisingly sympathetic to the work and to Rousseau, investigated the situation and was able to put his mind at rest. Moved by this friendly gesture, Rousseau addressed to Malesherbes four autobiographical letters

(LETTERS TO MALESHERBES) in January 1762. *Émile* eventually appeared in May of that year, a month after the publication of *The Social Contract* (printed by Rey).

But it was *Émile*, rather than *The Social Contract*, that was to cause Rousseau a great deal of trouble with the religious authorities, who found a long section in Bk IV, THE CREED OF A SAVOYARD VICAR, to be unacceptable in view of the ideas of natural religion and the attacks on the Catholic Church contained in it. On 7 June 1762 the book was denounced by the Faculty of Theology at the Sorbonne, and later that day the Paris *parlement* ordered Rousseau's arrest. Copies were publicly burned. Warned that he would be detained, Rousseau fled to Yverdon in Switzerland during the afternoon of 9 June. But matters did not rest there. A week or so later, both *Émile* and *The Social Contract* (published in April of the same year) were burned in Geneva, and under pressure from the Genevan authorities Rousseau was required to leave Yverdon, eventually finding a haven at Môtiers where Rousseau enjoyed the protection of Frederick of Prussia. Then in the August, the Archbishop of Paris, Christophe de Beaumont, published a pastoral letter, a decree, of censure and guidance regarding *Émile*, detailing why it was heretical and thus intolerable. In due course Rousseau wrote a vigorous reply, his LETTER TO CHRISTOPHE DE BEAUMONT (published in 1763), in which he defended his ideas and actions with great clarity. Such was the immediate impact of the publication of *Émile*; in the longer term, it shaped the rest of Rousseau's life, turning him into a hunted and stateless fugitive.

Émile contains many of Rousseau's most far-reaching ideas. Perhaps because of its considerable length and because it can appear diffuse and over-detailed, it is not as widely studied or appreciated as others of Rousseau's works on associated themes – which has a deleterious effect on the understanding of his thought overall. For in *Émile* we find what we do not find in his other writings: a thorough discussion of the way in which an individual can find, or make, a place for himself in society without suffering ALIENATION or the personal corruption and pain that this involves. Without an appreciation of Rousseau's ideas on this point, it is impossible to interpret his concerns in his other social and political works correctly: they will appear to describe the conflict between the needs and good of the individual and the demands that social and civil existence place on him as one that Rousseau never successfully resolved. However, in *Émile* is to be found a careful treatment of this issue which throws much light on his other works.

Émile describes the development of a typical individual, Émile, under the guidance of his tutor, Jean-Jacques (Rousseau himself). Émile's powers and dispositions gradually develop and unfold – from earliest infancy, through youth and adolescence, up to maturity and the assumption of his full place in society as a self-determining adult. Each of the five books covers a period of years in which, Rousseau thinks, certain significant clusters of phenomena occur together. Books I and II cover, roughly, birth to 12 years; Bk III, 12 to 15; Bk IV, 15 to 20; and Bk V, 20 to 25. No special weight should be attached to this chronology, nor to Rousseau's treating these issues in the form of a developmental narrative. Although he stresses the importance of doing things at particular times and in a particular order, he is primarily concerned to explain what is appropriate to, and good for, the several aspects of man's nature and potential – as competent individual looking after his own interests, as friend, as member of society, as lover, as citizen, and so on.

Fundamental to the whole work is Rousseau's belief that humans have an intact nature which, if allowed proper scope for development, will allow them to be useful, happy and good, for themselves and for others. It is man's interference with the normal course of nature that makes people corrupt, miserable and damaging to themselves and to others. He announces in the very first sentence: 'Everything is good as it leaves the hands of the Author of things; everything degenerates in the hands of man' (*E* I, 37; *OC* IV, 245). An explanation and a defence of this basic claim – that man is by nature good but is corrupted by society (*see* NATURAL GOODNESS) – constitutes, at root, the whole argument of *Émile*. (And it is restated in subsequent works.)

The goal of a good education, of a life scheme that will enable a person to remain in possession of his proper powers and to express them fully in all aspects of his life, is to keep faith with the integrity of nature. The disposition proper to individual nature is AMOUR DE SOI, an innate concern to preserve one's own existence and to have a fruitful life. But *amour de soi*, to begin with, is not a conscious concern, is not directed by a knowledge of what is beneficial or hurtful; and it can be deflected from its proper objective by events that may befall the weak and vulnerable child.

Initially an infant needs most of all nourishment, protection and the opportunity to flex his growing limbs, to begin to enjoy his power of existence. But even at this time, things can go awry. A child cries; tears are his first words – they bring attention, relief, aid. He has no other way of summoning assistance, but if this comes too easily, the child will come to believe that, at the pucker of a lip, the world can be bent to his service. Then, if relief is not forthcoming, he will become enraged; he will think that he has been disobeyed, denied, thwarted. His rage reveals his representing the world as wrongfully denying and spiting him. He will begin to feel that all human transaction is a battle of wills, for dominance and command – or else, servility and denial will be the outcome. This aggressive representation of human dealings, Rousseau thinks, must be avoided at all costs. If it is sustained, a child will become alternately imperious and servile, domineering and cringing, and these patterns perpetuated into adulthood and society spell man's downfall.

Above all, Rousseau recommends that the child be deflected from this path in his dealings with others. Otherwise, 'the idea of empire and domination . . . excited less by his needs than by our services' will be implanted, and 'moral effects whose immediate cause is not in nature begin to make their appearance' (*E* I, 66; *OC* IV, 287). This is how nature begins to be corrupted, not necessarily through ill-intentioned actions, by the work of man. To prevent this corruption, Rousseau suggests that up to the age of fifteen Émile should be insulated from contact with the wills of other humans, and hence from any tendency to combative conflict. Instead, he should concentrate all his energies on learning the real limits of his powers and abilities by engaging with his surroundings, gradually learning practical competences that will make him well able to look after himself as a living creature situated in the world. Command and obedience, duty and obligation, must be excluded from the ambit of his experience. Moral ideas and social relations, which involve negotiating with others for a footing in their concerns, should still be in abeyance at this point.

But this is less than half of what makes a whole person – and now Émile enters the next stage. If matters were taken no further, we should not have 'completed the man' (*E* III, 203; *OC* IV, 481). 'Émile is not a savage to be relegated to the desert. He is a savage made to inhabit cities. He has to know how to find his necessities in them' (*E* III, 205; *OC* IV, 483–4). He must now begin to consider himself in regard to others.

Rousseau thinks it is the onset of puberty, with the flood of feelings and desires towards others and the concern to find favour in a woman's eyes that this involves, that makes Émile's relations with others now of paramount concern. Rousseau is certain, however, that that first flood of sexual interest must be checked, or else rivalries, jealousy and intrigue will dominate Émile's first attempts to find a place for himself in the life of another (*E* IV, 214; *OC* IV, 494). His quickened interest in other people, especially in how they look on him, must be channelled elsewhere. Émile's imagination having been caught by other people, it should be directed towards caring for them in their weakness, through COMPASSION. In this way, he will find a footing in others' affairs in which there need be no rivalry or competition for precedence. Instead, he may learn to care for and respect others, who will, in turn, look on him with gratitude and esteem. The demands of AMOUR-PROPRE, which directs a person to ensure that he is well regarded and honoured in the affairs of men, will be met through the kinds of relationship that compassion establishes. His *amour-propre* need not, therefore, take on an exacerbated and inflamed character whereby he would think he was receiving his due only if he gained ascendancy over others or claimed for himself a place of invidious distinction in relation to them.

Émile has thus re-entered the human world, and will engage once more with the fraught issue of encountering the will and feelings of others, which was put into abeyance in his earlier years. But instead of this encounter being structured by fear, aggression and competition it is shaped by mutual regard, trust and cooperation. In this way, Émile achieves a place in human society that is as beneficial and creative for himself as it is for those he has dealings with. Human encounter is not a conflict leading inexorably to triumph or defeat, in which every party is disfigured by a malice that destroys him and his 'opponents'. It is, rather, a forum in which each more amply possesses and expresses his natural powers and can attain the full scope of his humanity.

There is, in this, no desertion or distortion of nature. It is proper to human nature to live, work and share with others in many ways and on many footings. The essential point is that such relationships should continue to benefit each person by enabling him to act constructively and creatively with and for other people. Conflict and competition may be common features of human intercourse, but they are not inevitable, nor are they appropriate to nature. The 'moral order', whereby persons are tied to each other by responsibility and title, is not inevitably a desertion or distortion of nature. This gives the lie to those who maintain that, for Rousseau, all social connection involves human beings in a loss of personal integrity, and plunges them into self-division and aggressive conflict with others.

In one of his finest passages, he works through these matters in Bk IV of *Émile*, with control, precision and focus.

In Bk V Rousseau returns to the issue of Émile's desire for an intimate companion. He uses the introduction of Émile's destined wife, Sophie, as an occasion for expounding on the character, dispositions and education of WOMEN. In coming to love Sophie, he is even more exposed to the dangers of loss of self-possession and of abandonment to the control of others than he was when seeking a place for himself in society generally. Rousseau insists that he must always retain his moral and personal integrity; only by doing so will he merit and retain Sophie's love. She cannot value someone who makes himself the plaything of her feelings; she was made to love men, not monkeys (*E* V, 404; *OC* IV, 761).

If their love is consummated in marriage and family, then, as the head of a household, Émile will become the member of a state. Rousseau thinks it essential that he learn about the nature and basis of the civil order, so he includes what is in substance a brief summary of the principal ideas of The SOCIAL CONTRACT (*E* V, 458–67; *OC* IV, 836–49). Finally, after a period of travel which Émile undertakes both in order to become better acquainted with the affairs of men and to test the endurance of his love, his education is complete. He has considered his 'physical relations with other beings', his 'moral relations with other men' and his 'civil relations with his fellow citizens', and he is now an adult and his own master (*E* V, 455; *OC* IV, 833). He is a competent, rational, loving and feeling being (*E* III, 203; *OC* IV, 481), fully constituted 'as a man and an integral part of his species' (*E* IV, 220; *OC* IV, 501).

Further reading: Bloom (163); Charvet, ch. 3 (23); Dent, chs 2–4 (24); Horowitz, ch. 8 (27); Jimack (167); Jimack (168)

Émile et Sophie (1781) [13]   It was probably in late 1762 that Rousseau began to write a sequel to Bk V of ÉMILE, about Émile and his new wife Sophie as they began their married life together. Although he returned to the material from time to time over several years, he made very little progress. It takes the form of two letters (the second uncompleted; both published posthumously, in 1781), supposedly addressed by Émile to his former tutor, guide and friend, Jean-Jacques (i.e. Rousseau himself), recounting what has happened to him since they parted.

The subtitle, *Les Solitaires*, gives some clue to the work's content: Émile and Sophie's life together is not to be an unbroken idyll of love. Despite Jean-Jacques' constant warnings of the dangers of city life, Émile and his wife move to Paris, largely to distract Sophie from the grief she suffers at the loss of their daughter and of her parents. The couple become deeply estranged. Sophie is unfaithful; Émile cannot control his pain and despair. All efforts at reconciliation prove hopeless; all trust is gone, and there is too much suffering on both sides for them to live in unity again. Émile decides to leave her and to leave France, and to take his chance as a wandering soul.

In the second letter he tells of how he sets sail for Italy, but on the way the ship is attacked by pirates and he is sold as a slave. He is brutally treated, but eventually rouses resistance among his fellow-slaves and persuades their master that they would work better for him if they were properly cared for. Émile is put in charge, and does the job so well that he is made the slave to the Dey of Algeria. The letter breaks off at the point where, it appears, Émile (rather like Joseph in Egypt) is about to become the valued adviser to a powerful king.

Written with vigour and flair, the letters make arresting reading, but it is doubtful that they add much to the principal ideas of *Émile*. Some critics have seen in them Rousseau's acknowledgement that even his most carefully fashioned product, the naturally good Émile, is destined to failure: human beings can never be happy, can never retain their goodness, however well schooled. Others have argued that Rousseau intends to show that there is one lesson that Émile had still to learn: what it is like to suffer desperately. Only once he had been purged by this fire would he know what it is to be fully human. Perhaps these two letters should be given a more central place in the evaluation of Rousseau's ideas.

Further reading: Shklar, Appendix (36)

Encyclopaedia, The (1751–65) (*Encyclopédie ou Dictionnaire Raisonné des Sciences, des Arts et des Métiers*)   Rousseau contributed about two hundred articles on music to Diderot and d'Alembert's *Encyclopaedia*, and one long article on political economy ((A DISCOURSE ON) POLITICAL ECONOMY). For the supplementary volumes, Rousseau's own *Dictionary of Music*, based on these first articles (*see* MUSIC: WRITINGS ON), was used for many additional and alternative entries.

The *Encyclopaedia* derived from a proposal to translate, adapt and extend Chambers' *Cyclopaedia*, or *Universal Dictionary of Arts and Sciences*, that had first appeared in Scotland in 1728. This robust piece of commercial opportunism soon turned into a very much more impressive and important undertaking. After one or two false starts, Denis Diderot took over the editorship, and with the principal assistance of Jean d'Alembert he conceived the idea of creating a comprehensive encyclopaedia of all aspects of human endeavour and achievement, showing the progress of man in the newly liberated environment of universal reason and ENLIGHTENMENT. But even Diderot's original conception was not equal to the work's ultimate form. In the prospectus of 1750 eight volumes of text and two of plates were announced, and subscriptions taken out. In the end, seventeen volumes of text (the last in 1765) and eleven of plates (the last in 1772) were produced, to be followed only a few years later by four supplementary volumes of text and one of plates.

It was, and remains, an astonishing achievement, a monument to that very industry its content celebrates. Art, music, architecture; mathematics, geometry, cartography; agriculture, metal-working, mining; economics, government, law – there is no area of human inquiry, artifice or labour that is not covered. Hundreds contributed to the various volumes, but it was the prodigious labour that Diderot devoted to the whole enterprise that provides the unity of purpose, the 'philosophy'. There is, throughout, a confidence that men are, or can soon become, masters of their own destiny; that they have the knowledge and skills to fashion the world and society to their convenience and advantage. The power of reason, in all its guises, has liberated people from the stultifying material and moral inheritance of the past, and equipped them to understand and act for their own interest and the interests of all in a world of which they now have mastery. As the embodiment of progressive confidence, the *Encyclopaedia* was not universally well received by the civil and religious powers. Various attempts at suppression were made, but the climate was in its favour and there were too many influential persons prepared to back the work to allow its continuing publication to be blocked.

Rousseau's entries on music constitute a small footnote to the changing musical culture of eighteenth-century France; and the article on political economy is an important part of his output on political and moral themes. But, inevitably, a great many of the articles now have no more than a historical interest.

Sources: No complete modern edn exists; there is a 2-vol. selection ed. Alain Pons (Paris, 1986).

Further reading: Darnton (242); Hubert (256); Lough (263); Martin (272); Oliver (197); Proust (326)

Enlightenment   The Enlightenment was a movement of ideas, a gradual set of changes in religious, scientific, social and political thought, that took place in France in the eighteenth century.

> The Enlightenment, by that name, was not a thing that any English speaker knew during the earlier nineteenth century. It is a modern word. When English speakers first began to need a word to describe the climate of opinion in the age of the Encyclopaedia, they used the German word *Aufklärung*, evidence enough that the notion had not yet reached the popular histories for schools. For three-quarters of the nineteenth century they did not think of the age as an enlightened age. Most of them thought of it with opprobrium as the age which ended in a nemesis of guillotine and terror. (Chadwick (283))

A 'climate of opinion' is, notoriously, a vague and ill-defined phenomenon, and people's assessment of it is inevitably subjective. None the less, Rousseau is so commonly held to be a signal figure of the Enlightenment that his place in that 'climate of opinion' needs to be considered. The major figures of the movement saw themselves as engaged in the business of clearing away mysteries, obfuscations, the clutter and rubbish of outmoded ideas and institutions which stunted man's progress. In their

112

place was to be put that which was transparent in its rational purpose and functioning, liberating and forward-looking. In particular, the Church's – specifically the Catholic Church's – control over learning, law, government and the affairs of men was to be overcome. Universal secular reason, the techniques and methods central to natural science, were to acquire sovereignty in its place; everything was to be investigated, explained, brought before the bar of rational evaluation in order to vindicate its credentials.

In general terms, then, the Enlightenment was committed to open, unimpeded investigation, unchecked by dogma or authority derived from sources which could not themselves sustain such investigation. In principle, anyone was at liberty to, and had the capacity to, conduct such investigations. No one was privileged, no one excluded. Society's wise and learned men ought to attain their position not by special dispensation, nor by dependence on some supposed hierarchy: theirs was a career open to talent. Thus there is a strongly egalitarian strand in Enlightenment thought, although Rousseau was exceptional in carrying forward extensive demands for EQUALITY in the social and political spheres. Although many of the movement's ideas were subversive of established orders, few other Enlightenment figures advocated such radical proposals.

The ENCYCLOPAEDIA is probably the most representative document of the Enlightenment. Its principal editors, Diderot and d'Alembert, and the innumerable and often distinguished contributors (for instance, Voltaire, Condillac, Holbach, Grimm, Rousseau) – often referred to as *philosophes* – are the movement's leading figures.

Except for his extensive essay on political economy (*see* (DISCOURSE ON) POLITICAL ECONOMY) Rousseau's contributions to the *Encyclopaedia* were all on music (*see* MUSIC: WRITINGS ON). But despite this narrow range he was, to begin with, closely involved with the project overall. However, his attitude towards the other *encyclopédistes*, and to the climate of ideas they were creating, went through drastic changes. His first mature work of social theory, the DISCOURSE ON THE SCIENCES AND THE ARTS, already takes a highly critical stance towards arts and letters as contributing anything worthwhile to human benefit and happiness. This essay did not at once signal a breach with his friends, though: it was seen more as an expression of paradox, as a demonstration of the free play of critical intelligence that the *philosophes* celebrated, than as a serious attack on them and their aspirations. Indeed, it can be read, rather, as a call for greater dedication to the pursuit of truth; as a statement that only the pretenders and charlatans should be criticized, not the undertaking itself.

This accommodation did not survive long. For personal reasons, but also because of widening differences in outlook, conflict gradually became deeper. Rousseau no longer saw increasing CIVILIZATION as leading to greater fulfilment and happiness; he did not believe that REASON was capable of proving the existence of God and sustaining religious belief – instead, it produced only disabling scepticism and cynicism. He came to feel that human affairs and social order depended more on virtue and loyalty than on knowledge of, and adherence to, rational principles of conduct. In these and other ways he became not only estranged from, but hostile to, the shallow confidence that everything could be explained, that human conduct was susceptible to purely rational direction, that all change was progress towards a better and happier future. Increasingly he came to value a sense of mystery, humility, submission as true to the deepest movements of the human heart.

Vague as such conflicts between reason and faith, knowledge and mystery, intellect and feeling, may be, Rousseau was giving voice, in his own way, to some of the deeper disquiets over the scope and power of science in relation to the nature of man, the universe and God which ramified during the nineteenth century and were to be addressed by people as diverse as Hegel and Matthew Arnold. What presents itself as 'enlightened' thinking, even in these days, is often a set of ideas that is controlling, restrictive, reductive and imperious and that, far from offering any enduring grasp of what we need to know in order to flourish, often simply misses or ignores anything not within its remit.

Although Rousseau is clearly not representative of this prevailing 'climate of opinion' – notwithstanding that he is often seen as such – there remain, of course, many important points of likeness. His emphasis on the moral dignity proper to every individual, leading to his idea of civil authority lying in the hands of 'the people' (*see* AUTHORITY), is plainly compatible with the elevation of the scope and rights of individual judgement that is implicit in the critical intellectual inquiries of the *Encyclopaedia*. However, it may be argued that by so stressing the inalienable titles of individuals, Rousseau undermined not only established structures of authority but also those ties of common loyalty and allegiance that he thought to be essential to any just and creative community. If we consider the 'age of Enlightenment' as the age in which the conception of the 'modern individual' came to full maturity, then Rousseau's ideas must surely have played some role in this.

Sources: DI
    Letter to d'Alembert on the Theatre

Further reading: Cassirer (239); Darnton (243); Gay (247); Hampson (252); Hazard (254); Kant (288); Keohane (260); Martin (272)

equality   Rousseau's treatment of the nature and importance of human equality falls into two parts: first, his criticism of inequality; second, his account of what equality is and why it matters.

His discussion of the foundation and character of inequality is primarily to be found in the DISCOURSE ON THE ORIGIN OF INEQUALITY, in which he distinguishes two forms: natural, and conventional, inequality. The former consists in differences in strength, health, quickness of mind and so on; the latter in differences of riches, honour, power and authority. It is his view that the former inequalities are inevitable, and normally benign or inconsequential; the latter, on the other hand, are illegitimate, pernicious and without justification. It is these to which he gives most attention.

Principally because, when in association with others, people are concerned to gain invidious ascendancy (*see* AMOUR-PROPRE), they seek to establish and maintain as much inequality of as many different kinds between themselves and others as they can, in order to gain a sense of themselves as superior over the negligible or contemptible others. Virtually any differentiating mark – such as wearing particular garments, having certain manners – can be turned to this purpose, providing only that the person or group will thereby be able to think of themselves as superior, more distinguished, a 'better class of person'. Wealth, privileges, social stations all take their primary significance from this malign desire to do other people down (*see* COMPARISON). These differentiating marks are esteemed as 'merits' even though they signify no real quality and function only as devices to procure the abjection of competitors.

These inequalities, Rousseau believes, are the principal sources of human misery and corruption. And even the 'superior' person is harmed, he contends, since, depending as he does on the good opinion of others to preserve any sense of his own worth, he has lost possession of himself, has become the plaything of others' estimates of him (*see* ALIENATION). Rousseau maintains, also, that there is no correlation between natural and conventional inequalities. It is a question 'fit perhaps to be discussed by slaves in the hearing of their masters' but 'highly unbecoming to reasonable and free men in search of the truth' (*DI* 44; *OC* III, 132), whether strength of body and mind, wisdom and virtue, are found in proportion to power or wealth.

What forms of equality does Rousseau think desirable, and why? First of all, there must be a basic equality of moral and civil position and standing, so that no one is in servitude or subjection. It is proper that none be the subject of arbitrary command, that all share equal authority and right to direct their own affairs and to determine the affairs common to all (*see* CITIZEN). Even in the best state, there may be some differences of property and wealth, but these, he argues, should never be allowed to become so great as to cause any one person to become dependent on the will and favour of some (specific) other person for his survival and security. For this will result in his enslavement to that other person, and his master too will be corrupted, in believing that in having dependants lies his own merit and value. Second, then, it is clear that a guaranteed basic equality in material provision, sufficient to relieve everyone of the need to curry favour from another in order to gain a livelihood, is something Rousseau thinks important.

Also in the best state there will be certain differences in power and position: not all members will, for instance, be governors, with the power to administer the law. But such positions will be established on the common authorization of all, acting in their equal sovereign capacity as members of the supreme authority in the state; government exists as a delegated function, on the approval of every person. Furthermore, those who occupy such positions have the task of defending and protecting the person and goods of all. They are (in theory at least) servants of the public good, in their function as governors of it.

These fundamental equalities, in moral and civil standing and in access to material resources, are valuable not merely for what they prevent – namely, servitude and destitution (in all their guises) – but for what they procure, and not just for each individual but for all as a community. It is only in relation to persons whom one values and honours as equals, Rousseau argues, that one can oneself receive that recognition and respect that is truly meaningful, that truly represents one's being honoured as a morally significant being. The tribute of slaves is an empty gesture, paid from fear or threat; it confers no true honour on its recipient. But those who know their own worth, and whom one recognizes as having worth, can by their respect of one establish that one counts as a human among humans.

The rich and powerful should not, therefore, resent or begrudge the diminution of their privileges, for the benefits that these conferred were only apparent. They can obtain in a community of equals that honour of themselves that they sought via the delusive allure of dominance (*see* DOMINATION).

Sources: *DI*, especially Pt 2
       DPE
       SC Bks I, II

Further reading: Charvet (331); Nesbit (138); Paul (295); Walzer (347); Williams (349)

Essay on the Origin of Languages (*Essai sur l'Origine des Langues*) [8] *See* ORIGIN OF LANGUAGES.

F

First Discourse   *See* Discourse on the Sciences and the Arts.

freedom (liberty)   The notion of freedom, or liberty, is central to Rousseau's social and political thought. To the enjoyment of freedom he attaches, probably, more importance than to any other aspect of human life. 'To renounce liberty,' he writes, 'is to renounce being a man, to surrender the rights of humanity' (*SC* I, ch. 4, 170; *OC* III, 356). He employs the notion in several distinct ways and contexts, which must be distinguished if his thoughts about this complex matter are to be fully understood.

First, two instances of Rousseau's notion of freedom that are somewhat distinct from its use in social and political contexts. He claims in the Discourse on the Origin of Inequality that human beings have a capacity (which distinguishes them from the animals) to check their immediate impulses or to take deliberate, non-impulsive action for the sake of future good: 'Man has some share in his own operations, in his character as a free agent. The one (a brute) chooses and refuses by instinct, the other (a man) from an act of free will; hence the brute cannot deviate from the rule prescribed to it, even when it would be advantageous for it to do so' (*DI* 53; *OC* III, 141). At a common-sense level, it is clear that humans frequently enjoy the power of self-determined choice of action, enabling them to withstand or overcome the 'dictates' of nature.

Related to this is Rousseau's argument that moral evil (and good) is imputable to man because he is the self-determining source of his own actions. He does not claim to *know* that man is 'free in his actions and as such is animated by an immaterial substance' (*E* IV, 280–1; *OC* IV, 587); this conviction is one of the 'articles of faith' of the Creed of a Savoyard Vicar. But he maintains that the evil that men do 'falls back' on them and cannot be imputed to God or laid at God's door as a complaint. For, in giving men freedom of this kind, God has 'put in man's actions the morality which ennobles them'.

These two notions of, or aspects of, human freedom are not uncontro-

117

versial or unproblematical, but they are somewhat marginal to Rousseau's central interest.

We move closer to these central concerns in the following, third, instance of freedom. It is a commonplace that our ability and opportunity to carry out our intended acts can be hampered or constrained by, for example, external obstacles, lack of resources or inadequate skills. All of these limit our freedom, our scope to do what we intend or please as and when we intend, or it pleases us, to do it. To increase individual freedom in this sense is simply to reduce or remove obstacles, or to increase relevant resources, knowledge, skill and so on. This kind of freedom is sometimes called 'negative' freedom, when it involves taking away con- straints or limitations (negations of freedom) thereby enabling a person more amply and successfully to express his desires and intentions in action. At a superficial level it is a familiar idea, one that we frequently employ when we bemoan loss of freedom and extol the benefits of increased freedom.

It is important, however, to distinguish between the kinds or sources of external obstacles that may impede a person doing as he chooses. In the case just considered, it is principally a question of the hardships and impositions of natural circumstances. As soon as we include impositions produced by the direct action (or inaction) of other people – threats, or poverty, for example – we change the character of the constraints, and the issue of human freedom takes on further dimensions. Rousseau was deeply concerned throughout his mature work with patterns of control, command and power between people, and it is in this connection that he makes his most significant claims about freedom.

Possibly his single most famous remark is: 'Man is born free; and everywhere he is in chains' (*SC* I, ch. 1, 165; *OC* III, 351). What freedom, and what enslavement, does he have in view here? The freedom is, in essence, this. No one, according to Rousseau, is born into a position whereby he is bound (*de jure* or *de facto*) to the obedience of the will of another, whereby he stands answerable to or accountable to anyone else for his actions. It is not intrinsic to the condition of man to be in such a position, whether it be moral, civil or any other kind of obedience or control that is at issue. (There is one exception: the case of God. But no man is God, and no man can claim the authority of God in his command or control of other men.) Each of us is, then, originally accountable to and for ourselves alone, the sovereign director of our own actions, beholden to, answerable to, no one else.

Rousseau dramatizes this conception of original or 'natural' liberty with his image of persons being, in the first instance, isolated, independent, not associated with others. But this picture of primitive isolation need not be

taken literally: its point is only to make clear that hierarchy and subordination, authority and control, are utterly alien to the original powers and
titles of human beings. Each person is his own sole judge and master;
there is no other human judge or master before whom he stands and must
acquit himself.

It is one's absolute self-sovereignty in governing and directing one's
own actions, accountable to none, that is central to Rousseau's affirmation
of the natural liberty proper to all men alike. It is clear, though, that
someone may enjoy perfect liberty of *this* kind, but still suffer extreme
restrictions on his freedom of action as a result of natural hardships or the
difficulty (providing it is not produced by human power or neglect) of
scratching a living. It is, in fact, limitations on freedom of this latter sort
which force people, according to Rousseau (*SC* I, ch. 6; *OC* III, 360), to
join together in material and civil associations in order, by pooling their
strength and skills, to overcome these obstacles. But as soon as they do
associate for this reason, the issue of the retention of their self-sovereignty,
of their natural liberty, becomes crucial.

Unless there is a perfect, more or less spontaneous, coincidence in the
plans and actions that each member proposes for the concerted action of
all, there is bound to be some compromise or limitation of individual
discretion in arriving at and carrying out the plans that concerted action
requires. A procedure (formal or informal) is required for achieving a
common purpose and strategy, which cannot be the design of one, non-
accountable, person alone. If this were so, everyone else would have been
denied scope for the exercise of their own judgement. They would have
renounced their own liberty.

This unlimited self-sovereignty can be called 'discretionary' freedom,
thus indicating that the individual enjoys total discretion in whether to act
or not. Is there any way in which consistent coordinated action with
others can be achieved without compromise of, or disappearance of,
discretionary freedom? Or does association with others involve the loss of
that type of freedom, and its replacement by a different type? Or does it
involve the loss of all types of freedom – if not totally, at least in large
measure? Rousseau's answers to these questions are complex, and the
subject of controversy. What follows is one possible interpretation.

The issue of arriving at a decision procedure in a way that would
respect the discretionary freedom of all who are to be subject to the rules
issuing from the implementation of that procedure might best be resolved
by ensuring that no decision procedure has authority without the individual discretionary consent of all to its implementation. So, then,
although someone might subsequently be required by another to do
something he did not want to do, at one remove he would himself have

authorized this control and direction of his actions. This is part of Rousseau's thought, but not the whole of it. For, first, he insists that there must be limits on the 'output' of any decision procedure, even if it is one whose power to control has been authorized. No directive can be binding which dispossesses a person of his moral title to respect, or which renders him destitute.

But there is a second, more important, point. A person may refuse to agree to establish a certain decision procedure for reasons of private interest about which he is very emphatic. It is conceivable that he might therefore simply be excluded from the association. But if the problem recurs, there can be no real prospect of establishing an association capable of concerted action. To end up making terms which approximate to acknowledging as dominant the claim of any one person's private interest would enforce everyone else's subjection to him. It is essential, therefore, that each person bring to the question of his dissenting from a proposal only concerns of a general kind which affect fundamental human interests and are common to all, not concerns exclusive to himself. Only if this is so will the procedure finally arrived at not contain a bias towards an individual or group to the detriment and limitation of others.

What this means is that the reasons for assent or dissent to any procedure must not express a person's unfettered self-sovereignty, his absolute discretion. Such reasons must derive from the common interests of all, interests shared with others as like human beings faced by common needs and predicaments. Assent to, or dissent from, the terms and conditions of association do not, therefore constitute the exercise of complete discretionary freedom, but the exercise of the liberty that each person has as one human among others working together to form a common union. This is not the liberty of a non-answerable, isolated being, but the liberty proper to one who seeks to establish a basis of common order acceptable and appropriate to all alike.

Since this liberty represents the basis of, and scope for, the unimpeded action proper to one who honours and respects the value and entitlements of all other persons alike, it might be called 'moral' freedom or 'moral' liberty. In one way, 'moral' liberty is a diminished liberty, as compared with 'discretionary' liberty. In the exercise of moral liberty a person is constrained by the requirement to honour and respect others (who, in turn, honour and respect him). No such 'constraint' with reference to others is intrinsic to discretionary freedom. If this last makes any demands at all, they are only those of acting with prudent foresight of personal good. But Rousseau would argue that this moral constraint does not represent the diminution or denial of anything valuable. Rather, it is a requirement that enables and enlarges: by observing it a person assumes his proper character as one who both gives and receives respect from other, equal, persons (*see* EQUALITY).

Such moral constraint does not license tyranny or the domineering control of others – which is more likely to be the upshot if absolute self-sovereignty is taken to be the only freedom worth fighting for, and if any diminution of it is felt as a trade-off reluctantly made. It is only if we recognize that our acceptance of the moral law of acknowledging the dignity of others is the condition by which we achieve any secure or worthwhile freedom for ourselves that, in Rousseau's view, we shall ever transcend a social structure pervaded by competition for mastery over others. While recognizing that acceptance of these conditions of liberty may seem to be a heavy burden and that its requirements are austere, Rousseau insists that unless these are indeed accepted and embraced the alternative liberty of unregulated discretion is delusive, making everyone the victim of the competition for domination and control over others.

This notion of 'moral', sometimes called 'positive', freedom attracts much adverse comment. It is objected that a condition subject to laws and to the requirement of honouring others must be one in which freedom is diminished, not one in which a new and better freedom is obtained; it is merely to play with words, and to disguise a (sinister) attempt to control the lives of others, to say that the imposition of laws is really the condition of true liberation.

Such cricitism normally focuses on this remark that Rousseau makes in *The Social Contract* (I, ch. 7, 177; *OC* III, 364): 'Whoever refuses to obey the general will shall be compelled to do so by the whole body. This means nothing less than that he will be forced to be free.' The complaint is that Rousseau here disguises techniques of social control, of enforcing subservience, as the conditions of freedom. But his thought here is, in fact, that obedience to the GENERAL WILL requires no more than honouring the equal human moral and civil standing of others: to be required to do this is no more than what the duties of morality demand. If these are not accepted, competition for personal ascendancy over others is all that remains. Presumably, those who think that the obligation to recognize the human rights of others represents a constraint on their own personal freedom find other people's very existence a burden, an imposition which enforces an unwelcome restraint. It is doubtful that the moral and civil law, in preventing one from doing things hurtful to others, diminishes any freedom worth having. There are many aspects of personal life which do not involve threats to the moral standing of others. In these aspects, a person retains his discretionary freedom – indeed, his use of it is better protected, Rousseau argues, because of the very existence of limits. Rousseau's account of these very complex issues, which permit no easy resolution, remains one of the most penetrating and challenging.

Sources: *DI*, especially Pt 1
    E, Bk IV
    SC, Bks I, II

Further reading: Berlin (330); Dent, ch. 5 (24); Fetscher (120); Green (284); Levine (128); Plamenatz (141); Remple (142); Taylor (299); Wokler (149, 150)

G

general will The notion of the general will plays a central role in Rousseau's account of the source of just and authoritative law in the 'ideal' state depicted in The SOCIAL CONTRACT. It holds the key to understanding how civil authority and power can be legitimate. This notion is a complex one, and its interpretation is highly controversial: what follows is one possible interpretation.

The SOVEREIGN BODY in Rousseau's state (as in any state) issues directions (laws) for the regulation of the common life of all members of that state (*see* AUTHORITY; LAW). Directives which have the form: 'Thou shalt [shalt not]...' may be understood as declarations of will. So the sovereign has a will, and laws are the expression of that will. According to Rousseau, such laws are legitimate, just and rightly command obedience when, and only when, that sovereign will is the general will.

For Rousseau, the sovereign body comprises all the adult members of the state. So the general will, as the will of the sovereign body, is, in some fashion, the will of all the members of the state. The crucial issue is to determine *how* the general will relates to, emerges from, the will of all the members of the sovereign body. 'The general will', Rousseau says, 'must be general in its object as well as its essence . . . it must both come from all and apply to all' (*SC* II, ch. 4, 187; *OC* III, 373). If we can determine what this means, we can determine in what way a directive coming from all the members of the sovereign body would be an expression of the general will. It will be so if it applies to all and comes from all.

The matter of it applying to all means that no one is exempt from, above or apart from, that directive (law); and that the law is expressed in general terms so that no specific individual or group is singled out by it. Some laws may impose differential requirements – say, on house-owners rather than on non-house-owners. But Rousseau holds that the primary concern of the general will is to impose requirements of the most broad and fundamental kind which attach to people simply as members, together, of the state. Devising more specific laws, and applying law to particular cases, is the function of GOVERNMENT.

123

The issue of the will 'coming from all' is more problematic. Rousseau makes a distinction between the WILL OF ALL and the general will, though he thinks that what the general will is can be worked out from the will of all (*SC* II, ch. 3, 185; *OC* III, 371); this distinction needs to be observed, therefore, in working out how the general will comes from all. Rousseau believes that there will be some basic directives to which each person has like reason to assent – like reason, because these directives concern the defence and protection of fundamental interests, such as personal safety, security of livelihood and moral dignity, that everyone shares. These common interests provide each person with a reason for welcoming such directives. A directive which favoured some but burdened others, on the other hand, could not offer the disadvantaged party the same reason (or, perhaps, any reason) for welcoming or assenting to it; though the favoured party might feel that *they* had a stronger reason for assenting to it than they would to a directive that offered to everyone equal reason for assent. It is only when each person has equal reason with every other to assent to the directive that, in Rousseau's view, that directive can properly be said to come from all in equal fashion and for equal reasons. Only on that condition is that directive an expression of a properly general will.

Thus it could readily appear to some – those who would be advantaged in the instance just described – that accepting a directive that benefits all alike in the same way and to the same degree would be to settle for less than they might wish or might get away with. Because this is so, it is only when the fostering and promoting of the interests that all people have in common is to each individual person a high, even paramount, concern that the law is likely to be, in fact, an expression of a truly general will. It is only when the promoting of the interests that all have in common becomes the interest of each member that we shall avoid narrow personal or sectional interests usurping the common interest, and the general will being replaced by, for instance, a CORPORATE WILL (perhaps masked, deceptively, as if it were the general will). This is why Rousseau thinks that we are not likely to be able to determine a genuinely general will if we are dealing with a people who do not already feel some sense of common loyalty, purpose and destiny, such that the good of all, and not just his own, matters highly to each (see *SC* II, ch. 7, 194–6; *OC* III, 381–2). Not all peoples are equipped to pass laws that will be just and equitable, or to establish a will that is truly general.

But given that a person or group may feel that they have more to gain from directives that favour them differentially, why should they submit to the requirements of the general will which favours all alike without differentiation? Why should common loyalty be their paramount concern?

Why should a person place the common interest above his own PARTICU-
LAR WILL, which conduces to his own private advantage (*SC* I, ch. 7, 177;
OC III, 363)? In response, Rousseau argues that a person gains for
himself only a delusive advantage if he places private advantage first. Not
only will the disadvantaged persons try to claw back from him what they
have been denied, so that social life will be driven by conflict and
aggression, but the fact is that there is no real personal profit in nullifying
and dispossessing others. It is only with equals and from equals that any
of us procures that respect and honour that we need. Our own moral
dignity is respected only by those whom we, in turn, equally respect (*see*
AMOUR-PROPRE; EQUALITY).

Rousseau would be the first to admit that there are many motives in
people which militate against the realization and acceptance of this state
of affairs. And this is another reason why it is only those who are
accustomed – and glad – to share and work with others in common toil
who have any real prospect of achieving a civil existence regulated by laws
deriving from the general will. It is also the reason only small states,
Rousseau thinks, have any real prospect of establishing just and equitable
laws for all which will be well observed. For only in such states can a real
sense of community, a real bond of mutual loyalty, grow up and be
sustained. In large states, the fate of many people will seem a matter of
indifference to many of the others.

The notion of the general will has been abused, particularly when it has
been equated with 'the people's will', as that concept was used in the
Terror. In fact, that 'people's will' was very far from being general, in that
it victimized certain individuals and groups. There is no reason to doubt
Rousseau's sincerity when he writes in the (DISCOURSE ON) POLITICAL
ECONOMY:

> The security of individuals is so intimately connected with the public
> confederation that . . . that convention would in point of right be dissolved,
> if in the state a single citizen who might have been relieved were allowed to
> perish . . . does not the undertaking entered into by the whole body of the
> nation bind it to provide for the security of the least of its members with as
> much care as for that of all the rest? (*DPE* 131–2; *OC* III, 256)

A will, to be truly general, must give voice to the interests which each
person has in common with every other. If any one person is neglected,
the will ceases to be general, the law is for that person tyrannical, and he
has no obligation to obey. It is through the general will alone that each
person, in common with every other, has justice done to him.

When Rousseau says that people should be forced to obey the general will he is saying only that they should be forced to honour the needs and dignity of all other persons. And it is in being so forced that a person is being forced to be free – that is, to do those things which it is proper to him to do as a morally responsible person acknowledging the human rights of others (*SC* I, ch. 7, 177; *OC* III, 364; *see* FREEDOM).

It may be because we have so seldom seen a general will in practice, rather than because the very idea of such a will is incoherent or pernicious, that people are apt to be sceptical about or wary of it.

Sources: *DPE*
      E, Bk V
      SC , Bks I, II

Further reading: Barnard (111); Barry (112); Crocker (117); Dagger (118); Dent, ch. 5 (24); Gildin (123); Jones (124); King (126); MacAdam (131); Masters, ch. 7 (69); Melzer (137); Riley (143)

Geneva Rousseau was born a citizen of Geneva. Although, driven by personal troubles and a youthful urge for adventure, he left in 1728 and, by his conversion to Catholicism, lost his titles as citizen, his tie to his native city remained powerful both in his feelings and in his imagination. In 1754, by which time he had achieved considerable eminence, he determined to return, to renounce Catholicism, to reclaim his citizenship and to re-enter the Protestant faith. He wrote a long eulogy to Geneva as the best of all birthplaces, and attached it as a dedicatory preface to the DISCOURSE ON THE ORIGIN OF INEQUALITY. Although this was no doubt in part intended to smooth his path in reclaiming his citizenship, it is clear that it also gave voice to genuine feelings and needs of Rousseau's – however inappropriate an object for these Geneva may have been. This loyal passion of a prodigal son stayed with Rousseau for nearly a decade.

In an article on Geneva (published in 1757) written for the ENCYCLO-PAEDIA, d'Alembert had recommended the introduction of theatrical arts into the city as an enhancement to its culture. Taking upon himself – to the irritation and disgust of many of the less ostentatiously self-important members of the city – the role of mentor, protector and proselyte of the glory and spirit of Geneva, Rousseau wrote his LETTER TO D'ALEMBERT ON THE THEATRE (1758), defending the purity of Genevan morals and the excellence of Genevan customs against what he believed would be the corrupting influence of a theatre and all that it would bring with it.

Rousseau continued to make great play with his status as a citizen of Geneva – indeed 'the citizen' became a standard form of reference to him. His LETTER TO CHRISTOPHE DE BEAUMONT, written in self-defence as well as in defence of ÉMILE after its condemnation in 1762, is prefaced with a long rehearsal of all the Archbishop's many titles and honours – against which Rousseau sets his own proud claim to the title of citizen of Geneva, as if that said all that needed to be said about his dignity and station.

This claim neither pleased, nor appeased, the Genevan authorities. Not only had they banned, and burned, *The Social Contract* and *Émile* in June 1762, following the example of the Parisian authorities, but they also banned his *Letter* when it appeared in 1763. Disgusted by this, Rousseau renounced his citizenship in May of that year, becoming literally, as well as metaphorically, a man without a homeland. Nor did matters end there. Rousseau had had protracted bad relations with the Genevan attorney-general, J.-R. Tronchin, who published in the September an anonymous defence of the actions of various Genevan councils against Rousseau, under the title, *Lettres Écrites de la Campagne* (*Letters Written from the Country*). In part, these letters were written with the general intent of bolstering the authority of the Genevan authorities against certain radicals, who were claiming that they were unjust and corrupt. Taking Rousseau as their inspiration and guide, these radical groups were using his mistreatment in furthering their objectives. Rousseau wrote at length, in his own defence, his LETTERS WRITTEN FROM THE MOUNTAIN, which not only detailed the injustices he had suffered but also criticized at length the actions of the government of Geneva on many issues. Working from information supplied to him by friends, Rousseau exposed widespread abuses, usurpation of powers and improper and illegitimate acts. This did nothing, of course, to placate his enemies. He became the object of further attacks, but it looked for a while as if the radical cause would triumph.

Despite the solicitations of friends, Rousseau avoided any further involvement, and within eighteen months he had left that part of Europe altogether. He never visited Geneva again, although he retained close links with certain people there, particularly the two who were to edit his works after his death, P. Moultou and P. A. Du Peyrou. By the time of his death, the storms of twenty years earlier having abated, Rousseau was willingly claimed by his native city as one of her great sons.

In order to compare with the reality Rousseau's image of Geneva in his writings, it is desirable to present some of the material facts. The population was about 25,000, of whom only about 1500 – the citizens and the bourgeois (burghers) – enjoyed political rights. The rest were called *natifs* (born in the city, but not of citizens or burghers) and *habitants* (resident aliens). These 1500 electors convened annually as the sovereign body called the *Conseil Général* (General Council) or *Assemblée du Peuple*. Although denied the right to initiate legislation (following the Mediation of 1738 which brought the civil uprising of that time, which Rousseau had witnessed, to an end), this body could elect four chief officers of state, the

127

syndics, and had the right of representation or protest – in theory, at least – against legislative proposals.

There were three executive councils – the *Grand Conseil* (Grand Council) (of 200), the *Petit Conseil* (Small Council) (of 25) and the *Conseil des Soixante* (Council of Sixty) – who shared in a complex fashion the responsibility for the affairs of state. Despite constitutional provisions to prevent it, the Small Council gradually assumed greater and greater powers, claiming for itself not merely an executive but a sovereign role as well. In addition, its membership assumed a patrician character, thus further subverting the sovereign authority of the General Council. It was particularly the Small Council that initiated attacks on Rousseau and that he, in turn, attacked as a usurpatory and illegitimate power. The fact that, under the terms of the Mediation, legislation was initiated not by the General Council but jointly by the Grand Council and the Small Council, added fuel to the claims of usurpation. Indeed, even the right of protest by members of the General Council came under attack – a point with which Rousseau took particular issue in his *Letters Written from the Mountain*.

The other relevant aspect of Genevan life is its Calvinist inheritance. In 1541, in the hope of creating an ideal Protestant commonwealth, Calvin devised for Geneva a constitution. This included a clerical and academic elite that had as much influence on the customs and culture of the city as did the political institutions that were also part of that constitution. In particular, Calvin established a form of 'moral police' known as the Consistory, whose concern was to promote private virtue by the punishment and exposure of transgressors. Although there is considerable debate over just how intense this Calvinist ethos was during Rousseau's upbringing, there is no doubt that his mind and feelings, and his beliefs about how a state should be ordered in order to establish public virtue and private decency, were much influenced by it.

Further reading: Cranston, vol. I (17); Green (8); Miller (18); Palmer (182); Spink (277)

God   *See* CREED OF A SAVOYARD VICAR; RELIGION (CIVIL).

goodness   *See* NATURAL GOODNESS; VIRTUE.

government   The term 'government' refers both to the task or function of government and to the body which carries out those functions. Rousseau devotes most of Bk III of The SOCIAL CONTRACT to a discussion of the tasks and office of government, and the different forms the body of government can take:

What then is government? An intermediate body set up between the subjects and the Sovereign, to secure their mutual correspondence, charged with the execution of the laws and the maintenance of liberty, both civil and political . . . The members of this body are called magistrates or *Kings*, that is to say *governors*, and the whole body bears the name *prince*. (*SC* III, ch. 1, 208–9; *OC* III, 396)

The most important points regarding Rousseau's conception of government are these. First, it is an executive, not a legislative, body. Acts of legislation are the province of the supreme authority in the state, the SOVEREIGN BODY (*see* AUTHORITY; GENERAL WILL). Government is 'simply and solely a commission . . . in which the rulers, mere officials of the Sovereign, exercise in their own name the power of which it makes them depositaries. This power it can limit, modify, or recover at pleasure' (*SC* III, ch. 1, 209; *OC* III, 396). From this stems the second point: that the government acts with delegated or derived power and authority, subordinate to the sovereign authority (of the whole people acting in their capacity as citizens).

Rousseau thinks that a state needs such an office as governor, for a number of reasons. All acts of legislation are general in character: they lay down what any citizen is to do or not to do. But there will be times and places where these general laws have to be applied to particular persons. This is not a proper function of the sovereign authority, if only because there can be no confidence that it would act justly in cases involving the interests of particular individuals. Also, it would be wholly impractical, and certainly ineffective, to assemble the whole body of the citizens to deliberate upon and determine the many everyday issues of civil administration and management.

Rousseau is well aware that in dividing sovereign legislative functions from subordinate governmental administrative and executive functions he is moving not only against the prevailing terminology of his time but against common ideas. In his view the functioning of legislative and executive bodies is hampered by serious confusion: a clear conceptual differentiation between the two is essential, if the sources of legitimate authority in the state are to be identified and explained. He is only too familiar with the situation in which legislative power is held by only a few persons – in theory, servants of the sovereign will of the whole citizen body – who for personal reasons muddy the distinctions that Rousseau is attempting to draw.

The third point central to Rousseau's idea of government is that there is no one form for the body of government to take that will be equally appropriate to the needs of all states and nations. Differences in size, in population, in dispersion, in geography – all have a bearing on what form of executive body will be fit to carry out and apply most satisfactorily the sovereign will of the people, and to administer the affairs of the state. Although sovereign authority is democratically constituted, after a fashion, in Rousseau's account, but, whilst acknowledging that it would appear that he had direct participatory democratic government in view (*see* DEMOCRACY), it would be a mistake to think that he automatically favours democratic government. He lays down some general rules aimed at determining the best form for government to take in any particular case, but at the same time he allows that there are many exceptions, and no one 'pure' form – democratic, aristocratic or monarchic – may be the best. If Rousseau has a preference it is for an elective aristocracy – not really so dissimilar to the representative democracy common in the West in the late twentieth century, though without the same distinction between legislative and executive function (see *SC* III, ch. 15, 240; *OC* III, 429).

The fourth point of major significance concerns the government's presence in the state as the locus of a sectional or factional will distinct from the general will of all the citizens and from the particular, private, will of individuals (*see* CORPORATE WILL). Rousseau is well aware that a body of persons, vested with special powers, will be apt to see a special advantage in its own maintenance and advancement, which will cause it to extend its power and claims at the expense of the common good. Checking the growth and usurpatory tendency of this sectional interest is essential: it is the existence of such powerful sections that represents the greatest threat to justice and legitimate authority, and leads to the subversion of the general will. Rousseau propounds no fail-safe procedure to prevent this from occurring; nor could there be one. What he remains convinced of is that this is an abuse of power, and leads in effect to the 'dissolution' of the state:

> The dissolution of the State may come about . . . when the prince ceases to administer the State in accordance with the laws and usurps the Sovereign power . . . the great State is dissolved, and another is formed within it, composed solely of the members of the government, which becomes for the rest of the people merely master and tyrant. So that the moment the government usurps the Sovereignty, the social compact is broken, and all private citizens recover by right their natural liberty, and are forced, but not bound, to obey (*SC* III, ch. 10, 233; *OC* III, 422).

It is unfortunate that Rousseau never makes it wholly clear who shall judge that such usurpation has taken place, short of an assembly of the whole people judging as common citizens alike. In modern states where no such thing can take place, this ringing affirmation of the inalienable sovereign rights of the people lacks clear and effective application.

Sources: *DPE*
     GP, chs 6–9
     SC, Bk III, and *passim*

Further reading: Gildin (123); de Jouvenel (66); Lemos (68); Masters, ch. 7 (69); Noone (140)

H

happiness Although Rousseau nowhere gives any definition of happiness, nor discusses it in any systematic way, he returns time and again, throughout his writings, to the matter of the nature and sources of human happiness.

He has no doubt that everyone wants to be happy. AMOUR DE SOI, although explained principally in terms of desire for self-preservation and self-maintenance, is also at the root of everyone's concern to be happy. It does not follow, however, that everyone wants happiness more than anything else, that they want to maximize their happiness, or that the enjoyment of happiness is the greatest good or is the motive behind all other pursuits. Thus, for instance, social or civilized man, in Rousseau's view, wants power and personal distinction more than he wants happiness – and not just because he is mistaken about the *sources* of his happiness. Equally, a good man, following his conscience, will want to behave justly more than he will want to make himself happy, if this would involve injustice. Of course, if he keeps faith with his conscience he will be self-content; but the enjoyment of self-contentment is not the motive for his action. Also, even if self-contentment is the 'supreme enjoyment', Rousseau knows very well that this does not falsify the familiar truth that often the wicked prosper and the good languish. There is more to human happiness than the comfort of a clear conscience (see *E* IV, 281–3; *OC* IV, 587–90).

In Rousseau's view, it is part of God's providential plan that those who are just and virtuous will also enjoy happiness, even if only in the survival of the soul after death. His principal point is that there is no insurmountable conflict between duty and interest – not just because to observe duty is the surest route to the furtherance of personal interest, but because God has so ordered human nature that the requirements of conscience (or duty) and the needs of individual good will harmonize. Rousseau thinks that this same coincidence between the demands of justice and the individual's own good can be procured in the ideal state. For, in such a state, the principles of just acknowledgement of the rights of all are the principles through which the individual himself receives recognition and honour as a bearer of human dignity. Thus the individual's good will be furthered, but it is doubtful whether this will in fact produce a coincidence between justice and happiness since more is required for happiness than only this.

In Bk V of ÉMILE, Rousseau suggests that reciprocal intimate love provides the felicity that gives life its whole value (*see* LOVE). Given the amount of time and attention people devote to trying to secure this, it would seem that the view is widely shared. In regard to his own life, though, perhaps with a certain resignation or sense of defeat, Rousseau turned more and more to the pleasures he found in an almost trance-like absorption in nature, and in the simple enjoyments of games and fun with children and peasants. He says, in the end, that happiness is beyond us, and that we should instead make do with contentment, peace of mind, inner and outer tranquillity. It is not entirely clear what distinction he is drawing here: perhaps he has in mind the anxious aspirations that can colour a person's attempts to gain happiness for himself and that open him up to pain and disappointment, sometimes leaving him even worse off. It is hard not to detect a trace of personal bitterness in this doctrine of settling for inner stillness and contentment (*see* THE REVERIES OF THE SOLITARY WALKER).

In Rousseau, we do not find the notion of happiness put to extensive and systematic use in moral and social theory (as we do with, for example, utilitarian thinkers); nor do we find any very profound meditations on the sources and character of temporal felicity. It is the rights and dignity of the individual, rather than the promotion of general happiness, that take precedence in his social theory.

Sources: *E*, Bks IV, V
       RSW, Second, Third, Fifth, Seventh–Tenth Walks

Further reading: Grimsley (187); Grimsley (249)

I

inequality *See* Discourse on the Origin of Inequality; equality.

J

Julie, ou La Nouvelle Héloïse (1761) [9]   In April 1756 Rousseau moved, with Thérèse Levasseur and her mother, to the Hermitage, a cottage in the forest of Montmorency lent to him by Mme d'Épinay. It was his long and solitary walks in the forest that provided him with the setting for an extraordinary imaginative outpouring. As he walked, he became obsessed with imagined figures whose looks, lives and loves wholly absorbed him (see *The Confessions*, Bk IX). In the winter of that year, in a fever of erotic ecstasy, he wrote the first of the imaginary letters between Julie, her lover Saint-Preux, and her friend and cousin Claire. These were to form the foundation for the first two parts of his epistolary novel, *Julie*. Rousseau appears to have felt rather equivocal about this work, since it involved deserting his persona of man of high principle, scourge of fashionable society who would have nothing to do with the frivolities of love, courtship and illicit passion. None the less he persisted with it, and in the summer of 1757 he completed the third part of the novel and some of the fourth (as he conceived it at that time, the work was to finish at the end of Part IV).

Then, fiction and reality seemed to come together in his life. He fell in love with Sophie d'Houdetot (Mme d'Épinay's sister-in-law), whom he had met briefly the previous year, and seemed to find in her the personification of many of the traits of his novel's heroine, Julie. Sophie was living at Eaubonne, only a few miles from the Hermitage, and Rousseau and she spent many days walking and talking in what was, for Rousseau at least, a state of amorous rapture. The relationship did not endure: Sophie remained loyal to her lover, Saint-Lambert, who had been away when Rousseau first met her. Rumours of Rousseau's infatuation soon reached him, and although at first Saint-Lambert seemed to tolerate his intense devotion to Sophie, the atmosphere between them became progressively more fraught. Rousseau became convinced that people were doing their best to slander and ridicule him; his suspicions fell on Mme d'Épinay and her lover Grimm (his then friend). By December 1757 relationships had deteriorated so badly that Rousseau left the Hermitage and moved to Mont-Louis, nearby.

During this time, he was proceeding with further episodes. A fifth and then a sixth part were written, from which the intense eroticism of the first four is noticeably missing. It is possible that his own amorous disappointments determined him to recover the position that his uncontrolled feelings had caused him to desert, and that he wished once more to assume (through the figure of Wolmar, whom Julie marries) the mantle of judge and legislator of the manners and morals of society.

The work was almost complete by the end of 1758, but extensive recopying and polishing for publication meant that it did not appear for a further two years (being published in London in December 1760, in Paris in January 1761 though printed by Rey in Amsterdam). During 1760 Rousseau copied parts of the book for Mme de Luxembourg (to whom he was also reading it), adding some extra pages, *Les Amours de Milord Édouard Bomston*, which describes the exploits of a fairly minor figure in the novel itself who goes to seek love and fulfilment in Rome.

Julie was an astonishing success. (At least seventy-two editions were produced in French before 1800, and about half as many in English translation.) Rousseau now enjoyed tremendous popularity and his work was more avidly read than at any other time in his life. This acclaim was not to last, however. Eighteen months later he was overtaken by the catastrophes that followed the publication of ÉMILE and THE SOCIAL CONTRACT, and he was obliged to flee Paris for Switzerland, living in virtual exile for the next ten years.

The original title for Rousseau's novel was to be *The Letters of Two Lovers, Living in a Small Town at the Foot of the Alps*. Why he changed his mind and chose to echo the medieval story of Héloïse is not clear, since Rousseau's Julie hardly compares with her predecessor. The principal protagonists are Julie; her cousin Claire; Saint-Preux, originally Julie's tutor but soon her lover; Julie's parents; and, later on, her future husband Wolmar. The action proceeds through exchanges of letters amongst these characters, and opens with a crisis: Saint-Preux confesses his love for Julie, who is at first dismayed and appalled, but then ill-advisedly attempts on her own to overcome her lover's ardour. Julie is depicted as a woman of intense moral seriousness, but one whose very intensity will betray her. She cannot treat this relationship lightly, and is insensibly drawn into ever closer intimacy with Saint-Preux as she attempts to argue him out of his attachment.

Julie's father returns from the army, and disparages Saint-Preux for his importunity. Julie sends the young man away for a time, but they continue to correspond, and their communications become more and more passionate. Saint-Preux returns and threatens to kill himself unless Julie comes to him. When she learns that she is to be betrothed to the

Baron de Wolmar, an old comrade of her father's, she gives herself to her lover in an ecstasy of passion and despair. Their illicit liaison continues for some time until a new figure comes on the scene – an English peer, Édouard Bomston. Out of jealousy, Saint-Preux challenges him to a duel; but this is averted when Julie tells Lord Édouard what is going on and he generously offers Julie and Saint-Preux the use of one of his estates. He even extends the invitation to Julie's father, but he will have nothing of it: in a rage, he strikes Julie, who miscarries Saint-Preux's child.

Julie's mother discovers her daughter's illicit correspondence, and, whilst grieving that this unique love can never be accepted, is none the less deeply shocked and falls mortally ill. Julie becomes convinced that she is responsible for her mother's death, and in her turn falls ill with smallpox. Saint-Preux leaves for Paris in the company of Lord Édouard; Julie recovers, and pledges herself to Wolmar although she still considers herself the spiritual bride of Saint-Preux.

Some years elapse (we are now at the beginning of Part IV), during which Saint-Preux has been at sea with Admiral Anson's expedition, which he joined at Bomston's instigation. Claire, in the meantime, has been married and widowed, and is left with a daughter; and Julie, now Julie de Wolmar, has two sons. Although she does not realize it, Wolmar knew of her liaison before their marriage; and he now conceives the idea of employing Saint-Preux as a tutor for their boys at his model estate of Clarens. Wolmar believes that, once they encounter each other in changed circumstances, both Julie and Saint-Preux will be purged of their early infatuation and thereby freed from the burden of their past.

In his attempt to control (or manipulate) their lives, Wolmar decides to go away for a week and to leave the two former lovers alone. Julie and Saint-Preux go for a trip on Lake Geneva, get caught in a storm and are trapped in the spot where, ten years before, Saint-Preux had suffered extremes of passion. Julie resists his renewed declarations, seeming finally to have left all passion behind her. But having saved one of her children from drowning, she contracts pneumonia, and in her dying moments, while resigning her soul to the mercy of the Almighty, she confesses that she has never ceased to love Saint-Preux. Claire, meanwhile, has fallen in love with Saint-Preux. The novel ends with she, Saint-Preux and Wolmar all living on the estate together, united in adoring memory of the departed Julie, sanctified in death.

Debate has raged over how this work of Rousseau's should be interpreted. Some see it as disjointed, the first four books being given over to the story of a tragic, illicit passion told with great intensity, but with the reality of these feelings denied in the last two books, in which Julie undergoes a spiritual conversion and, in purity and faithfulness, dedicates her life to God. Others see this end prefigured from the start: we are intended all along to recognize that Julie and Saint-Preux are led astray by their feelings, and that it is only by the purification and regulation of these feelings by the demands of duty and conscience that human life can be redeemed. Yet others see Rousseau working out, in a different medium, many of the same themes that preoccupied him in his more theoretical works – themes such as the individual in relation to society, the need to abolish the separate self and to assume an identity borrowed from the community.

Whatever the controversies of interpretation, despite a certain stiltedness of idiom and artificiality of manner *Julie* succeeds in creating an atmosphere of genuine erotic and passionate intensity. Readers of such writers as Richardson or Laclos will appreciate *Julie*.

Further reading: Anderson (154); Crocker (155); Ellis (156); Gossman (158); Green (8); Horowitz, ch. 6 (27); Jimack (160); Jones (161); Shklar, chs 4, 6 (36); Tanner (162)

justice Justice, as generally understood, is the rendering to each person of what is due to him. The essential question to determine is what is owed to each and why, and how this can best be rendered to him.

Rousseau nowhere gives such a general definition of justice, nor does he list the various things that are owed to people in different contexts or the reasons why they are owed. But from his writings emerges a clear view of what he thought were the basic requirements of justice to each and all. Fundamentally, he holds that the rules of justice emanate from God and are implanted in each person's CONSCIENCE, although it may require the enactment of positive law to ensure obedience to these requirements (*see* LAW).

These rules of basic justice demand the following: that no one be harmed in his life, liberty, possessions or moral personality either by deliberate ill will or by neglect or indifference. 'Moral personality', in Rousseau's view, is the fundamental human need for each person to be recognized and honoured by others as one who matters and has value and dignity in his own right. This entails that, for instance, in any matter that affects him his views shall be consulted, or he shall become more fully involved in the determination of the issue – and not just by the grace or at the discretion of others but because that is his proper right and title as a person with the same significant standing as anyone else. Even if the individual might be better off materially under paternalistic rule, such rule represents a fundamental human degradation and injustice, since it makes the individual the inferior of another, subject to that other's direction (no matter that it may be benign). So, not to harm someone in his 'moral personality' requires that such forms of rule be removed (or not instituted in the first place). Each person must, rather, have the title and scope to contribute to common affairs on the same footing as anyone else, and to determine his own affairs, where others are not affected, by his own discretion.

Procuring justice for each and every person in a society in all these respects is the primary purpose of civil association, of establishing the civil state. Rousseau thinks that the operation of the GENERAL WILL is the means whereby justice is most comprehensively procured for all persons, not only because of the principles that will issue from it (the laws) but also because of the manner of functioning of the general will, in which each person takes part as an authoritative member of the SOVEREIGN BODY (see AUTHORITY). Justice is done to each person's moral personality largely through his joint equal standing, with everyone else, as a legislative member of the sovereign body, in which no one defers to or is subordinate to anyone else, and each functions as an equally honoured and empowered individual (see LEGISLATION).

One of Rousseau's primary concerns is to show that there is no basic conflict between the demands of justice and each individual's own good. He argues that it is only by honouring the good and dignity of others that an individual can receive that honour and regard for himself that he needs and wants as a person among persons. To commit injustice towards others degrades and subjugates them. And, in so doing, the unjust person also precludes himself from receiving from others the kind of respect and care that would truly benefit him and give him the human standing he wants.

Rousseau argues that we commit injustice towards others, making them suffer fundamental ills, not only by actively hurtful acts but also by negligence or indifference. But he is realistic enough to realize that concern for the lot of others, which alone can consistently motivate people to care for others' good, is not indefinitely extensible. It is only within fairly small societies, in which there is a generally felt community of interest, mutual loyalty and commitment, that each person can expect to receive his just due. In large societies, where no such unity of sentiment exists, Rousseau thinks that justice will become largely an empty word. Many people will be mistreated or ignored just because, in a large society, it is impossible for the individual to have such a powerful sense of community that another's sufferings are felt (nearly) as acutely as his own (see COMPASSION). It may be true that there is a universal, God-given rule requiring us to render justice alike to all. But to make this rule effective as an instrument for procuring actual justice it should work through the sentiments and institutions of fairly small, independent and close-knit communities.

In articulating these fundamental elements of what is due in justice to each person, Rousseau was propounding his conception of basic human rights, to be denied which is to be denied human dignity.

Sources: *DI*, Pt 2
   E, Bks IV, V
   SC, Bks II, III

Further reading: Masters, ch. 6 (69); Perelman (342); Shklar, ch. 5 (36)

L

language   *See* ORIGIN OF LANGUAGES.

law   In Bk 2, ch. 12, of The SOCIAL CONTRACT, Rousseau distinguishes four different categories of law as relating to the organization of a civil society. He also uses the term 'law' in an extended, or metaphorical, sense when he talks, for instance, of the 'laws' of the heart.

The first category of laws concerns 'the action of the complete body upon itself', where 'the whole people decrees for the whole people'. These political, or fundamental, laws are 'properly speaking only the conditions of civil association. The people, being subject to the laws, ought to be their author: the conditions of the society ought to be regulated solely by those who come together to form it' (both quotations: *SC* II, ch. 6, 192; *OC* III, 379). Such laws, as the epithet 'fundamental' implies, are the most basic and decisive for the whole shape and organization of the civil association. It is by their terms that the basic standing of each member, as CITIZEN, is determined; it is these laws that lay down the rights and duties which each shall have as a member of the association. And it is by means of these laws that the primary purpose of the association – to defend and protect the person and goods of each member – is most directly to be achieved.

Such laws are acts of the GENERAL WILL, from which they take their form and derive their authority. Such laws must be general in character, not only in not naming particular persons, but also in primarily addressing people in respect of their most widely shared and common characteristics, e.g. as needing physical safety and sustaining (although Rousseau does allow that qualifications for membership of different classes of citizenship can be specified (*SC* II, ch. 6, 192; *OC* III, 379)). Any act which commands a particular person, or a particular matter, is a decree of magistracy, not an act of law (*see* GOVERNMENT).

Second, Rousseau identifies a class of what he calls 'civil laws'. These should secure citizens against dependence on other, specific, persons, but should make them very dependent on the whole association for the protection and enjoyment of their civil titles. For if individuals were obliged to depend on specific others for their security or sustenance, then they would, in effect, become enslaved to these persons and denied their civil recognition. It is only when the general laws of society protect individuals in their livelihood and civil standing that they can be relieved from this servitude to other people. It is, as Rousseau frequently says, only through the maintenance of general law that each person alike can enjoy equal liberty.

The third class, criminal laws, concerns sanctioning obedience to the first two classes of law: criminal laws are 'less a particular class of law than the sanction behind all the rest'.

The final class that Rousseau here identifies is, perhaps, an instance of extended sense of 'law'. These laws are those that mould people's characters, attitudes, loyalties, feelings – namely, 'morality . . . custom . . . public opinion', which in turn shape people's outlook and aspirations in the most fundamental ways. He says that 'manners and morals' are, in fact, the 'keystone' of all good and effective legislation and of the successful establishment of a just and happy society. His point here is twofold. On the one hand, without the cultivation and maintenance of attitudes of mutual loyalty and fraternity and of a sense of common destiny, individuals will be apt to see in the demands of law only something being exacted from them, which they will baulk at or attempt to evade. They will not realize that the provisions of law are, in fact, the conditions of their personal liberty, that it is these that permit the possibility of a good society. On the other hand, such attitudes are a prerequisite for the enactment of just and equitable law in the first instance. For where such concern for the common weal is absent, or shallow, it will be particular or sectional interests that find expression in devising rules for the common conduct of all; and, failing to be acts of any properly general will, these will only be 'law' in name, not in nature.

Rousseau is not thinking here of any censorious or intrusive 'moral police' (though he may have had the Consistory in mind; see GENEVA). He is more concerned with the social and psychological preconditions against the background of which law proper can be not just obeyed, but embraced as the primary medium through which the central objectives of civil association are realized. The twentieth-century citizen probably attaches less importance to this than Rousseau did, even perhaps finds the idea of regulation by public opinion objectionable. But, if so, then our perception of law as furthering commonly desirable objectives is also diminished.

Finally, Rousseau believes that there is a law of justice to all implanted by God in each man's CONSCIENCE (see CREED OF A SAVOYARD VICAR; JUSTICE). Were each person to heed these inwardly knowable laws, there would be little or no need of civil law and sanction. However, this is not the case, and 'in default of natural sanctions, the laws of justice are ineffective among men: they merely make for the good of the wicked and the undoing of the just' (*SC* II, ch. 6, 191; *OC* III, 378). Thus, conventional positive law is required 'to join rights to duties and refer justice to its object'. Rousseau is here stressing that we cannot be under a moral obligation to behave justly to others unless we have some realistic hope of mutuality, and that one of the primary purposes, particularly of the criminal law but also of civil association, is to procure this. A criterion of good law for Rousseau is that it should procure mutual justice; and this requirement underpins the proper functioning of the general will in declaring fundamental laws.

Sources: *DI*, Pt 2
       E, Bks IV, V
       SC, Bks II, III

Further reading: Friedrich (121); Gildin (123); Horowitz, ch. 7 (27); Masters, chs 4, 6 (69)

legislation Rousseau makes a sharp distinction between acts of legislation, and administrative and executive acts (or decrees). Acts of legislation are those which concern the formulation, authorization and promulgation of LAW. Such acts are the expression of the GENERAL WILL, and establish the basic terms and conditions for the civil association that is to be instituted. Rousseau invariably stresses that legislative acts must be general – that is, they must not target specified individuals or groups, or address particular issues. This is because it could not be expected, if this were to happen, that any properly general will could be declared. Particular or sectional interests would be bound to obtrude, and certain individuals would either profit or suffer unjustly.

Administrative and executive acts are the function of GOVERNMENT; they may apply to particular individuals, but do so only under the general terms and rules established by legislation. There can be, Rousseau thinks, no absolute guarantee that such acts will not improperly disadvantage certain persons. For a good state, it must be a central issue in devising an appropriate institutional structure to try to check such potential abuse, while at the same time leaving to the office of government, and to the governors, sufficient powers to discharge their necessary tasks successfully.

These functions are not always as clearly differentiated in practice as they may be conceptually. This can give rise to confusions about the sources of authority and power in society, which Rousseau thinks should be avoided.

Although, in the optimal case, acts of legislation, as the acts of the sovereign body, should be the declaration of the whole body of the people acting to regulate its common affairs in a general way by fundamental laws, Rousseau thinks that a body of people may be ill equipped to carry out this task satisfactorily for themselves. It is in order to resolve this problem that he introduces the figure of the LEGISLATOR, and it is the nature and function of this figure, rather than the abstract points about the notion of legislation, that are of particular interest here.

Sources: *GP*, chs 1–5
    SC, Bk II

Further reading: Masters, chs 7, 8 (69)

legislator   The figure, or function, of the 'legislator' in Rousseau's political theory strikes many people as one of its most curious, and unconvincing, elements. But in introducing this quasi-divine creature, he was addressing a central issue for all political theory.

In Rousseau's view, the most urgent issue facing any prospective civil state is that of devising the most just and most beneficial fundamental laws that will comprise the basic terms of association for each member of that institution (*see* LAW): 'The people, being subject to the laws, ought to be their author; the conditions of the society ought to be regulated by those who come together to form it' (*SC* II, ch. 6, 193; *OC* III, 380). If and when 'the people' do instigate and authorize the law, they are all alike members of the SOVEREIGN BODY, and their legislative will is the GENERAL WILL.

But having established how things ought to be, Rousseau goes on to raise difficulties for himself:

> But how are they to regulate them? Is it to be by common agreement, by a sudden inspiration? Has the body politic an organ to declare its will? Who can give it the foresight to formulate and announce its acts in advance? . . . How can a blind multitude . . . carry out for itself so great and difficult an enterprise as a system of legislation? Of itself the people always wills the good, but of itself it by no means always sees it. The general will is always upright, but the judgement which guides it is not always enlightened. (*SC* II, ch. 6, 193; *OC* III, 380)

It is these and other allied problems which '[make] a legislator necessary'.

The legislator is said to be a semi-divine or divinely inspired person of 'superior intelligence beholding all the passions of men without experiencing any of them', whose 'happiness would have to be independent of us

144

and yet ready to occupy itself with ours' (all quotations in the entry are drawn from *SC* II, ch. 7; *OC* III, 381: 'The Legislator'). He is neither governor nor, strictly, sovereign; for although he may propose laws he cannot enact or authorize them, and once he has completed his work he either leaves or returns to the status of a common citizen. But somehow – by his superhuman intelligence, his sympathetic impartiality, his extraordinary foresight – he can not merely devise an appropriate body of fundamental laws, but also prevail upon the 'blind multitude' to exercise their sovereign authority by enacting this very code. He is unable to appeal either to force (since he has none) or to reason (since the multitude is 'blind'); so he 'must have recourse to an authority of a different order, capable of constraining without violence and persuading without convincing' (that is, without producing reasons capable of affording complete rational conviction).

What authority is this? It is divine authority, speaking in the name of God (or of the gods) and thereby making people think that the same God-originated decrees that bind each person in conscience are also to be found in the laws of the state. But invoking divine authority is notoriously the recourse of every trickster and fraud. What will show that wisdom, not trumped-up nothings, is being offered?

Rousseau has identified an important issue, but he appears to be setting himself an impossible problem here. When he says that 'the people always wills the good, but . . . by no means always sees it' he formulates the issue in a somewhat misleading way, appearing to suggest that although there is, here, a well intentioned body of people eager to do the right thing, it is somehow unable to hit on that right thing. The legislator helps them with this. But if we ask just why they are unable to hit on the right thing, we see that this formulation of the problem misrepresents its true nature.

In Rousseau's view, what makes it hard for the right rule (law) to be identified is that people neither see nor feel that their own individual good is, and must be, tied in with everyone else's good if a just and beneficial social state for any of them is to result. A mere multitude, in which each is concerned with his own separate affairs, cannot see how the common interest is, and must be, their own best interest. This is not so much because they intend to distort or subvert the general will to their own advantage (so that it becomes, in effect, only a sectional will in place of the general will) – though this can happen. It is rather that no one has any sense of the way in which the good of each and the good of all stand or fall together. Each 'finds it difficult to realize the advantages he might hope to draw from the privations good laws impose'.

The legislator's task, then, is in essence that of creating a sense of common loyalty, common destiny, to unite these unconnected persons so that the 'yoke of public happiness' is experienced by each as the condition for his own happiness. Isolated persons lose, or overcome, their separateness to a degree, and share each other's needs and good as their own (see DENATURING). The very achievement of this sense of common life gives people the 'vision' they require to see the good. It is not a question of a cognitive act that is separate from the volitional act. The right orientation of the will, towards the common good of all, is at the same time the overcoming of the obstacles to understanding what is the right thing to do.

It is Rousseau's view that it will take some special inspiration or motivation to make persons used to considering their advantage from the viewpoint of solitary, independent beings alone, enlarge their sense of the demands that life rightly makes on them to take on board a concern for the common good of all. It is that inspiration which the legislator attempts to provide by claiming to speak in God's name.

When Rousseau allows that this claim can be fraudulent he is merely acknowledging that not all such appeals can create and sustain an adequate bond of common union. The legislator cannot, by himself, and unaided by other facilitating conditions (which Rousseau discusses at length in SC II, chs 8–10, all of which concern the 'fitness of the people' to receive laws), create an enduring social spirit. At most, he can open the way to the possibility of it, by bringing people to think of themselves as 'one people' with a shared destiny. Many other factors will contribute to the survival (or disappearance) of that spirit.

We are ourselves now so accustomed to living under common laws that we forget that it took many centuries for any sense of common dependence, let alone common union, to emerge in England or America (to the extent that it has emerged, or survives, anyway). Civil wars, for example, occurred during the process. Rousseau makes his concerns seem more problematic than they are by speaking as if the 'birth of a nation' could be brought about after just a short gestation. In fact, the pangs of delivery may take hundreds of years, but a major part of what is going on during that time is what Rousseau is describing – that is, the formulation and consolidation of such a sense of shared life and cause that it is possible for laws that honour each person alike to be formulated and accepted by all alike, rather than seen as an outrageous imposition, as embodying the requirements of a common good and as such to be resented or hated, because no such good was believed in.

Throughout his political writings Rousseau stresses the need for bonds of shared sentiment, if people are to concern themselves with their fellows. This is what the legislator is endeavouring to introduce. Given our modern wariness of rampant nationalism, which this emphasis can lead to – and of which Rousseau too was well aware – it is all too easy to overlook the fables and heroic events that sustain a country's sense of identity, and that make citizens do things for their fellows that reason unaided might fail to direct them to do. Liberalism is perpetually embarrassed by the often non-rational preconditions that make the appeal to reason in public affairs possible, and sometimes effective. Rousseau is not so shame-faced (*see* CONSIDERATIONS ON THE GOVERNMENT OF POLAND).

Sources: *GP*, chs 1–5
        SC, Bk II

Further reading: Dent, ch. 6 (24); Horowtiz, ch. 7 (27); Kelly (125); Masters, ch. 8 (69); Matthews (135); Shklar, chs 4, 5 (36); Waldmann (147)

Letter on French Music (1753) (*Lettre sur la Musique Française*) *See* MUSIC: WRITINGS ON.

Letter to d'Alembert on the Theatre (1758) (*Lettre à M. d'Alembert sur les Spectacles*) [7]   In the autumn of 1757 an article on GENEVA appeared in vol. VII of the ENCYCLOPAEDIA, written by Rousseau's friend and one of the editors of the *Encyclopaedia*, Jean d'Alembert. In addition to relating the history and describing such aspects of the city as its constitution and manufactures, d'Alembert had proposed establishing a theatre there. Rousseau saw in this, probably rightly, the influence of Voltaire, who was living outside Geneva and had recently put on theatrical performances at his house. These had been discouraged by the Consistory, Calvin's 'moral police', and Voltaire had used the opportunity of d'Alembert's fact-finding visit to the city to push his own case against this controlling moral censorship. Rousseau determined to reply to d'Alembert's article, focusing particularly on the issue of establishing a theatre, and defending the customs and morality of Geneva and its citizens.

     Rousseau's *Letter* (in which he uses for the first time the motto *Vitam impendere vero* ('Dedicate life to truth') as his own) appeared in October 1758 – d'Alembert, with pleasing impartiality, himself having acted as censor and declared it fit for publication. Rousseau's veiled accusation against Diderot, in the preface, of having betrayed their friendship, by casting doubt on his sincerity and goodness, marked the final rupture between these two men, although Rousseau's relations with d'Alembert continued on an amicable, if rather remote, footing. The *Letter* attracted enormous attention, and over four hundred articles and pamphlets were written in response to it. The population of Geneva appear to have been generally pleased by Rousseau's polemic in their defence.

     The *Letter* begins by commenting on d'Alembert's statement that the pastors of Geneva were Socinians – that is, that they rejected all revelation

147

as inessential to Christianity, and the doctrine of eternal punishment as incompatible with God's justice. Rousseau objects that, while he himself admires the tolerance and equity of the pastors – which such beliefs might well be conducive to – d'Alembert had no right to impute such views to them and that, in doing so, he has laid them open to accusations of heresy.

Turning to the main business of his *Letter*, he criticizes, on a variety of grounds, d'Alembert's suggestion that a theatre be established. He argues that a theatre can only flourish if it provides amusement. But if it does so, it distracts people from finding pleasure in their personal and civic duties, and thus weakens the habits and sentiments that make them the good people they are, capable of sustaining a just and beneficial community. The theatre is not an agent of moral improvement; it must pander to existing tastes, and in fact consolidates them. It engenders no real passion, but ersatz feelings that diminish any real effort that people might invest in important concerns.

In an extensive critical discussion of Molière, particularly of his play *Le Misanthrope*, Rousseau principally objects that the main character Alceste, who is good and honest and a lover of men, is made to look ridiculous and contemptible. Philinte, the smooth man of the world, on the other hand, is shown as his superior and as getting the better of him. Rousseau insists that this play is a work of genius, as fine a piece of theatre as one could hope to find. But in it virtue and goodness are made mock of, and so it can hardly be maintained that the theatre can improve morals.

Rousseau believes that undue prominence is given in plays to the 'love interest', and this panders to the preoccupations of women in an unacceptable way. What will happen, as far as the pleasures and wishes of women are concerned, if a theatre is established? They will require finery, and will always be wanting to go out to see and to be seen. Once again, all pleasure will be removed from the necessary and beneficial tasks of family and community; expense and idleness will take their place.

It is absurd to hold that careful legislation can guard against all these ills. If it is to have any real effect, legislation must secure obedience, and this it can do only if people see and share the real concerns that legislation is intended to foster. But, as his whole argument has shown, establishing a theatre, going to the theatre, the very content of plays – all militate against that sense of common life and republican loyalty which obedience to law needs to draw on. Sitting shut up in the dark as isolated individuals makes no contribution to – indeed, works against – the central and permanent need of persons living together to sustain a just and properous community. As an alternative, Rousseau would favour public festivals in which people gather in the open air to celebrate events significant for them as part of their civic and cultural inheritance.

For all the flair that Rousseau deploys in writing the *Letter*, his case carries little conviction. It is, of course, essential that those sentiments that equip a society to sustain itself as just and humane are not neglected, but it is hard to believe that the theatre, even in Geneva, would be a major instrument for their dissolution, or that it could become a symptom of their decay.

Further reading: Bloom (205); Polizer (208); Robinson (199)

Letter to Christophe de Beaumont, Archbishop of Paris (1763) (*Lettre à Christophe de Beaumont*) [15]   Immediately after the publication of ÉMILE, Rousseau was in trouble. Particularly because of his ideas on a 'natural religion' and his attacks on revelation and the Catholic Church contained in the CREED OF A SAVOYARD VICAR, which appears in Bk IV, the work was denounced by the Faculty of Theology at the Sorbonne in June 1762 and a warrant for his arrest was issued. Copies of the book were burned in Paris (and, a little later, in Geneva), and Rousseau fled France, staying for a while at Yverdon before being compelled to leave there and settle at Môtiers under the protection of Frederick of Prussia.

The Archbishop of Paris, Christophe de Beaumont, published in August of that year a *mandement*, a pastoral letter of instruction and guidance (a decree) to his priests and members of the Church explaining in detail why the *Creed* was unacceptable, irreligious and sacrilegious. Rousseau obtained a copy of it and, inflamed by the attacks not only on his ideas but also on his sincerity, he set about replying to it. Completed by November 1762 and published in March 1763, his *Letter to Christophe de Beaumont* was banned in Geneva. Disgusted at this further mistreatment by the city he had so idolized and of which he had felt so proud to be a citizen, he renounced his citizenship in May of that year.

Rousseau's *Letter* contains some of his most vigorous writing. In the first part he gives a general statement of the primary ideas that have shaped all his work. In the second, he criticizes and rebuts objections that the Archbishop has made against views expressed in the *Creed*.

In all his diverse writings, Rousseau claims at the beginning of the *Letter*, he has always written with the same basic opinions. Over the years people have formed the most contradictory opinions, both of his views and of himself, but he has never changed, so why should action only now be taken against him? Nor can he understand on what authority such action is taken. A Genevan has a book published in Holland – Néaulme was chosen as (nominal) publisher, in an attempt to avoid problems of censorship. And now it is burned in Paris, without trial, without right of defence.

He outlines some of these 'same ideas upon which he has always reasoned'. Principal among them is that man is by nature good, but corrupted by society. Man is designed to be well and to do well, but is endlessly perverted from this course (see AMOUR DE SOI; AMOUR-PROPRE; NATURAL GOODNESS). Only the doctrine of original sin (see SIN (ORIGINAL)) is laid against his thesis. But, Rousseau goes on, the arguments for this doctrine are muddled and indefensible. Is his crime, then, that of not having reasoned as badly?

Turning to the Archbishop's criticisms, he replies that his views have been distorted or misrepresented; that the objections are muddled, and based on circular reasoning. He insists again, as he does in the *Creed*, that we need to separate Christian belief and conviction from subservience to priests, to one Church, to the dogmas of one specific creed. All that the latter give rise to is tyranny and the sacrifice of blood on the altar of God. But, Rousseau maintains, charity is not murderous; it cannot be blasphemous to urge peaceableness, purity, simplicity, in place of fanatical bloodthirstiness. (It is important to recall that the Inquisition was still at work in Spain.) However, should he, albeit incredibly, be mistaken on these points, he has made them in good faith, with complete sincerity. To do such a thing, Rousseau protests, is not a crime requiring punishment.

The *Letter* ends on a note of self-aggrandizement. Were there any truly enlightened government in Europe, he says, it would erect statues to the author of *Émile*, and he would not be hunted and persecuted. This remark attracted the particular contempt of Voltaire, whose tendency to humour and patronize Rousseau had by now turned into a settled hatred.

There is nothing of importance in the *Letter* that Rousseau does not express elsewhere in greater depth and detail. It is, however, notable for its fluency, its tight polemical development, and the rhetorical power of his comments on religious intolerance – which might well be more often restated, since they are still not widely heeded (see RELIGION (CIVIL)).

Further reading: Green (8); Grimsley (176); Grimsley (187)

Letters to Malesherbes (written 1762; published 1779) (*Lettres à Malesherbes*) [10]   Rousseau had completed the manuscript of *Émile* in 1761, and through the offices of Mme de Luxembourg it was to be printed in Paris by Duchesne (although under the name of a Dutch publisher, Néaulme, in the hope of avoiding problems of censorship). Rousseau became disturbed about the slowness of the printing process, and suspected Jesuit interference (he was also quite ill at this time). Eventually, the censor, Malesherbes, was contacted: he made inquiries on Rousseau's behalf, setting his mind at rest in the most considerate way. This was the beginning of an enduring friendliness between the two men which survived despite the great differences in their positions and the dangers to which Malesherbes was exposed through his support of Rousseau (*see* ÉMILE).

Moved by Malesherbes' generosity, Rousseau wrote four autobiographical letters to him in January 1762, in which he set out to explain his conduct and some of the principal events of his life. Here can perhaps be seen the first expression of the self-disclosing impulse that was to come to the fore over the next fifteen years, finding its fullest development in THE CONFESSIONS, but also leading to such pieces as ROUSSEAU JUDGE OF JEAN-JACQUES: DIALOGUES and the REVERIES OF THE SOLITARY WALKER. By now Rousseau's major theoretical works were finished. For most of the rest of his life his writings were given over to self-articulation and self-defence.

These letters were not intended for publication. They appeared, though, in 1779, when they were included, without permission and quite inappropriately, as notes to J.-A. Roucher's poem, *Les Mois* (Roucher had tried, unsuccessfully, to procure their publication in the *Journal de Paris*).

In the First Letter Rousseau defends himself against the charge that he is a misanthrope who seeks notoriety by affecting a love of the country and of solitude. Such accusations had been made against him when he decided to leave Paris in 1756 and settle at Montmorency. In fact, he says, it is rather that he hates the deception and falseness that he always finds amongst people in cities. His own unquenchable spirit of liberty and his desire for open self-expression finds scope only in the serene and unoppressive surroundings of the country.

The Second Letter recounts some of the events of his early life, including for the first time the story of his 'illumination' on the way to Vincennes and of the myriads of ideas that crowded in on him at that moment (*see* DISCOURSE ON THE SCIENCES AND THE ARTS; THE CONFESSIONS). In particular, he mentions man's NATURAL GOODNESS, and the works that he has based on this, one of his primary ideas. The Third Letter concerns his present state of mind. He began really to live and to enjoy true happiness, he says, only when he moved to the Hermitage in 1756. There he had been able to take simple delight in walking, play with his dog and cat, people his world with delightful figures of imagination – in short, fully to enjoy his own lazy and dreamy nature. In such surroundings he has come to feel the presiding presence of an infinite and benevolent creator. After days given over to contemplation and simple pleasures, he returns in perfect contentment to his quiet home.

The Fourth Letter summarizes how he should, he thinks, be understood. He has disclosed his true sentiments, and now he can be seen for what he is. It is held against him that, being solitary, he is useless to men.

151

But his works set an example; he wishes to benefit all men, not just a particular few, and he would hate to get caught up in partisan intrigues and quarrels. Above all, he hates injustice and inhumanity; he treats all persons as equals. His is, in fact, an exemplary life, or so he declares.

Further reading: Grimsley (176)

Letters to Sophie   *See* MORAL LETTERS.

Letter to Voltaire on Providence (or *On Optimism*) (written 1756; published 1759) (*Lettre sur la Providence*) [5]   Soon after Rousseau's move to Montmorency in early 1756, Voltaire sent him a copy of his *Poème sur le Désastre de Lisbonne* ('Poem on the Lisbon Disaster'), dealing with the moral and religious significance of the earthquake that had devastated Lisbon and killed several hundreds of people. In the poem, Voltaire scorns the idea of a beneficent deity who so orders things that all is for the best in this best of all possible worlds. This shallow, blind optimism of Leibniz, Pope and others prevents people from seeing that the human lot is really one of pain, desolation and destruction. No providential plan or beneficent hand is to be seen in it.

For no very clear reason, Rousseau decided to write a reply to Voltaire concerning the views expressed in his poem. This *Letter* was never intended for publication, but copies were made and in 1759 an edition was printed, without Rousseau's permission, by Formey in Berlin.

Rousseau argues that much of the evil in the world is of our own making. Also, much of that evil prevents greater evil, or may have good consequences overall. We cannot always see the whole design. In none of the events that have provoked Voltaire's scorn of the deity are there sufficient reasons for despair. No metaphysical subtleties can make him, Rousseau, doubt his deep feeling of beneficent providence. Those who cast up the goods and ills of human life forget, he argues, to add, on the plus side, the sweet sentiment of existence. They attend only to the events that happen in a person's life, and overlook the value of having life at all.

He agrees that one should not properly say that 'all is good'. Rather, what one should say is that everything is good for the whole. Furthermore, if, as God promises, men shall enjoy eternal life, the profits and losses of three score years alone cannot be the decisive measure of His goodness and beneficence. Speaking more personally, Rousseau says it is odd to find Voltaire, who lives in comfort, seeing evil all about him, whereas he, Rousseau, who lives in poverty and obscurity, sees only a providential order and the blessings of God.

Interspersed among these rather unremarkable points is an attack on religious intolerance and savagery (*see* RELIGION (CIVIL); CREED OF A

SAVOYARD VICAR). The relevance of this (albeit entirely sound) line of thought – which Rousseau was to return to over and over again – to Voltaire's poem is somewhat doubtful. Voltaire made no direct reply to this *Letter*; he does not appear to have been offended by it – the ultimate breach between the two men was to have other causes. Rousseau was pleased to think, however, that Voltaire's *Candide* (1759) represented his considered response to the points he had made.

No doubt Rousseau was already meditating on the ideas for the *Creed*, in which is to be found his best account of the nature of God's providence, when he wrote this *Letter*. But the *Letter*, by itself, adds little to our understanding or appreciation of his later views.

Further reading: Goldbery (186); Grimsley (187); Leigh (338)

Letters Written from the Mountain (1764) (*Lettres Écrites de la Montagne*)
[17]   In June 1762 the Genevan authorities had followed the example of those in Paris, banning and burning *Émile* (adding, for good measure, copies of *The Social Contract*). Rousseau was stunned. However absurdly, he had believed that the latter work, at least, would be well received in Geneva, for he thought he was enunciating and defending in it the principles that informed the Genevan constitution. This was the beginning of his final rupture with his birthplace. His LETTER TO CHRISTOPHE DE BEAUMONT of 1763, in which he defended the ideas of ÉMILE – particularly those expressed in the CREED OF A SAVOYARD VICAR – was generally well received by the Protestant clergy of Geneva. However, this too was banned under pressure from the French *résident* (consul), and in May of the same year Rousseau, disgusted, renounced his citizenship of the city.

A few weeks later some Genevan citizens handed in a remonstrance to the syndics (*see* GENEVA), protesting against the impropriety of the treatment Rousseau had received. In part they were using his case as an opportunity to reopen old conflicts between the main body of the citizens and the *de facto* patriciate which occupied the positions of importance in the Small Council and other governmental bodies. Rousseau attempted to keep himself removed from these political struggles, but in September 1763 he was made the object of a direct attack. Jean-Robert Tronchin, the attorney-general of Geneva, wrote, anonymously, five *Lettres Écrites de la Campagne* ('Letters Written from the Country'), defending the actions that the Small Council had taken against Rousseau. Tronchin was acclaimed as having saved Geneva from conspiracy and rebellious uprising.

Rousseau determined to write a reply to Tronchin's *Letters*. Using information about the constitution and political history of Geneva that his friends had collected for him, he had soon completed his combative response, the *Letters Written from the Mountain*. Published in December 1764, they caused considerable uproar. Whether in response to these *Letters* (in the fifth of which he is denounced), or because of his now deep detestation of him, Voltaire took the opportunity to publish (also anonymously) a short pamphlet, *Le Sentiment des Citoyens* (*The Sentiment of the Citizens*), in which he exposed to the general public the fact that Rousseau had abandoned his children. Rousseau was driven to distraction; his long descent into madness may, perhaps, date from this time.

The Genevan authorities united in condemnation of the *Letters Written from the Mountain*. Even those who wished to continue to attack the ascendancy and excessive powers of the Small Council regarded them as too dangerous to be used in support of their case. And even living where he was, at Môtiers in the principality of Neuchâtel, Rousseau was not safe. Slowly, the tide of opinion turned against him, and he was soon forced to flee once more, this time to England.

There are nine letters in all. The first part is taken up with a general defence of Rousseau's ideas and an attack on the actions taken against him; the second is more concerned with the history and present state of Genevan political life, and its desertion of the true principles of the constitution.

In the First Letter Rousseau says that, like any man, he can make mistakes in his writings. But should he not then be corrected in open argument, rather than condemned, his works banned? It cannot be said that he has any pernicious intention. In the CREED OF A SAVOYARD VICAR he attacked only cruel and fanatical religions, expressed no irreligious feelings or attitudes. On the contrary, he spoke up for gentleness, beneficence, toleration – this is hardly to be a seditious or pernicious writer. If there is some issue of religious doctrine that he has got wrong, he says in the Second Letter, then God should be his judge. In so far as it is a question of his having flouted the laws of the state, then the case is all on his side. For, in attacking him and his works, both the Genevan state and its Church have deserted their avowed principles of liberty and toleration. And it really cannot be argued that he writes as an atheist, he says in the Third Letter. It is true that he has attacked miracles as incredible and unnecessary to the Christian religion, but it is also the case that God has revealed his power and goodness to man better in the law and order of nature than in any specific miraculous intervention.

The next three letters are principally devoted to criticizing the propriety of the actions taken against him. How can he be accused of secret machinations against the state when he published *Émile* openly, in his own name? And, furthermore, he was condemned without due process; no charge was publicly laid, nor was he given any hearing where he might defend himself. In all cases, he goes on, the various governmental and legal officers and bodies have exceeded their powers. Many worse offences have gone unnoticed; why was his work singled out? It is clear, he concludes, that it is French influence that has caused him all this trouble. It is particularly strange that his ideas in *The Social Contract* should be attacked. For has he done anything in that work other than hold up Geneva as an example before the whole of Europe? If it were – incredibly – true that his ideas attack the foundations of all governments, how is it that only Geneva retaliates? Since he is not alone in proposing this kind of view, why should he be the target of specific censure?

The second part begins with the Seventh Letter. Here, and in the last two letters, Rousseau argues that gradual changes in the Genevan political structure have led to the usurpation of sovereignty by the governing councils, so that liberty has been sacrificed. He attacks in detail the various abuses that have crept into the political system, maintaining that the citizens have been deprived of their fundamental rights – prevented not merely from taking part in legislative acts, but from protesting against legislative proposals. What has come about, Rousseau says, is a state divided against itself; the bourgeoisie and the councils are now in opposition, whereas the latter should be the servants of the will of the former.

On nearly all points it would appear that Rousseau has the best of the argument – not that that was of any avail to him. The work is a fine exercise in polemical defence, but its general interest is limited: the points that he addresses, the arguments that he adduces, are all constrained by the particular purpose for which he was writing. And there are no points of theoretical significance in it that he has not argued elsewhere, unfettered by the exigencies of conflict.

Further reading: Green (8); Spink (277)

Lettres Morales   *See* MORAL LETTERS.

Lévite d'Éphraïm, Le   *See* POETRY AND MISCELLANEOUS PROSE.

liberty   *See* FREEDOM.

love   In the DISCOURSE ON THE ORIGIN OF INEQUALITY (70–1; *OC* III, 157–8) Rousseau distinguishes what he calls the 'physical' and the 'moral' ingredients in the feeling of love. The 'physical part' is just the 'general desire which urges the sexes to union with each other'. The 'moral part' is 'that which determines and fixes this desire exclusively upon one particular object'. In his view this 'moral part' is a 'factitious feeling, born of social usage', which gives rise to jealousy and vindictiveness and is one of the primary causes of ALIENATION and inequality among men. This element in the feeling of love feeds on notions of relative merit and beauty, which are largely invidious, causing both men and women to seek exclusive preference for themselves to the detriment of others. Natural man, by contrast, is a stranger to these feelings; he is 'confined merely to what is physical in love', and so is relieved of violent fits of passion and dispute (see SEX).

Rousseau returns to this point in *Émile* Bk V (429–31; *OC* IV, 796–9). But in this later context he is anxious to show the character of 'true love' between humans, and does not adopt the same disparaging manner towards the 'moral part' of love. He has said, indeed, that reciprocal love holds the whole value of life, so he must show how there can be a bond of loving union between persons which is 'moral' in character yet does not degenerate into jealousy and anger and breed vindictiveness and conflict.

By calling the bond 'moral', Rousseau means that it is mediated through ideas of what is proper, right or fitting, what is owed or deserved by each to each, whether these be sound or unsound ideas (see MORALITY). His task must be, then, to show what specific character these ideas should have if the bond is to be a sound, creative and benign one, and if it is not to introduce inequality, enslavement and other distortions into human relationships. His view is that both Émile and Sophie, his representative lovers, should recognize that it is not to their own good, nor to the good of the one each loves, to become so enslaved by the bonds of love that his or her entire life and being becomes disposable at the whim of the beloved. It is essential that each lover retain a strong sense of his or her value as an independent person, that he or she recognize that there are values and goods that matter just as much as submitting to the will of the loved one.

If this is not done, Rousseau argues, they will, anyway, debase themselves and make themselves no longer interesting or worthwhile as persons to be loved. Someone who, in passion, forsakes all he believes to be good nullifies himself has nothing about him that could be of value to anyone else. A lover can have no cause to forsake his virtues for the sake of his beloved; by so doing, he will only degrade the basis of his love and make himself of no worth to that person. It is Émile's 'esteem of true goods, frugality, simplicity, generous disinterestedness, contempt of show and riches' (*E* V, 433; *OC* IV, 801) which make him attractive, interesting and estimable. It cannot be appropriate, therefore, for him to cease to be all these things by enslaving himself to Sophie (however powerful, Rousseau admits, the temptation to do this may be) (see also JULIE).

His discussion of this matter is one more proof that he does not consider all social relations between persons as automatically engendering their disfigurement and misery. Although this is very often how things turn out, it is not inevitable (*see* AMOUR-PROPRE). Providing only that there can be equal respect and regard, based on a recognition of the value and honour of the persons involved, then, so far from this representing any loss of humanity for them, it is the means by which they achieve their full humanity in association with others.

It may be noted that Rousseau's own experiences of love hardly measured up to his prescription. He appears to have been incapable of bringing together the 'physical' and 'moral' parts: those he had sexual relations with he did not love, and those he loved he did not have – was incapable of having – sexual relations with. Furthermore, his only real love (for Sophie d'Houdetot) was marked by a signal failure to retain any sense of his own personal worth: he abandoned himself to transports of helpless passion. The real Sophie, as well as the imagined Sophie in *Émile*, behaved with a great deal more integrity and honour than did Rousseau (or than did Émile). Indeed, Rousseau seems to suggest that it is principally the incapacity of men to respond appropriately to the upsurge of love's passion that is responsible for most of the human deformation and misery that infuses intimate relationships.

Sources: *DI*, Pt 1
       E, Bks IV, V
       La Nouvelle Héloïse
       RSW, Sixth, Eighth, Ninth Walks

Further reading: Schwartz (35); Shklar, chs 3, 4 (36); Starobinski (37)

luxury Throughout his mature writings, Rousseau adopted a hostile attitude towards luxury. In the DISCOURSE ON THE SCIENCES AND THE ARTS, for instance, he mentions it as one of the signal evils of increasing civilization.

He has three principal grounds for his hatred of luxury. First, it is a primary vehicle for the expression of AMOUR-PROPRE in its excessive or distorted character. Luxurious possession is principally nothing more than conspicuous consumption, having meaning for the possessor only in that it enables him to think he has the better of others who languish in indigence. It expresses an aggressive desire to do down others as inferiors and confers no real benefit on the possessor, whose self-worth is measured only by his ascendancy over others. Those others, therefore, in effect possess his soul, since he depends on their deference rather than on his own real merits to sustain a sense of his own value (*see* ALIENATION; ARTIFICIAL). Thus:

I could prove that, if we have a few rich and powerful men on the pinnacle of fortune and grandeur, while the crowd grovels in want and obscurity, it is because the former prize what they enjoy only in so far as others are destitute of it; and because, without changing their condition, they would cease to be happy the moment the people ceased to be wretched. (*DI* 101; *OC* III, 189)

And he makes similar points in *Émile* (IV, 351–4; *OC* IV, 685–91), saying that what matters to people about luxury is that it is their exclusive possession: it has meaning to them in terms only of others' lack of it. The rich man never enjoys; rather, he has always to be showing other people how much he is enjoying himself. And that is an empty pleasure.

Second, Rousseau argues that the production of luxury goods involves great chains of labour and materials. Not only is such production destined merely for ostentation, but it involves a person's livelihood being dependent on fashion and caprice, and his dependence on others for the materials that he requires and for a market for his products (see *E* III, 195–202; *OC* IV, 469–80). The worker in a luxury trade may be highly skilled, but he has enslaved himself to empty and idle ends and is incapable of exercising his gifts at his own discretion and according to his own talents:

> See, therefore, how little solid are all those brilliant resources and how many other resources are necessary for you to take advantage of them. And then what will become of you in this cowardly debasement? . . . How will you – more than ever a plaything of public opinion – raise yourself above prejudices which are the arbiters of your fate? How will you despise the baseness and the vices which you need to subsist? You depended only on riches, and now you depend on the rich. (*E* III, 197; *OC* III, 472)

Finally, Rousseau argues that luxurious indulgence and luxury production lead to the neglect of what is really good and essential to human need and welfare. Although food, housing and clothing are basic essentials, which every person requires, in order to service the ostentatious tastes of cities the countryside is impoverished, and many people are deprived of these basic necessities. The desire to outdo others causes people to despise what they really require. No one needs expensive dress, exotic foods, but the taste for what is simple and wholesome will be killed. In the death of that taste lies, also, the death of the possibility of human beings collaborating in a just and equitable fashion such that each and all can have their human needs met by common labour for a shared good. Where it becomes more important to have precedence than anything else, to meet basic needs for oneself, let alone for all, will seem irrelevant.

Rousseau's strictures on luxury acquire particular significance if considered against the background of the continous debate, taking place in eighteenth-century France, about the possibility of reconciling private interests and the advancement of public good. Not only the influential Englishman, Bernard Mandeville but also the physiocrats argued that avarice and the desire for luxurious living stimulated economic activity and material prosperity, and should not be thought of as inimical to the good of others. (Such ideas find a more sophisticated and complete expression later, in the writings of Adam Smith.)

Rousseau joins others such as the Abbé de Mably and Morellet in arguing that such an idea was completely mistaken and pernicious. The envisaged harmony, or mutual fertilization, of individual private material interests is, in their view, quite implausible. Instances of private interests leading to effective and mutually profitable cooperation are the exception rather than the rule. Exacerbated *amour-propre* finds profit only in another's ignominy – and this will ensure that conflict of interests will be the norm. But not only this: the pursuit of narrow individual profit concentrates the heart on the fortunes of oneself alone, making it impossible that justice and equality for all be valued as the first principles of society. It is a mistake, too, to think that rational conviction as to the good of these virtues is sufficient to ensure that they are fostered. When the love of luxury is predominant, the individual will never learn to feel that his own good is bound up with the well-being of his fellows.

Rousseau's ideas on luxury, though representing one small part of his thinking about the needs and goods of the individual in relation to a humane civil community, engage with his immediate predecessors' and contemporaries' similar notions on the subject.

Sources: *DI*, Pt 2
      DSA
      E Bk IV

Further reading: Martin, ch. 9 (272); Shklar, ch. 3 (36)

M

magistrate *See* GOVERNMENT.

master Rousseau talks at many points of the role of being master of men, of having power, command, over them. In his view such a position is almost invariably unjust and illegitimate, and the desire for mastery of others is corrupt and damaging. In terms perhaps more familiar from the writings of Hegel and Marx, Rousseau discusses the mutual corruption of master and slave (*E* II, 85; *OC* IV, 311); and how someone who 'thinks himself the master of others . . . still remains a greater slave than they' (*SC* I, ch. 1, 165; *OC* III, 352).

Many of the recurrent principal ideas that pervade his mature writings converge in his assessment of the master–slave relationship. Rousseau thinks it is through the pressures of excessive AMOUR-PROPRE that we are caused to seek mastery over others. In being able to make others submit to our will we demonstrate to ourselves, we think, our potency and significance as human beings. By enforcing subjection on them, we convince ourselves that we count for something, are undeniably important presences, in the lives of others. But, he argues, this is a delusion. Such an aggressive response to other people is born of fear and insecurity, and the relationship it establishes can do nothing to assuage that. For the recognition others pay me when they are in servitude to me in no way comprises an acknowledgement by them of my value and importance. They pay it only as a tribute exacted from them, as lip service paid only for fear of a whipping. I am to them only a feared and hated superior power; I am not honoured and respected as a person. My own nullification of others precludes my securing the very human respect I wanted.

Furthermore, so long as I require others' subjection as a proof of my own power and importance, my sense of my own worth lies at the disposal of others. They have only to escape my control for me to see them reviling or ignoring me; and, in so doing, they reduce my own sense of personal significance to nothing. I am, in this way, enslaved to those I enslave, and – in significant respects – more of a slave than they (*see*

160

ALIENATION). For it is inconceivable that a slave should believe that his potent reality as a human depended on his subjection to his master; that relation, in fact, is a denial of his reality. But for the master, his sense of personal significance does require others' obedience. And he is dependent in other ways as well: his needs and tastes are such as to require the work of many hands to equip him with what he believes he requires. He is, thus, defenceless, weak and unable to conserve his life from his own resources. Even when, apparently, he is at the pinnacle of power, he is hedged around in innumerable ways, needing to retain his position, to cajole and threaten, to demand or exact service somehow.

It is not only practically more sensible, but humanly and morally more valuable and creative, to establish with others relations of equality and cooperation, instead of supremacy and command. By doing so, each person more completely belongs to himself, depends on his own power and resources, and can both give and receive recognition of value (*see* COMPASSION).

Rousseau presents powerful and enduring insights into the inner meaning of the desire for mastery over others. It may be that his account is coloured by his need to console himself for not enjoying a powerful and prestigious position in society himself – for he enviously denigrates the persons and lives of those who do. None the less, the depth and pervasiveness of people's desire to gain control over their fellows is hard to exaggerate; and it is equally hard to exaggerate the malign character and consequences of this. Where, perhaps, Rousseau's account is weak is in his apparently supposing that the master would patently suffer from the ill-effects of his dependence on others (*see* DEPENDENCE): usually, people so arrange their lives that they stand on a footing of equal regard with some, then act in concert with them so as to achieve mastery over others. (Rousseau has, of course, other objections to such forms of sectional interest.) It is perhaps the fact that any one individual can thus insulate himself from any direct dire effects of his craving for supremacy that gives Rousseau's views on the matter less force than they otherwise might have. What has caused people to accept at some level the demand for human equality – and this is quite contrary to Rousseau's own views on how it might come about – has not been their pleasure in experiencing egalitarian human intercourse, but some more or less rational conviction that such an arrangement is proper and due to humans.

Sources: *DI*, Pt 2
       E, Bk IV
       SC, Bk I

Further reading: Shklar, ch. 3 (36)

morality Rousseau deploys the concept of morality in two, connected, ways. In one, the commonplace way, he uses it to speak generally of the principles, criteria and goals that comprise a person's, or a society's, standards of proper conduct. But first, the more unusual usage.

At the beginning of the DISCOURSE ON THE ORIGIN OF INEQUALITY, Rousseau distinguishes two kinds of inequality: 'natural or physical'; and 'moral or political', which 'depends on a kind of convention, and is established, or at least authorized, by the consent of men' (*DI* 44; *OC* III, 131). Since he goes on to be consistently critical of inequalities of this second kind, it may be wondered how he can refer to them as 'moral'. But this is a simple misunderstanding. 'Moral' here does not signify morally good, justified or appropriate. Rather, it indicates the character and basis of the inequality, no matter whether it be of an acceptable or of an unacceptable kind.

The inequality is 'moral' in character when it is articulated and sustained in moral terms – that is, in terms of the differences in titles, rights, duties, responsibilities, obligations that one person has in relation to another. Thus, for instance, if I am stronger than you, this is a 'natural or physical' inequality not merely in that it originates in differences of natural inheritance, but in that the character of the inequality is a matter of physical phenomena only: I can move greater weights, defeat you in a fight, and so on. On the other hand, if I am your father and you my child this is (as normally understood) not merely a physical relationship that I have with you, but a moral relationship also. I have certain duties in relation to you, and you to me; I have certain titles to direct and control you, and you have certain obligations to obey and follow my direction. We not only *understand* our relative positions in terms of our having these rights and duties towards each other, but also *act* in relation to each other on the basis of these notions.

To give an example of a 'moral' relationship that Rousseau would criticize: a feudal lord may (take himself to) have the right to dispossess one of his serfs of his house or land, and the serf may (take himself to) be obliged to submit to this. The character of their transaction is constituted through these differential titles and obligations. (In this case, Rousseau would probably say that the 'moral' relationship masks a more direct power relationship. But the lord possesses superior power not merely physically – in fact, he may well be weaker. Rather, he possesses this superior power only through the consent and cooperation of others who will execute his commands; and this rests on moral relations.)

Thus, to explain his notion of a 'moral or political inequality', Rousseau goes on to say that it 'consists of the different privileges which some men enjoy to the prejudice of others; such as that of being more rich, more honoured, more powerful, or even in a position to exact obedience' (*DI* 44; *OC* III, 131).

It is in an allied sense that, when Émile begins to establish relationships with other people (ÉMILE, Bk IV), Rousseau says 'he begins to sense his moral being' over and above his character as a 'physical being', the scope and limits of which he has already explored, according to Rousseau's educational plan, in his earlier years (*E* IV, 214; *OC* IV, 493; *see* EDUCATION). Émile's concern with his 'moral being' is his concern with the 'position' he will hold among men; what honour, recognition, standing or titles he should receive, and what he should afford to others. In a similar vein Rousseau talks of a person's 'civil' being, in terms of his standing as a citizen among citizens (see *E* V, 455; *OC* IV, 833). And one could also talk of a person's 'collaborative' being, when he functions as a 'hand' in a joint practical undertaking where what matters about him is how he functions as a cog in the whole 'machine'.

The assumption of 'moral being' – that is, coming to understand oneself and other people, and one's relationships in terms of titles, obligations, responsibilities and so on – is for Rousseau a crucial element in human development. It is in this area that both AMOUR-PROPRE and COMPASSION play their most significant role, as providing ways in which we may find a footing with, and come to terms with, other people (for our, and their, good or ill). It is a mistake to suppose that, for Rousseau, once a person has assumed the character of a 'moral' being, his 'natural' being has been left behind and his life is automatically distorted. True, distortion often does occur if these moral relationships involve control and domination; but relations of equality and mutual care are, equally, moral relations, and Rousseau sees these as unequivocally good and in accordance with nature (*see* NATURAL GOODNESS). The only way in which 'nature' is transcended in moral relationships is that people are no longer, to themselves or for each other, simply physical creatures encountering one another on physical terms.

In this same way Rousseau argues in The SOCIAL CONTRACT (Bk I, ch. 8) that in entering the civil state a 'very remarkable change' takes place in man, whereby justice is substituted for instinct, and human actions acquire the morality they formerly lacked. 'Natural liberty', which depends solely on the strength of the individual, is replaced by 'civil liberty', which is limited by the general will (*see* FREEDOM); and possession, which is the effect of force or the right of first occupancy, is replaced by PROPERTY, which is a 'positive title'. Rousseau adds that a man acquires, in the civil state, 'moral liberty, which alone makes him truly master of himself' (*see* VIRTUE).

Acquisition of moral being, holding a position in the 'moral order'

(*E* IV, 235; *OC*, IV, 522), is primarily a matter of recognizing oneself as, and of being recognized as, a bearer of rights, duties and titles which equip one to enjoy a certain standing with others in society (and in the state). To possess moral being, in this way, is not a matter of being virtuous, excellent or otherwise commendable as a person. It is to have a certain status, and to act in terms of one's possession of that status; human excellence is a comparative matter and depends on other grounds.

Partly because it is in this way that Rousseau understands a person's moral character, he consistently denies that there is any morality in a child's actions. A child can have no grasp (or no proper grasp) of the ideas of titles, obligations or responsibilities, and so it cannot be that he intentionally flouts these and acts wickedly. It is only with the 'age of reason' (*E* I, 67; *OC* IV, 288) that we come to knowledge of such things, and that conscious evil can then be imputed to us. He does not deny that a child can do damage; but, since he cannot know the moral significance of what he is doing, the damage that he does is not, alone, proof of badness in him.

To return to the commonplace use of the notion of morality. Rousseau often speaks of the morality of the times, meaning the standards of behaviour generally observed or esteemed (nominally, at least); and sometimes of 'true' morality, meaning those standards which, in his view, are truly good, just and appropriate. In this broader sense, 'morality' covers both titles and obligations but also virtuous excellences in a person. Rousseau sometimes characterizes 'true' morality in terms of familiar forms of action, such as serving one's country, obliging friends, relieving the unhappy; sometimes in terms of obedience to the promptings of CONSCIENCE; and sometimes in terms of behaving in ways suitable to the condition and circumstances of man – a precept which, he says, if rightly understood, comprehends all the others (*E* V, 445–6; *OC* IV, 819).

Sources: *DI*
        E, Bk IV
        SC Bk I

Further reading: Blum (21); Charvet, ch. 3 (23); Dent, ch. 4 (24); Shklar, ch. 2 (36)

Moral Letters (or *Letters to Sophie*) (written 1757–8; published 1861) (*Lettres Morales*) [6] In early 1756 Rousseau left Paris to live at Montmorency, in a cottage called the Hermitage lent him by Mme d'Épinay. While taking long walks there in the woods, he was taken over by powerful erotic fantasies which, in due course, took shape as the plot for his novel JULIE, OU LA NOUVELLE HÉLOÏSE. Soon after he had begun to draft the opening letters of that epistolary novel, there came into his life the near-incarnation of his dream heroine, Julie. This was Sophie d'Houdetot, Mme d'Épinay's sister-in-law, with whom Rousseau fell passionately in love (see *The Confessions*, Bk IX). Rousseau wrote the *Moral Letters* for Sophie's edification over the winter months of 1757–8. These six short letters were not published in his lifetime – and it is unclear whether he intended them to be published, anyway; some appeared in 1861, the rest in 1888.

In the *Letters*, Rousseau sets out to give Sophie the benefit of his mature understanding of the nature and sources of virtue, and of the way of life that best conduces to the possession and exercise of virtue. Outlining the occasion for his enterprise, he explains that on their walks together Sophie has often asked him for moral guidance. Now in all sincerity, he turns to this task, and is hopeful that it will be of benefit, since Sophie has all the advantages and opportunities for living a virtuous life. The object of human life, Rousseau goes on, is HAPPINESS, but no one can agree on how it is to be found. Sages and philosophers engage in endless disputes about it. Those who live in cities impoverish others; all walks of life present obstacles. It is only in your own heart that you can find what you need for happiness; modern wisdom and learning provides no clue.

This same attack on the confusion and emptiness of reason and philosophy continues in the Third Letter. All we can be sure of is that we are, that we exist. We cannot advance by reason beyond this point; we must instead trust to sentiments, to our deepest and clearest feelings.

These feelings disclose that there is in us a love of virtue and order. In each of us there is an interior voice which, if listened to with humility and care, will lead us to act well and to be well. Its promptings are proper to the needs of our souls, and lead us to do what is fine and honourable. This inner principle of CONSCIENCE will direct us to love justice and to follow truth, overcoming all prejudices. This inner feeling precedes reason, and is a better guide to life. In the Sixth Letter Rousseau offers advice on how we can make ourselves ready to hear this voice and follow its guidance. We must learn to do without the world, to be on our own without boredom. We should take time off in the country, in stillness and solitude, and do simple good works for those about us – the poor, the oppressed. The great danger faced by people in Sophie's position is idleness, which causes them to seek amusements and luxury. These blind and deafen the soul, and make us heedless of the promptings of humanity.

There is little in these letters, which are really more of a curious love gift than works of serious intent, that Rousseau did not discuss elsewhere – in particular, in THE CREED OF A SAVOYARD VICAR – in more depth and detail.

Further reading: Grimsley (187)

musical composition [23]   Rousseau's first great passion was music, and the bulk of his creative output in the 1740s and early 1750s was in musical composition and in writing about music (*see* MUSIC: WRITINGS ON).

Although he received a few lessons from Le Maître in 1729, Rousseau was almost wholly self-taught, both as a practitioner and a composer. In his early days he certainly overreached himself; he has left an amusing account of one episode of youthful hubris when a farrago of nonsense that he wrote for presentation at Lausanne, under his own direction, was saved from fiasco by just one good tune (*The Confessions*, Bk IV). He clearly had some genuine, if slight, musical talent, on the basis of which he could probably have made a living as a composer and teacher – particularly after his great success with the opera *Le Devin du Village* ('The Village Soothsayer') in 1752. But although from time to time throughout the rest of his life he composed small pieces – mostly cantatas, songs and ballads – musical composition remained for him only a diversion.

His first efforts were in the field of opera, combining solo singing, choruses, recitative, declamation, interludes, ballets, and so on. Towards the end of the 1730s, while he was still living with Mme de Warens, he apparently composed a lyric tragedy, *Iphis et Anaxarette*, but had the good sense to throw it on the fire (some part of the text survives, but none of the music). The subject matter (taken from Ovid) concerns the love of Iphis, an officer of the court of King Ortule, for Anaxarette, Ortule's daughter. In standard fashion, despite her love for Iphis she is pledged to Philoxis, a foreign prince. The work breaks off at the point where preparations are being made for the unwelcome marriage.

Rousseau's next composition in this genre is a curious work, *La Découverte du Nouveau Monde* ('The Discovery of the New World'), of which, again, we have the text but no music. This was completed while he was tutor to the children of de Mably at Lyons in 1740 or 1741. It is an allegorical drama in which the European powers invade the Antilles, but are reconciled with the native Indians and live together in peace under the rule of Queen Isabella of Spain. It is possible, if with difficulty, to see in this a germ of his later interest in the clash between civilization and native simplicity.

In 1743 Rousseau began work on a further opera, *Les Muses Galantes* (roughly modelled on Rameau's *Les Indes Galantes* of 1735), but progress was interrupted by his leaving for Venice. As soon as he returned to Paris he resumed work on it: text and music were completed in early 1745. Some of the music was played at the house of La Pouplinière, and the whole was performed before M. de Bonneval, master of the King's entertainments, and an audience that included Richelieu and Rameau. Rameau declared that the work had some fine parts – not by Rousseau –

and some dull parts – by Rousseau. Not surprisingly, these comments did nothing to establish good feeling between them, and they were to engage in public dispute a few years later.

Richelieu, on the other hand, was enthusiastic about the work, and tried to get it put on at Versailles. But neither there, nor at the Opéra where it was rehearsed, was it performed. (Once more, the text survives, but most of the music is lost.) Richelieu now recommended that Rousseau produce a shortened adaptation of Rameau and Voltaire's joint work, *Les Fêtes de Ramire*, for performance before the King. This Rousseau did, not at all pleasing Rameau (though Voltaire seemed happy enough), and it was performed at Versailles in December 1745. (The text is very short; the music has not survived.) The little opera concerns Fatime, a princess, who is languishing in prison, her royal house having been conquered. Ramire, the son of her conqueror Alphonse and not a brutal man, has fallen in love with her. Venus, as usual, conquers Mars, and Ramire lays down his arms before the charms of Fatime. The empire of love triumphs over the rage of war.

Whereas none of these early labours of Rousseau's amounts to much, his next work, his single glorious musical triumph, entitles him to an honourable mention in musical history. In April 1752 he went to stay with his friend François Mussard at Passy. While there, he wrote within a few weeks the words and music of *Le Devin du Village*, completing it in Paris by early May. Duclos, the Royal Historian, had the work accepted by the Opéra, where it was rehearsed in late June. The Master of the King's Entertainments, M. de Cury, demanded that it be presented at court, and on 18 October it was performed at Fontainebleau before Louis XV and Mme de Pompadour. It was a tremendous success, and Rousseau was summoned to appear before the King to receive a royal pension. However, he returned to Paris, pleading illness (and, later, republican sentiments). *Le Devin* was then put on at the Opéra, and published in 1753. It remained in the repertory for at least fifty years. Mme de Pompadour herself took the part of Colin in a private performance at her country home of Belle-Vue, in March 1753.

Collette, the heroine, is a shepherdess whose lover, Colin, a shepherd, has forsaken her for the lady of the manor. She seeks the aid of the village soothsayer, whom she wants to make Colin think she has fallen for someone else. Colin becomes intensely jealous, realizes that it is she that he really loves, and returns to her. They are reunited and live happily ever after. The music is charming – delicate, simple, melodious – and devoid of the elaborate devices and decorations which, in Rousseau's view, made so much French music stilted and lifeless. Although a slight piece, it is still performed from time to time, and has been recorded. (An adaptation of *Le*

Devin was produced in London in 1770 by Charles Burney under the title, *The Cunning Man*.)

In both the DISCOURSE ON THE SCIENCES AND THE ARTS (1750) and the *Letter on French Music* (1753), Rousseau was developing ideas on social and political issues that were to set him at odds with the 'high culture' and manners of Paris and the court. He appears to have resolved that he could not keep faith with his true genius if he remained part of this life, and in 1755–6 he turned his back on the capital and on the possibility of a musical career. Although he did not wholly give up composing, he now confined his output to the small scale, writing mostly motets, airs and songs. In 1774 he began another opera, *Daphnis et Chloé*, but did not complete it.

He produced only two further musical pieces of note. The text of his brief monodrama, *Pygmalion*, is simple. In this 'lyric scene' the sculptor languishes, devoid of inspiration. He throws himself at the feet of his statue of Galatea and begins to work on it. But she appears to be alive: he pours out all his heart and love for her, and, indeed, she comes to life. Rousseau wrote this piece at Môtiers in 1762; eight years later it was performed at Lyons, with music by his friend Coignet, as part of the celebrations that marked Rousseau's return to Paris from 'exile' at Monquin. It was later performed at the Opéra in Paris. Some have seen in it a remote precursor of Schoenberg's *Pierrot Lunaire*.

The second substantial musical achievement was a collection of around one hundred songs, ballads and poems that Rousseau had set to music (some with more than one setting), often at the request of friends. Mostly composed in the 1770s, these pieces were assembled after his death, appearing in 1781 under the title, *Les Consolations des Misères de ma Vie* ['The Consolations of the Troubles of My Life'], *ou Recueil d'Airs, Romances et Duos de Jean-Jacques Rousseau*. The title was the editor's, though based on a note left by Rousseau on one of the songs.

Finally, a musical curiosity. A melody that Rousseau wrote for one of the interludes to *Le Devin*, which came to be known as 'Rousseau's Dream', has been widely used as a hymn tune. It appears both in the Methodist Hymn-Book, where it is a variant tune for 'Lo, He comes with clouds descending', and in *The Scottish Psalter* (1929), where the words, 'Lord, a little band and lowly', are to be sung to it. An adaptation of the same melody was used by Weber in his incidental music to *Turandot*; and this, in turn, was taken up by Hindemith and used as the basis for the second movement of his *Symphonic Metamorphoses on Themes by Carl Maria von Weber*.

Further reading: Blom (191); Cucuel (192); Jansen (194); Pougin (198); Strauss (200)

music: writings on [24]   There are four principal groups of writings. First, Rousseau's *Project for a New Musical Notation* (*Projet Concernant de Nouveaux Signes pour la Musique*), which was subsequently published, with additions, as the *Dissertation on Modern Music* (*Dissertation sur la Musique Moderne*) in 1743. Second, the entries he wrote on musical topics for the ENCYCLOPAEDIA, under the editorial direction of d'Alembert. These connect with the third group of works, Rousseau's contributions to the Querelle des Bouffons, which includes his *Letter on French Music* (1753) but also a number of shorter pieces, some written in response to Rameau's criticisms of his views. (For Rousseau's *Essay on the Origin of Languages*, relevant to this phase of his work, *see* ORIGIN OF LANGUAGES.) Finally, there is his *Dictionary of Music* (published in 1767), roughly based on the articles that he had written earlier for the *Encyclopaedia*. (Several of these were, in their turn, included in the supplementary volumes to the *Encyclopaedia*.)

When, in 1742, Rousseau finally decided to break with Mme de Warens and to strike out on his own in Paris, he took with him his play *Narcissus* (*see* THEATRE) and his *Project for a New Musical Notation*. Within a few days of his arrival in Paris, on the strength of some letters of introduction from influential friends in Lyons he was invited to present this project before the Academy of Sciences, on 22 August. Although he was listened to with interest, the project was not accepted. Among those who criticized it – justly, Rousseau thought – was Rameau. (The two were to cross swords later.)

The *Project for a New Musical Notation* seeks to replace standard musical notation with a numerical scheme, so that instead of a patterned arrangement of notes on the stave there is a linear arrangement of numbers (with dots above and below to indicate octave changes), together with other symbols. Thus, a note sequence might run: Ut c 1 3 5 1 3 5, with the dot above the second 1 indicating that it, and the following notes (me and soh), are in the higher octave, until a dot below indicates reversion. ('Ut' is doh, in the key of C.)

The representational scheme used in any musical writing is wholly conventional, and Rousseau claimed that he had instructed pupils successfully in his. But his scheme is not as clear as the familiar one: the 'shape' of a melodic line cannot, for instance, be taken in at a glance with the same ease as the familiar notation allows. In any event, he wrote in defence of it to the *Mercure de France*, and revised and extended the original project for publication as his *Dissertation on Modern Music* (1743). Very few copies sold, however, and his scheme never caught on.

Over the next few years Rousseau was occupied mainly with composition, and did not return to writing on musical topics until 1748–9. Having been asked by Diderot to prepare articles on music for inclusion in the

Encyclopaedia, he eventually wrote over two hundred, which appeared gradually, as the volumes of the *Encyclopaedia* were published.

The range of Rousseau's contributions is impressive (particularly since he was largely self-taught). He covers such topics as adagio, arpeggio, concerto, fugue, major key, plainchant, rhythm, semitone and syncopation. He also wrote on melody and harmony, his ideas on which were to become very significant (see below). Rameau had given to harmony and harmonic relationships a central place in his account of the structure and significance of music, seeing in harmony a metaphor for the interpretation of the universe (compare the medieval notion of the 'harmony of the spheres'). In his articles for the *Encyclopaedia* Rousseau largely followed Rameau's lead. Later, however, as a result of his time in Venice as secretary to the French ambassador (1743–4) when he had grown to love Italian music, he disputed the priority of harmony over melody.

At that time, Italian music was very little known in France. French operatic tradition was dominated by the seventeenth-century composer Lully and by Rameau. In 1752, however, a travelling opera company from Italy (the *Bouffons*, as they became known in France) had come to Paris, putting on performances of *opera buffa*, including works by Vinci, Scarlatti, Jommelli and, particularly, Pergolesi, whose *La Serva Padrona* made a great impression on Rousseau. When they returned in 1753, the question of the comparative merits of Italian and French opera had become a burning issue. Grimm, at that time still a close friend of Rousseau's, had opened the proceedings with a contentious pamphlet, his *Lettre sur 'Omphale'*, in which he criticized Destouches' *Omphale*, an opera in the tradition of French lyric tragedy. Grimm's aspersions were met with equal hostility, and now Rousseau joined in his support. Soon all Paris was divided. The supporters of Italian opera, who collected near the Queen's box, were known as the *coin de la Reine*, and supporters of French opera became the *coin du Roi*. Pamphlets and letters were published in great numbers. In 1753 Rousseau weighed in with his most substantial, and the most influential, contribution to the argument, his *Letter on French Music*.

Here Rousseau argues for the primacy of melody in all beautiful, expressive and moving music – which, he says, must be rooted in the sounds and accents of the spoken language of its nation of origin. The Italian language is flowing, full of resonance, with clear accentuation. The French language, by contrast, is harsh, thin, monotonous, without colour or modulation. This makes it impossible to set the French language to music melodiously, so composers have had recourse to harmony as a way of disguising the essential unmusicality of the material at their disposal. Rousseau concludes: 'The French have no music and cannot have; or, should they ever have that would be so much the worse for them.' (Several of the ideas in this *Letter* connect with Rousseau's uncompleted *Essay on the Origin of Languages*, which was probably begun before the *Letter*.)

Rousseau's *Letter* did nothing to soothe the feelings of the supporters of French music. So great was the outcry that greeted it that Rousseau claimed that it distracted people from an incipient rebellion provoked by Louis XV's dissolution of the Paris *parlement* (at whose hands Rousseau would, in due course, suffer himself). Among those offended by the *Letter* was Rameau, who was named in it as one who wrongly, unmusically, promoted harmony above melody. Relations between Rousseau and Rameau had already deteriorated, particularly because of Rameau's adverse reaction to Rousseau's *Les Muses Galantes*, although as recently as 1752 Rousseau had himself unstintingly praised Rameau's admittedly uncharacteristically Italianate *Platée*. Rameau mounted a series of increasingly bitter attacks on Rousseau's work, but although Rousseau did respond to some of these (as in his *Examen des Deux Principes Avancés par M. Rameau*), his concerns were rapidly moving away from music towards the major social and political theories of his maturity.

Although, when he first moved to Montmorency in 1756, Rousseau had intended to work up his *Encyclopaedia* articles into a form suitable for his planned *Dictionary of Music*, his work on it – involving extensive revision of his earlier material as well as the addition of many new entries – proceeded only very slowly. When it finally appeared in 1767, it enjoyed considerable success, and brought Rousseau a steady income during the last decade of his life. It was translated into English in 1770. Some articles were taken from it for inclusion in the supplementary volumes of the *Encyclopaedia*.

The successful setting to music of French words cannot, after all – as Rousseau maintained it was – have been impossible. Many operas, including his own, highly popular, *Le Devin du Village*, have been written in that language. Gluck, whom Rousseau came to know and admire in the 1770s, wrote occasionally to French libretti, and believed that Rousseau did not so much show the impossibility of French music as the need for new possibilities to be opened up. One of Rousseau's last writings on music is his *Observations sur l'Alceste de Gluck*.

See also MUSICAL COMPOSITION.

Further reading: Cranston, vol. I, ch. 14 (17); Kisch (195); Oliver (197); Robinson (199); Wokler (204)

N

nationalism In ch. 3 of the CONSIDERATIONS ON THE GOVERNMENT OF POLAND Rousseau writes:

> It is national institutions which shape the genius, the character, the tastes and manners of a people; which give it an individuality of its own; which inspire it with that ardent love of country, based on ineradicable habits, which makes its members, while living among other peoples, die of boredom, though surrounded by delights denied them in their own land. Remember the Spartan who, gorged with the pleasures of the Great King's court, was reproached for missing his black broth. 'Ah,' he said to the satrap with a sigh, 'I know your pleasures, but you do not know ours!'
>
> Today, no matter what people may say, there are no longer any Frenchmen, Germans, Spaniards, or even Englishmen; there are only Europeans.

This passage shows clearly the centrality of the idea, the sentiment, of nation and country to Rousseau's political thinking. Nor is his concern here confined to discussions of legislation and government for specific nations (such as Poland or CORSICA); rather, the idea of national, or patriotic, zeal and loyalty is fundamental to his thinking about civil society in general.

For Rousseau, the major problem in the way of securing any just civil society lies in the confined interests of men, which make them indifferent or actively hostile towards the welfare of others, despite the fact that each person needs the assistance of others and cannot survive well on his own. These confined interests do not comprise merely a narrow egoism which tries to claim everything for itself and will not willingly yield anything to others. They include also AMOUR-PROPRE, which perceives the destitution and ignominy of others as a benefit to the superior person, as a proof of his magnificence.

It is Rousseau's view that no stable and successful society can be achieved if these sentiments remain unmodified, and if the law serves only as a check or limit to their excess. It is, anyway, unlikely that just law will be devised if such are the prevailing sentiments; every person or group will

172

struggle for ascendancy, and although common law will be devised it is likely to contain provisions that conduce only to the benefit of a few. Also, in so far as law demands the accommodation of the interests of others, there will be an incentive to evade its requirements, which will be seen as unwelcome impositions. He argues, therefore, that it is essential that the horizons of human interest be widened, so that others' good or ill comes to be felt by the individual as part of his own good or ill, just as a friend's condition is a matter of personal concern to one.

However, this extending of concern cannot, Rousseau thinks, be indefinite. We are not susceptible to sharing in the weal and woe of simply anyone, however remote from us in time, place and situation, merely in virtue of his being, as we are, a member of mankind. But we can identify with the predicament of those with whom we have some sense of shared life, destiny, culture and history; those in whose fortune we see something of ourselves, and with whose well- or ill-being our sense of the quality of life is bound up. (There can, of course, be no precise determination of the outer limits of our extended concern.) In so far as we can thus identify with others, living under common law with them and making common cause for protection and welfare will not now appear as an exaction but as the embodiment of that course of life that we should ourselves wish for.

It is the country or nation that provides the most powerful and compelling object of loyalty for extended sentiments that will be strong enough to provide an effective source of action for all its members, without which society scarcely exists, let alone has any chance of surviving. Patriotism, or nationalism – not as empty words but as substantiated in tastes, manners and customs that are practised in one place among one group – comprises for Rousseau those public virtues by which alone a civil society may prosper and endure. At his most extreme, he argues that children's games, festivals and public acts of all kinds should be directed towards celebrating and reinforcing the sentiments of common life and destiny which each citizen should have as a member, with others, of a proud, individual nation. Thus, in ch. 4 of the *Considerations* he writes:

> It is education that must give souls a national formation, and direct their opinions and tastes in such a way that they will be patriotic by inclination, by passion, by necessity. When he first opens his eyes, an infant ought to see the fatherland, and up to the day of his death he ought never to see anything else. Every true republican has drunk in love of country, that is to say love of law and liberty, along with his mother's milk. This love is his whole existence; he sees nothing but the fatherland, he lives for it alone; when he is solitary, he is nothing; when he has ceased to have a fatherland, he no longer exists; and if he is not dead, he is worse than dead (*GP*, ch. 4, 176; *OC* III, 966).

Nowadays, such remarks win Rousseau few friends. We think only of the imperialism, the xenophobia and the savagery that nationalistic exaltation has produced. But, for all that, it is hard to deny that Rousseau is here examining a central issue of political theory and practice. No state can survive long if the bulk of its members see no good in its laws and practices beyond their being unwelcome necessities generated by the need to accommodate others. And whilst we may think that national groupings do not provide the best focus for the cultivation of sentiments of loyalty to a common good experienced as part of one's own good, to ignore or to denigrate the kinds of extended loyalty that go beyond the bounds of the narrow self is to court the disintegration of the state.

Sources: DPE
GP
PCC
SC, Bks II–IV

Further reading: Barnard (151); Cohler (152); Dent, ch. 6 (24); Kedourie (258); Viroli, ch. 4 (38)

natural goodness Almost as famous as Rousseau's epigrammatic remark, 'Man is born free; and everywhere he is in chains' (*SC* I, ch. 1, 165; *OC* III, 351; *see* FREEDOM), is his frequent refrain that man is by nature good but is perverted and corrupted by society. This view is expressed particularly in ÉMILE and ROUSSEAU JUDGE OF JEAN-JACQUES: DIALOGUES, and in his LETTER TO CHRISTOPHE DE BEAUMONT, in which he specifies it as perhaps the paramount idea that has pervaded and structured the whole of his work, and that he has always consistently maintained.

According to the common interpretation of his thinking here, Rousseau is maintaining that men are born, if not exactly virtuous (for that involves knowledge of good and the conscious will to do it), at least predisposed towards VIRTUE – benign, loving and tender in their innate sentiments and dispositions, naturally moved to cherish all those they encounter. Aggression, malice, spite and envy are strangers to the untainted human heart as it leaves the hands of its maker. These malign dispositions enter only because other people pervert and destroy the natural innocence and integrity of the individual. His is not the final responsibility for these faults; even in his evil-doing, he is really the hapless and abused victim of the ill-will of others, who make him a monster and then recoil from him.

It is often said that this depiction of primitive innocence is part and parcel of Rousseau's psychopathic denial of his own anger, envy and vindictiveness, which led him always to represent himself as the injured

174

but well-meaning victim of others' malice – a habit to which he was, undeniably, unduly prone (*see* PARANOIA). One might well wish to discredit such a righteous self-representation, but it is not Rousseau's psychological inadequacies that are at issue here, but what he really said and whether or not this is defensible.

Not the least of the problems with this familiar interpretation is that it lays Rousseau open to charges of massive inconsistency. How, if man is naturally good, can society corrupt him? Society is only other people, so unless they have (latent) tendencies towards evil-doing, or we have (latent) evil dispositions to be awakened, how can society engender corruption? Rousseau believes that some kind of benign society and state is possible – which THE SOCIAL CONTRACT is devoted to explaining. But how can he hold such a view if society inevitably corrupts? Rather than concluding that Rousseau adds gross inconsistency to his psychopathy here, we should begin to wonder whether this familiar interpretation is adequate.

A crucial passage for understanding Rousseau's thought on this topic occurs in *Émile* (IV, 212–13; *OC* IV, 491–2), where he is distinguishing man's 'natural' from his 'alien' passions. Here he acknowledges the sense of 'natural' meaning 'innate', born in us either actually, or potentially, as part of our inheritance. But this is not the sense that interests him, the sense in which he intends the term. Rather, the significant sense in which passions are 'natural' is that they are 'instruments of our freedom; they tend to preserve us.' Those passions that, on the contrary, 'subject us and destroy us' are 'alien' – that is, they are contrary to our nature and 'come from elsewhere . . . we appropriate them to the detriment of nature.'

Rousseau is deploying here a framework of ideas that goes back at least as far as Aristotle. In Aristotle's view it is proper to understand the constitution of things, particularly animate things, teleologically – that is, in terms of their having components and an organization which tend towards their preservation and maintenance, towards the goal of promoting their good, their intact life and well-being. This is how the natural constitution of a thing is identified; anything in it which blocks such tendencies, or veers towards the damage or destruction of that thing, is contrary, alien, to its nature. On this account, it would be possible for there to be dispositions or potentialities in a being that are innate but contrary to its nature. Or, again, there could be dispositions that are both innate and natural in this sense, but that are deflected from their properly natural tendency (by chance or design) and come to be damaging or hurtful to the being in question.

From this emerges Rousseau's primary paradigmatic notion of what is both 'natural' and 'good'. The 'good' in question is the self-preservation and fruitful life of the creature – here, a person. And what is natural are passions (and, connectedly, actions, circumstances and so on) which conduce to that good, either immediately or indirectly, either instinctively or by conscious design. The clearest instance of what is natural and good in this way is AMOUR DE SOI, 'the source of our passions, the origin and principle of all the others, the only one born with man and which never leaves him so long as he lives'. Derived from this love of ourselves is the tendency to love what preserves us. Thus it is, in this way, natural to man to love 'his nurse and his governess'. At first, Rousseau goes on, this attachment is merely 'blind instinct'; what turns it into a sentiment, a passion, is the growing awareness of their 'intention manifested . . . to be useful to us'; this inspires in us 'sentiments similar to those they manifest'. So, in the same sense of what is natural, our affection for those who aid and sustain us and our gratitude for their help (*see* COMPASSION) are also natural sentiments. These all come from, and aid and abet, our self-preservation and the fullness of our life.

Amour de soi is the source of *all* our passions; 'all others are in a sense only modifications' of it. This means that even hurtful and enslaving passions are 'if you wish . . . natural'. But some modifications 'alter the primary goal and are at odds with their own principle. It is then that man finds himself outside of nature and sets himself in contradiction with himself.'

What Rousseau has in view is this. A child's anger at frustration, his rage at not getting his own way, can cause him to see other people not as supporters but as malign persecutors spitefully thwarting him (*see* AMOUR-PROPRE). This, then sets him in competition for control over them and locks him into a perpetual struggle for dominance in a context pervaded by threats and fear. If this pattern of expectation and response becomes consolidated, as it can through mishandling of the child's needs and reactions, then, so far from his being moved by passions which preserve him and tend to his freedom, he is moved by aggression, fear and anger which not only are intrinsically hurtful but also create a situation that blocks any self-enlarging or mutually creative development (*see* ALIENA-TION). The child's original tendency to rage is not, itself, alien. It is an element in his self-assertion, his making a claim on life. But, through mistakes or misfortunes in dealing with this reaction, there has developed in the child an attitude towards life, himself and others that has set him at odds with his own purpose of having a fruitful life for himself with others, so that he finds he is 'in contradiction with himself'.

Given this background, it can be understood why Rousseau says that love, gentleness and beneficence are natural dispositions, and that cruelty, spite and greed are unnatural. This is not because he thinks that everyone is, so to say, born a saint until spoiled by others, but because the former dispositions grow out of, accord with and further the well-being of an individual, whereas the latter thwart and conflict with the pursuit and achievement of that well-being – something that no one would want to happen unless they had been subjected to distorting or deforming circumstances. It is not that Rousseau assumes that no one will have a tendency to harm others as his primary principle; but by means of this two-step argument, by showing how the latter dispositions are hurtful to the individual, he concludes that they are alien to his being.

Although this passage in *Émile* concerns the passions specifically, its burden may be generalized to all those cases where Rousseau talks of what is natural to or for man: in effect, he maintains that there is a basic integrity in the constitution and purposes of human beings which conduces to their own well-being and fullness of life, for themselves and with others. (And it is via his belief in this proper integrity of the human constitution that Rousseau arrives at his belief in God's providential order – not vice versa (*see* CREED OF A SAVOYARD VICAR).) Human beings are not, he thinks, fundamentally divided against themselves: where we find this to be so, we must suspect some externally engendered deformation. He then explains how morally evil traits and dispositions set a person in contradiction with himself, and how morally good traits follow from and develop his proper integrity. Thus he concludes that moral wickedness is unnatural and originates in external influences.

Although Rousseau's teleological conception of human organization may not convince, and he may not be thought to show successfully just how cruelty, malice and so on are contrary to personal good (let alone the good of others), his argument is well conceived.

Sources: DI
         E, Bks I–IV

Further reading: Charvet, chs 2, 3 (23); Clark (332); Dent, chs 3, 4 (24); Dent (166); Howells (255); Masters, ch. 3 (69); Melzer (29); Shklar, ch. 2 (36)

nature 'Nature' is one of the most pervasive of all Rousseau's themes. Man is 'naturally' good; the 'state of nature' is benign and tranquil; a 'natural' education is creative and constructive; immersion in 'nature' is healing and uplifting. Rousseau is not alone, of course, in making the appeal to nature a touchstone of much of what is good, benign, beneficial, true and edifying, in contrast with the ills that social artifices and pressures, enforced labour, commerce – and civilization itself – impose on men. Then, as now, nature is widely seen as the healing alternative that will relieve us of the pains that, having deserted her bosom and ignored her teaching, we now suffer.

Rousseau applies the idea of nature and of what is natural to many aspects of life. He conceives the character of man as naturally intact and creative (*see* NATURAL GOODNESS); he depicts man's primitive and undisrupted relation to nature (*see* STATE OF NATURE); he grounds healthy educational development on respect for nature (see EDUCATION; ÉMILE); he describes God's relation to the created world, and man's involvement in it, in the CREED OF A SAVOYARD VICAR. As far as the natural world itself is concerned, Rousseau was among those who instigated the shift in sensibility from the desire to 'tame' nature, to make it bear the imprint of man's design, towards the appreciation of the wild, the untouched and the terrifying in nature, which is characteristic of Romanticism.

This aspect of Rousseau's sensibility is, perhaps, best seen in the Seventh Walk of the *Reveries of the Solitary Walker*. Here he writes of one of his botanical expeditions:

> I made my way far into the crevices of the rocks . . . and I finally reached a corner so deeply hidden away that I do not think I have ever seen a wilder spot. Black fir trees were mingled and intertwined with gigantic beeches . . . through the few gaps in this dark wall one could see nothing but sheer rock faces and fearful precipices which I dared only look at lying flat on my face. From the mountain gorges came the cry of the horned owl, the little owl and the eagle, while from time to time some more familiar birds lightened the horror of this solitary place. (*RSW* Walk 7, 117; *OC* I, 1070–1)

The whole panoply of favoured terms – 'wild', 'gigantic', 'fearful', 'horror' – which serve both to fire and to express the Romantic imagination, finds employment in this passage. (The episode ends in bathos. No sooner has Rousseau started priding himself on being a new Columbus than he hears a familiar clicking: pushing through the bushes twenty yards from his silent peak, he finds a stocking mill hard at work.)

Rousseau's response to nature was not always of this sublime kind. In his delight in plants (*see* BOTANY), it is their charm and sweetness that he stresses. He argues that the study of minerals and animals soon leads to thoughts of 'the foul vapours of the pits', or of 'stinking corpses, livid running flesh, blood, repellent intestines'. It is only botany that gives continuous, pure, refreshing joy: 'Bright flowers, adornment of the meadows, cool shades, streams, woods and green glades, come and purify my imagination of all these hideous images' (*RSW* Walk 7, 114; *OC* I, 1068).

For Rousseau, communion with nature removes one from the hateful society of competitive men, and sets one free to rejoice openly in a world that yields its secrets to anyone who gives it honest attention, unclouded by self-interest or mercenary purpose. This same sense of communion, leading to a stilling of the proud and greedy ego, is central also to his quietly ecstatic reveries on and around Lake Bienne, which he recounts in the Fifth Walk. The 'ebb and flow of the water, its continuous yet undulating noise', or a 'stream murmuring over the stones' in a lovely river produce a state of semi-hypnosis: 'From time to time some brief and insubstantial reflection arose concerning the instability of the things of this world, whose image I saw in the surface of the water, but soon these fragile impressions gave way before the unchanging and ceaseless movement which lulled me and without any active effort on my part occupied me so completely' (*RSW* Walk 5, 87; *OC* I, 1045). In such a state, one becomes aware of the simple pleasure of existence as a feeling, living thing, freed from all suffering and from all striving for success and advancement.

Rousseau forcefully evokes the influence of nature, and its stirring, redemptive power. He occupies a significant position amongst those who established the importance of natural beauty and majesty as meeting a basic spiritual need in humans.

Sources: *DI*, Pt 1
　　　　　RSW, Second, Fifth, Seventh Walks

noble savage   'Noble savage', or 'savage', is what Rousseau habitually calls man in the STATE OF NATURE, as characterized in his DISCOURSE ON THE ORIGIN OF INEQUALITY. This peaceable, innocent and untroubled being occupies a central place in his imagination and in his arguments.

In one of his long notes to the *Second Discourse*, he suggests that orangutans, the 'inhabitants of the woods', should be regarded as 'savage men':

> One cannot see ... why the author [of the *Histoire Générale des Voyages*] refuses to give the animals in question the name of savage men, but one may readily guess that it is becaue of the stupidity of the creatures, and also because they did not talk – a poor reason for those who know that although the organ of speech is natural to man, speech is not natural to him. (*DI* (Cranston) 157; *OC* III, 210 n. 10)

He is prompted 'to doubt whether those very different animals resembling man ... were not in fact real savage men, whose race, dispersed since antiquity in the forests, with no opportunity to develop any of its potential faculties, had not acquired any measure of perfection, and was still found

179

in the primitive state of nature' (*DI* (Cranston) 155; *OC* III, 208). It has even been suggested that, although he had no real notion of evolution, Rousseau did not believe in the fixity of species, since he held that changes in life circumstances would produce not only changes in ability (such as the development of speech; *see* ORIGIN OF LANGUAGES), but also changes in appearance and bodily conformation. These same changes could, in turn, transform civilized man into a vampire.

Despite his obviously favourable attitude towards the peaceable disposition and the simple life of the 'noble savage', Rousseau has no doubt that such a creature, and such a life, are not fully human, in that the full range of human capacities and potentialities is not developed. In *Émile* he writes: 'Although I want to form the man of nature, the object is not, for all that, to make him a savage and to relegate him to the depths of the woods . . . The same man who ought to remain stupid in the forests ought to become reasonable and sensible in the cities' (*E* IV, 255; *OC*, IV, 551). And: 'Now, needs change according to the situation of men. There is a great deal of difference between the natural man living in the state of nature and the natural man living in the state of society. Émile is not a savage to be relegated to the desert. He is a savage made to inhabit cities' (*E* III, 205; *OC* IV, 483–4).

So despite his apparent longing, in some of his references to natural man and the noble savage, for a lost paradise, it is plain that he does not think such a state feasible for modern man. The belief, long-held, that Rousseau nurtured an uncritical longing for a reversion to some idealized primitivism is slow to fade, however. But he did not, in fact, see an unbridgeable dichotomy between the natural, pre-social, benign and true, and the artificial, social, hurtful and corrupt. For him, it is indeed possible to live in society while remaining faithful to human nature. (*See* AMOUR-PROPRE; COMPASSION).

Source: *DI*, especially Pt 1

Further reading: Cook (80); de Jouvenel (83); Lovejoy (92); Lovejoy (212); Meek (96); Plattner (99); Wokler (104); Wokler (105); Wokler and Frayling (107)

Nouvelle Héloïse, La   *See* JULIE, OU LA NOUVELLE HÉLOÏSE.

O

opera   *See* MUSICAL COMPOSITION.

Origin(s) of Inequality   *See* DISCOURSE ON THE ORIGIN OF INEQUALITY.

origin of languages   The *Essay on the Origin of Languages* appears never to have been completed to Rousseau's satisfaction. In 1765 he contemplated having it published along with some other short pieces, but the work did not appear until 1781 in the collected edition of posthumous works. Controversy still attaches to its date(s) of composition, to its connection with others of his works, and to its place in the context of his intellectual development. It is probable that Rousseau began to prepare it in conjunction with his remarks on language included in the DISCOURSE ON THE ORIGIN OF INEQUALITY (begun in 1753); then he modified and extended it with a view to including it in the *Examen de Deux Principes* (1755), his reply to Rameau's criticism of his *Letter on French Music* (*see* MUSIC: WRITINGS ON). In 1760–1, after further work, it assumed its more or less final form.

Thus, the *Essay* comprises material prepared over seven or eight years, which no doubt accounts for its broad approach and the multiple allusions to other ideas that Rousseau was concerned with over the same period. There are references to *Le Lévite d'Éphraïm* (*see* POETRY AND MISCELLANEOUS PROSE), and a discussion of pity (the consistency of which with related material in the *Second Discourse* and *Émile* is much debated; *see* COMPASSION). The first eleven of the *Essay*'s twenty short chapters concern, primarily, the origin and character of different languages; the rest, music, particularly the issue of the relation between melody and harmony which so preoccupied him in his disagreements with Rameau.

Rousseau begins by saying that gesture is the most natural and powerful form of communication, best suited to conveying physical needs. Speech, he says, is most appropriate to the arousal and expression of passions. Love, hatred, pity and anger necessitated the first vocalizations, which were accentuated, song-like and inarticulate. Vocabulary was first of all wholly figurative. The world was apprehended in the image of it

181

formed by passion, and described accordingly. Unknown persons aroused fear and dread, and were thus called giants.

Words acquire a literal meaning only later, as languages develop and are shared among many people and used for less emotional purposes. As language progresses, it becomes more precise and less passionate; ideas of reason replace sentiments of the heart; accentuation disappears and monotony takes its place. These changes are accelerated by developments in writing. Ideographic symbols are replaced by a cosmopolitan alphabet which fixes speech, and analyses its structure and components, making it more regular and exact at the cost of expressive flexibility. The perfection of grammar and precision leads to a loss of vigour.

Rousseau explains these changes by reference to differences in climatic and material circumstances between southern and northern peoples. Southern peoples, who live in warm, lush surroundings, have little need to associate in groups larger than the family and are widely dispersed. They live without settled agriculture and the associated problems of ownership, legal requirements and so on. Although the first to be populated, southern regions were the last to form nations, to quit their primitive liberty and indolence. Only occasional need, such as finding water for the animals, brought such people together, thereby giving rise to the development of amorous relations between them. Their first speech would have been soft and voluptuous, suited to the demands of love, not to those of need.

In the inhospitable north, on the other hand, everything is dictated by the necessity for survival; the primary need is for help, not for love. Speech, correspondingly, is harsh, abrupt and demanding, intended not to caress and to seduce, but to convey need accurately. So urgent is the need to survive that others are always seen as potential predators towards whom a hostile commanding posture must be adopted. Speech is crude and shrill, yet clear and articulate in its precise impositions.

He then turns to the issue of the relation between speech and music. Since vocalization not pressured by need is an expression of passion, so men's first speeches were songs, full of rhythm, accent and melody. Melody in music imitates passion, mirrors these intense vocalizations of feeling. Melody is speaking music; it imitates the inflections of the voice. Harmony, on the other hand, has nothing in common with our passions; it enforces patterns and structures which constrain passionate utterance. Under the rules of harmony, song and speech are forced apart and into conflict with each other. Nor can harmony be defended by comparing it with a palette of colours: for colouring is an imitation of nature, while music is a medium of human expression. Music moves us not as a mere physical experience, but as understood and felt as the sign of the speaking soul of another human. Just as the passionate expressiveness of speech was lost under the harsh requirements that necessity inflicted on northern peoples, so has the same fate overtaken their music. Volume and sustainment are what were needed in their speech, and the only musical elaboration that these allow is harmony and counterpoint. All vigour, all spontaneous flow and force of melodic expression, are lost under the complex systems that these techniques require. Turning to the forms of language suited to government, Rousseau states that law and rule were born of a harsh necessity that removed men from their native circumstances of primitive ease, in which their only occasion for utterance was when amorous persuasion was called for. But all that has disappeared: force regulates the relations of men, who now demand not love but money. All eloquence is gone; the only aim of language is imperious control.

Many themes central to Rousseau's mature work are evident in this *Essay*. He insists on the primacy of feeling, of sentiment, of the heart, before reason, intellect, the head. He argues that the complexity and precision of language, suitable for sophisticated scientific inquiry and cultivated letters, are not signs of progress and superiority but of degeneration. Under the pressures that have caused them to develop grammar, logic and precision of speech and writing, men have been forced further away from their natural state and mode of life. Furthermore, government, law, property rights and so on are signs of man's disinherited state, not of his achieving full human status in a developed society. Finally, Rousseau emphasizes that narrow self-interest and hostility towards others have obliterated the sweet and passionate bonds of love that are proper to people and make for the betterment of their lives.

In his discussion of the origins of language in the *Second Discourse* (*DI* 58–64; *OC* III, 146–52), Rousseau is principally arguing that the mind of primitive man neither has, nor requires, general and abstract knowledge, but that he is governed by his immediate desires and sensations. With great acumen he sees that general ideas, which involve abstraction from particular experiences and objects, are different in kind from the original sensations that influence action, and that they require sophisticated intellectual judgement: 'The definition of a triangle alone gives you a true idea of it: the moment you imagine a triangle in your mind, it is some particular triangle and not another, and you cannot avoid giving it sensible lines on a coloured area.' Such abstract definitions necessarily require the use of words in propositions; a language of response to sensations would remain tied to the immediate particular circumstances. Rousseau declares himself unable to conceive either what needs could have provoked such an intellectual development, or by what means it could have taken place. The *Essay* may be thought to provide his answer to these problems.

In these strikingly original pages, Rousseau identifies and articulates one of the central problems facing any empiricist theory of language and thought (such as may be found in Locke), insisting on the distinction between sensations and judgements with a clarity not found again until the writings of Kant.

See also ÉMILE.

Sources: *DI*, Pt 1
        Essay on the Origin of Languages

Further reading: Cranston, vol. I, ch. 14 (17); Derrida (210); Grimsley (211); Wokler (213); Wokler (214); Wokler (215)

P

paranoia   Paranoia is the name given, with varying degrees of precision, to a mental disorder involving an elaborate structure of feeling and beliefs that are rooted in projected aggression. The manifestations of paranoia are many and various. Best-known are delusions of persecution, stemming from the belief that one is the victim of a secret and devious plot in which the plotters, who are privy to one's every move unless the most elaborate precautions are taken, are intent upon humiliating or tormenting one, or inflicting other terrible harm. The victim feels himself to be wholly innocent, the outraged and violated object of others' malice, harbouring (he believes) nothing but good, loving and generous feelings untainted by any hint of evil or disagreeableness. Other patterns of belief and response that have a paranoiac character include the idea that all gestures of kindness or friendliness are traps, intended to seduce or inveigle one into weakness; and the insistence, by the sufferer, that all actions be based on mood and feeling, without regulation by any sense of duty or responsibility – with the corresponding devaluation of all actions undertaken out of duty.

In all cases the paranoiac is unwilling or unable to admit to any feelings of anger, hostility or hatred. Such feelings (that he undoubtedly has) do not disappear, however, but are 'projected': that is, it is not the individual who is angry (he believes), but all those about him, who are also hostile and malicious towards him, and wish to thwart him. He, who has never felt a moment's hostility, cannot understand why he should be so ill-served, so abused. It is the individual's own unacknowledged anger that has engendered his conviction that those who come into contact with him wish to attack and harm him.

Rousseau himself suffered chronically – as well as acutely from time to time – from such delusions and related problems. His constant protests of innocence often accompanied by shrill, self-righteous denunciations of others; his perpetual fear of plots, his morbid suspiciousness; his frequent representation of others' magnanimity as tricks intended to impose upon

185

him, to control and constrain him – all these are clear signs of paranoiac disturbance.

These belief patterns came to dominate his life at two periods in particular. First, though, during the breakdown of his relations with Mme d'Épinay in 1757–8, when he was probably overcome with guilt over his passion for Sophie d'Houdetot, Rousseau may not have been entirely wrong in supposing that Diderot, Grimm and others were making mock of him and spreading malicious gossip. But his reaction to such little as he heard, or guessed, about this was certainly excessive. Much more serious was his breakdown in England in 1766–7. The preceding years of genuine persecution by Church and state; the exposure to the world of his abandonment of his children; his extreme isolation in a strange country – all of these may have contributed to a loss of stability which persisted, with occasional remissions, for nearly ten years. His accusations against Hume, his conviction that he was the hapless victim of an entrenched plot pervading most of Europe, were virtually without foundation and disclose only extreme mental disorder.

Many detect in Rousseau's work little else than the demonstration of his paranoiac predisposition. ROUSSEAU JUDGE OF JEAN-JACQUES: DIALOGUES (written 1772–6) and parts (especially the second half) of THE CONFESSIONS clearly show him contending only half-successfully with his disturbed feelings. But it would be quite another thing to suppose that his major theoretical works are little more than elaborate exercises in self-vindication against a persecuting world. It is true that in most of these works Rousseau was preoccupied with the hostility and aggression – often disguised, he thought – that people show towards each other in society. Thus he writes: 'Insatiable ambition, the thirst of raising their respective fortunes, not so much from real want as from the desire to surpass others, inspired all men with a vile propensity to injure one another, and with a secret jealousy, which is the more dangerous, as it puts on the mask of benevolence, to carry its point with greater security' (*DI* 87; *OC* III, 175). But should these judgements be seen as nothing but a morbid distortion produced by his hatred of men?

The answer is probably No. Even if, for instance, Rousseau's depiction of ordinary society as ordered to secure some men's profit in the destitution of others, and his diagnosis of the depth of the need for invidious precedence, are exaggerations, it cannot be denied that his account of man in society possesses exceptional power, even in its horribleness, and identifies some central aspects of social relations. One of the major features of delusional beliefs is their repetitive unoriginality. But though he may have repeated himself (if seldom in just the same words), Rousseau's ideas are never boring and never unoriginal. He has perceived something that goes very deep in human social relations: the potential for others to be represented as threats to be fended off, kept down, or otherwise controlled. There are, in society, many relationships and institutions embodying attitudes of aggression and fear – however disguised or modified by convention or by our habituation to them – that may be said to embody paranoiac attitudes.

In ÉMILE Rousseau gives a penetrating account of the sources of this aggression. Every infant, he believes, because of his inability to look after himself, is bound sometimes to experience the frustration of his desires. The child's rage at this makes him represent those around him as persecutors, intent upon thwarting him. It thus appears to him imperative that, to gain control of his situation and the satisfaction of his wants, he impose his will upon others in order to counteract the will that they, he feels, are imposing on him. Out of such elementary patterns of response, Rousseau argues, emerges the importance that people attach to ascendancy, power and command of others. And thus it is that such hierarchical patterns of domination and servitude both feed on, and intensify, the rages and resentments that humans feel against each other. It is only shallow thinking that can deny the depth and intensity of hatred that informs human affairs. It can be seen as being to Rousseau's credit that he did not minimize this.

Sources: C, Pt 2
   Hume, *The Concise Account* (336)
   RJJ: Dialogues 1, 2

Further reading: Dent, ch. 2 (24); Hofstader (287); Klein (290); Solomon (344); Starobinski (37)

particular will   In Bk III, ch. 2, of *The Social Contract* Rousseau says that we can distinguish in a magistrate three wills: his CORPORATE WILL, which he has as a member of the GOVERNMENT; his GENERAL WILL, which he has as a citizen; and his private, particular or personal will, which 'tends only to his personal advantage'. Each of these three notions of will needs to be understood alongside the other two.

It is Rousseau's view that each person has a strong (but not necessarily dominant or exclusive) sense of himself as a separate individual, not tied by sentiment or obligation to others in any way. Guided by this view of himself, the individual will form a conception of what is in his private or personal interest – that is, of what will be of advantage to him as and when he considers himself only as such a separate, particular individual. A person's particular, or private, will, then, comprises his desire to advance his personal advantage, so understood. Such a desire is closely related to AMOUR DE SOI.

As Rousseau stresses in *The Social Contract*, a person's particular will may be in conflict with the general will 'which he has as a citizen'. Thus he writes: 'His particular interest may speak to him quite differently from the common interest: his absolute and naturally independent existence may make him look upon what he owes to the common cause as a gratuitous contribution, the loss of which will do less harm to others than the payment of it is burdensome to himself' (*SC* I, ch. 7, 177; *OC* III, 363). Because of this conflict, individuals may be unwilling to do what they are required to do by the general will. Or it may be that they attempt to subvert the general will, substituting their own particular will under the guise of it. In both cases, civil society will perish.

The sharp contrast that Rouseau appears to make, particularly in *The Social Contract*, between particular will and the general will, between the individual as having absolute and natural independence and the individual as citizen, between personal interest and the common interest, leads critics to suppose that Rousseau believes that it is only by leaving the particular will behind and by 'substituting a partial and moral existence for the physical and independent existence nature has conferred on us all' (*SC* II, ch. 7, 194; *OC* III, 381) that men can become satisfactory citizens, and that civil society can be instituted and flourish (*see* DENATURING). This gives rise to the belief that Rousseau desires to see men in society become nothing more than occupants of a social role dispossessed of their individuality and particular character.

This criticism is misplaced. First, Rousseau makes it clear that not all of an individual's powers, goods and liberty are under the control of the general will and law (see *SC* II, ch. 4, 186; *OC* III, 373). This view would make no sense if nothing were left of a person as an independent individual once he became a citizen, the occupant of a social role. Second, although Rousseau draws a line between private interest and common interest (the interest that a person has as a citizen), it would be absurd to suppose that the advantages that a person enjoys as a citizen are not in his interest but in conflict with it. What happens when a person assumes the status of CITIZEN is that he acquires a new, additional 'self' or 'identity' different from the self or identity that he possesses as an absolute and independent being. As a citizen, a person is tied to others in common cause, under like laws, such that certain things will be to his advantage or disadvantage that would not be at issue if he had no connection with others. Or, if they were at issue, they would be viewed in a wholly different light (for example, as a 'gratuitous contribution'). We are obliged, then, to compare advantages and disadvantages not from the constant standpoint of an unchanging identity (a sheaf of self-constitutive concerns), but from different standpoints. Then, we are obliged to ask what reason we may have for adopting one or another standpoint. Rousseau explains in *SC* I, ch. 8 (*OC* III, 364) that to adopt the identity of a citizen is self-enlarging, ennobling and enabling in a way that retaining a particular individual identity could never be. By coming to live and have being as a member with others of a just and prosperous society, an individual's being is enlarged and the scope of his life possibilities is widened.

This is not a matter of making a choice that excludes all other options, any more than it is when a person chooses to be a parent, a teacher, or a particular individual. It is, rather, a matter of the range of objectives, rsponsibilities and rewards available to a person in each of several modes of activity and self-expression. Certainly, Rousseau thinks that self-actualization as a citizen should have priority over one's particular existence. But this is not to say that one's particular existence should be obliterated. When one becomes a parent one does not automatically cease to value what one valued when not a parent, or cease to be able to function as someone who pursues these goods. Conflict may occur, obliging one to establish priorities. But in describing the conflict between the particular and the general will, Rousseau is saying no more than that such is the nature of human activity when we respond to several conflicting goods which represent different ways of being, different identities to be enacted.

Sources: *DI*, Pt 1
 E, Bks I–III
 SC, Bks I, II

Further reading: Dent, ch. 3 (24); Horowitz, ch. 7 (27); Masters, ch. 1 (69); Shklar, chs 1, 5 (36)

perfectibility In the DISCOURSE ON THE ORIGIN OF INEQUALITY Rousseau says that, even in their natural or primitive condition, human beings have two faculties that distinguish them definitively from the brutes. One of these is free will (*see* FREEDOM); the other is 'the faculty of self-improvement', which he calls perfectibility. With most of the lower animals, the repertory of behaviours and possibilities for action is limited and fixed. With, for instance, nest-building in birds, the behaviour appears to be solely under the direction of instinct, and there is little or no variation amongst individuals. If, through natural accidents, suitable materials were not to hand, the species would perish. Higher animals may be taught a few tricks; and ethologists have seen innovative decisions of various kinds made, say, by apes. But the range of variations, and the spontaneous capacity to adapt to circumstances, is very restricted.

With humans, on the other hand, the plasticity of response is very great. Human beings' instinctual routines are very few; instinctual desires permit great variation in how they are satisfied. Humans can learn how their environment works, and can adapt their behaviour to it for their advantage, as well as modifying that environment for further advantage. Virtually all human behaviours are learned or acquired, and few become so consolidated as not to allow modification if need (or taste) requires it. Our capacity for all such flexibility and adaptability, our ability to increase our stock of knowledge and to apply it in infinitely various ways, Rousseau puts down to perfectibility.

In the *Second Discourse* Rousseau views our possession of this capacity, which is exclusive to humans, as a mixed blessing. On the one hand, we owe to it our capacity for agriculture, building, science, letters and manufactures – even our very society – and without it, except in the most propitious circumstances, human life would be scarcely sustainable. But, on the other hand, it is this capacity which 'draws man out of his original state, in which he would have spent his days insensibly in peace and innocence ... [and] which ... makes him at length a tyrant both over himself and over nature' (*DI* 54; *OC* III, 142). Because man can change himself and his surroundings, he can erect and sustain social conditions that are damaging to himself, whereas, if he were limited by finite possibilities intrinsic to the species, this would not have been possible for him. Our perfectibility, then, is the source of both our virtues and our vices.

Rousseau's (only half-meant) suggestion that an 'insensible' existence in peace and innocence would be the best for man should not be taken too seriously. In order, in the *Second Discourse*, to consolidate his point that ordinary human society discloses a scene of mutual hostility, of 'wants, avidity, oppression, desires and pride' (*DI* 45; *OC* III, 132), he will use any rhetorical resource in order to draw an adverse contrast with other, more benign and harmonious, possibilities for human existence. But there can be no doubt that, were the capacity for self-improvement not exercised, human existence would hardly rise above that of the beasts; and Rousseau would be the first to agree that no fully human life had thereby been attained. His principal concern in the *Second Discourse* is to show that, as things stand presently, a limited existence has been traded for a corrupt and damaging one. It remains to be shown how a fully human life, which requires all faculties to be developed, memory and imagination in full play, reason active (see *DI* 86; *OC* III, 174), can be achieved in society. It is to the task of showing this that *Émile* and *The Social Contract* are devoted. Perfectibility may open the way to vice and error; but without it there can be no virtue or wisdom either.

Source: *DI*, Pt 1

Further reading: Horowitz, ch. 3 (27); Masters, ch. 3 (69); Shklar, ch. 2 (36)

philosophy In the DISCOURSE ON THE SCIENCES AND THE ARTS Rousseau lists Descartes, along with Bacon and Newton, as one of the great 'teachers of mankind', a 'sublime genius' (*DSA* 25; *OC* III, 29). And it is clear from the rest of his writing that, even if he often disagreed with their views, he had a proper admiration for other great philosophical writers such as Plato, Montaigne and Hobbes. However, in general he evinced a contempt for philosophy and philosophers – though possibly only because he felt that those who professed the discipline or claimed the name had perverted it from its proper character.

His complaints against philosophy, as he believed it was commonly practised, were many. Philosophy raises doubts, questions and problems without end, and so far from advancing truth usually breeds confusion, error and uncertainty. In many cases, Rousseau argues, this is the deliberate purpose of those who call themselves philosophers, and who are more anxious to gain a name and applause for their ingenuity or speculative imaginativeness than to advance inquiry. Their aim is to show themselves cleverer, sharper, more subtle than others, without regard to whether or not their views are better-founded. AMOUR-PROPRE deforms philosophical investigation just as much as it deforms any other kind of human social activity. The cavils of philosophers often lead to disabling scepticism, destroying the necessary and sustaining confidences of ordinary people and offering nothing in their place. Social beliefs and religious convictions are all subjected to corrosive criticism, and there remains nothing to live by.

Nor are philosophers to be trusted or honoured in matters of moral conduct. Craving distinction and well versed in the arts of sophistry and casuistry, they will always find a hundred reasons for not aiding those in need or relieving the hurt of others. So far from philosophy broadening his mind or his sympathies, it concentrates the soul of the philosopher more narrowly within himself and provides him with endless means of rationalizing in order to excuse his indifference and hardness. In this case, too, it is people's simple, uncritical sentiments that are the surer guide to life – for all that such unsophistication attracts the scorn of the learned and subtle reasoner.

It may be that Rousseau's own scorn of philosophers arose from his discomfort in the presence of the *philosophes*, the Parisian intellectuals who,

191

with their quick wit and their sharp argumentativeness, often left him feeling slow-witted and foolish. But some of the points that he makes about philosophy and philosophers are telling, and are applicable not only to his own day.

Source: DSA

Further reading: Grimsley, ch. 1; Conclusion (26); Masters, ch. 2 (69); Shklar, ch. 3 (36)

pity *See* COMPASSION.

poetry and miscellaneous prose [25] Quite early in his life Rousseau wrote a number of poems, one of which was his first publication of any substance. He also wrote a few short (often incomplete) prose pieces, some of which have survived. None of these constitutes more than a minor element in his overall output.

The first of his poems, *Le Verger de Madame la Baronne de Warens* ('Mme de Warens' Orchard') was written in 1738 and published the next year under a London publisher's imprint, but was in fact printed in Annecy or Chambéry. Rousseau wrote this pastoral rhapsody of *c*. 250 lines when he was contemplating the beauties of life and of meditation in Mme de Warens' orchard. He invokes nature, science and the arts as the nourishment of the soul, and names the philosophers, poets, writers and historians who inspire him and raise his mind to higher concerns.

The *Épître à M. Bordes*, an epistolatory poem written to one of Rousseau's friends, was probably completed in 1741 when he was living in Lyons as tutor to the de Mably family. It was printed in the *Journal de Verdun* in March 1743. In these unoriginal 150 lines written in the heroic style Rousseau extols Bordes as a learned and brilliant man; he insists that he, Rousseau, is not to be seduced by riches and pride and, out of his republican spirit, will only honour true merit. He also, however, praises fulsomely some Lyons dignitaries. A longer poem, but one that expresses similar sentiments, is the *Épître à M. Parisot*, written to another Lyons friend. It probably dates from a year or so later, but was not published until 1776. The only other poem of any substance is *L'Allée de Sylvie* ('Sylvie's Walk'), written in 1746 at Chenonceaux, when Rousseau was staying there with the Dupin family. (His play *L'Engagement Téméraire* dates from this same period; *see* THEATRE.) Published in the *Mercure de France* in September 1750, this poem invokes the beauties of walking and of the country, which make Rousseau wish to relinquish the vain pomp and strivings of humanity and put his trust in God's beneficence.

Although some have seen in these works the germs of his later republicanism and love of nature, in none of them does Rousseau rise above the use of set poetic formulations to express the most conventional sentiments.

Le Lévite d'Éphraïm (*The Levite of Ephraim*), which he called a prose poem, is one of his strangest achievements. Rousseau fell asleep on the night of 8 June 1762 while reading the Book of Judges, chs 19–21, which tell the story of the Levite of Ephraim. He was woken at about two in the morning by a messenger from the Prince de Conti, saying that he would be arrested as a result of the complaints made about his recently published ÉMILE. Rousseau got up and packed his belongings, and by four in the afternoon he was on his way to a (temporary) refuge at Yverdon in Switzerland, where he arrived on the 14th. During the journey he began to write this prose poem. He completed it on arrival at Yverdon, and although it was not published in his lifetime (appearing first in a collection of his posthumous works published in 1781), it was always, he said, one of his favourite pieces (*C* XI, 541; *OC* I, 586).

In it, Rousseau retells the story of the young Levite more or less as it appears in Judges. The Levite took a woman of Bethlehem as his concubine, and although he could not marry her he promised to live with her in freedom and happiness. When she left him and went back to her family, he followed her, demanding her return and calling her his 'wife'. They left her family home together to return, stopping the night in Jebus. Here the townspeople demanded vengeance for the Levite's effrontery in taking her away, intending to violate him sexually. The old man in the house where the Levite and his 'wife' were staying offered to give the townspeople his own daughter in order to assuage their rage, but instead the Levite pushed his own woman out into the crowd. The next morning he found her dying outside the house. He took her body home, divided it into twelve pieces, and sent one piece to each of the twelve tribes of Israel. They then rose up to avenge the outrage the Levite had suffered, and attacked the tribe of Benjamin (who had been responsible for the killing) in an attempt to right the evil, leaving 26,000 men dead. The Levite too died, and was buried with parts of his mistress's corpse.

One can, perhaps, imagine that Rousseau found in this bizarre and brutal story some image of the kind of vengeance that he thought should be his for the wrongs inflicted on him over *Émile*. But it remains hard to understand why he should think this one of his most worthwhile works.

Of Rousseau's miscellaneous prose pieces, the most complete is *La Reine Fantasque* ('The Capricious Queen'), probably written in 1756. It was published, without Rousseau's approval, in 1758, and then again in 1769 in an edition corrected by him. It is almost a fairy story, concerning a wise king and a contrary queen who have no heir. The queen conceives; the king wants a son, but his capricious wife immediately declares that she wants a daughter. She gives birth to twins, one boy and one girl. The king ends up doting on his daughter, the queen on her son . . . Decked out with fairies, druids and the like, the piece is no more than a light-hearted fancy.

Les Amours de Claire et de Marcellin is a fragment of only a few pages. It dates from the summer of 1756, and it is possible that Rousseau would have continued with it had he not become absorbed in writing *La Nouvelle Héloïse*. Marcellin, who is betrothed against his will, falls in love with Claire. To put off his marriage he swallows several doses of emetic, and languishes in danger of his life. Meanwhile Claire, who has inherited some money, buys off Marcellin's fiancée . . . and there it ends. A further fragment, from around the same period, *Le Petit Savoyard*, also includes a character called Claire. It takes the form of the autobiographical story of one Claude Noyer, who tells of the daily affairs in his family and district. His sister Claire becomes the object of the attentions of the debauched Marquis d'Argentière . . . but what might have ensued we have no idea.

La Vision de Pierre de la Montagne was written in 1765 when Rousseau was at Môtiers, and was published that year in Geneva. Its occasion was the troubles that Rousseau was suffering over his attendance at church and other such trials to which he was subjected. (Violent objection had been taken to his attending communion, given his supposed atheism.) Written in numbered sentences, it concerns the imagined vision of Peter the Seer about his errant brother Jean-Jacques (i.e. Rousseau himself). The accusations levelled against Jean-Jacques are denounced; Rousseau gives a farcical recital of the unjust charges laid against him, and flatly states his own assessment of his case, taking a few side-swipes at his accusers.

Finally, *Le Persifleur* ('The Mocker'): planned in 1747-8, this was intended to be a periodical, which Rousseau and Diderot would take it in turns to edit. It never got beyond a draft of an advertisement, written by Rousseau, outlining the aims of the magazine and the merits of its editors. In it, he gives a portrait of himself that is intended to demonstrate that he is fit to produce such a journal and to merit the interest of his readers. He is, he says, two persons; sometimes he is fashionable and sophisticated, at other times harsh and misanthropic. He is a chameleon who assumes such varied colours that his character cannot be fixed. Such a diverse talent makes him able to appreciate and to comment on all aspects of life. Although in his later, serious, autobiographical writings Rousseau was also to insist that he had a volatile, many-coloured character, it would be a mistake to take this early piece as a sober attempt at self-analysis. He is merely trying to intrigue potential subscribers.

Further reading: Blum (21); Ellrich (206); Kavanagh (207); Rex (209)

Poland   *See* CONSIDERATIONS ON THE GOVERNMENT OF POLAND.

Political Economy   *See* (A DISCOURSE ON) POLITICAL ECONOMY.

Polysynodie   *See* ÉCRITS SUR L'ABBÉ DE SAINT-PIERRE.

power   Power consists in the capacity to produce effects; and, in the case of relations between persons, the effects will be changes in the life, attitudes and behaviour of the possessor of power and of those upon whom he exerts his power. Rousseau nowhere offers any precise definition of power, or of what it is for one person to have greater power than, or to have power over, another. It could, none the less, be said that he is more preoccupied with power than with any other single issue, not only in all his major social and political works but also in his autobiographical writings – though there from a different perspective. He subjects to the most penetrating analysis and criticism the basis, character and function of power relationships, both between individuals and within the institutions of society and of the state (including those who hold powerful positions).

In the great majority of cases, Rousseau believes, people desire superior power over others for two principal reasons. First, in possessing superior power a person can make others comply with his wishes and designs so that he can better secure, through their compliance, the objectives that he seeks. Power is, in this way, useful instrumentally to its possessor. The second, and more important, reason why superior power is desired is because its possession is believed to be a proof of personal superiority and distinction, a testimony to prestigious ascendancy over others. By commanding others, subordinating them to one's will, the individual comes to know and feel himself to be a person of substance, one who has significance as a person and as a presence. This sort of concern for the possession of superior power is closely bound up with the concerns of (excessive) AMOUR-PROPRE.

Power over others, whether as instrumentally useful or as a proof of personal significance, need not be exercised through brute force. Wealth, honours, prestige, fashionable 'visibility', all place a person in a position to secure the deference or subordination of others. Social processes and civil institutions are often structured in such a way as to establish and consolidate relationships of DOMINATION and subordination, of potency and impotence.

Rousseau is uniformly hostile to the existence of relationships of

195

unequal power. For instance, by being subordinated to others, the subjugated and oppressed are, in various ways, deprived of liberty – the opportunity to carry out their own purposes on their own decisions – and are made dependent on others for the enjoyment of fundamental needs and rights. Moreover, in being identified by others as inferior or insignificant beings, they will be apt to regard themselves in the same way and to consider themselves contemptible and their lives and needs worthless. In the case of those who enjoy superior power, Rousseau is not content merely to say that their behaviour is unjust and their superior standing illegitimate – though he does believe this. Rather, he tries to show that their superior position is, in certain ways, merely apparent and that, while seeking to enjoy domination over others, they are, in fact, enslaved. He hopes thus to demonstrate why the appeal to justice should be heeded by those who seem to profit from injustice.

To the extent to which my sense of my dignity and importance is dependent on the deference and servility of others, goes his argument, I am required at all times to shape my behaviour in ways that will continue to command others' esteem, or fear, of me. So far from my being able to do as I please, unaffected by the demands that others place on me, I am obliged to check and modify my life so as to capture and retain their compliance. I am 'trapped' by the constraints that the retention of my superior position impose on me:

> Your freedom and your power extend only as far as your natural strength, and not beyond. All the rest is only slavery, illusion and deception. Even domination is servile when it is connected with opinion, for you depend on the prejudices of those you govern by prejudices. To lead them as you please, you must conduct yourself as they please. They have only to change their way of thinking, and you must perforce change your way of acting. (*E* II, 83; *OC* IV, 308–9)

Nor, in Rousseau's view, is this dependence on others confined to the modification of outward behaviour. The need of others' esteem and subordination enters into the powerful man's own self-esteem, and he is thus – in the constitution of his own self-regard – at the mercy of the feelings and appraisals of others.

He does not think, of course, that human beings can survive very long, or procure a very full life for themselves, if they continue to rely on their 'natural strength' alone. But it is essential that when people unite in order to take advantage of concerted action this should not give rise to relationships of domination and subordination. A central purpose of the political structures and procedures which Rousseau outlines in THE SOCIAL CON-

TRACT is to enable people to act in concert, but in a way that does not enforce servility or impotence on any. In this way will be avoided not only the overt disadvantages which the oppressed and dispossessed suffer, but also those more subtle ills which, according to his account, those on the 'pinnacle of fortune' suffer.

The strength of Rousseau's account of the significance of power relations in society is twofold. First, he demonstrates a clear insight into the pervasiveness of such relationships, identifying how they shape (or warp) not only people's behaviour, but also their feelings, aspirations and self-judgements. Second, he shows how giving up the desire to achieve domination promises a relationship with others that will be creative and constructive for all parties, and that it should not be regarded by those who 'step down' from their positions of ascendancy as comprising, for them, nothing but a loss inflicted on them by the intransigence of the subjugated classes. In such arguments Rousseau prefigures the better-known views of Hegel and Marx.

Sources: DI
E, Bks I, II

Further reading: Lukes (339); Shklar, ch. 3 (36)

prince *See* GOVERNMENT.

Profession de Foi du Vicaire Savoyard, La *See* CREED OF A SAVOYARD VICAR.

progress If we understand by 'progress' the idea that changes in society, productive techniques, educational practices and so on are all moving towards an ever-improving condition, then Rousseau is emphatically critical of progress.

He often writes, in for instance the DISCOURSE ON THE ORIGIN OF INEQUALITY, as if the changes in human circumstances that caused men to come to live together in settled communities represented already a decline in the prospects for human happiness and fulfilment. More specifically, he identifies such 'technological' advances as metallurgy and agriculture as prime causes of the miserable and corrupt condition of human beings, since the skills that these new developments required made property ownership of crucial significance, and removed people irrevocably from their primitive condition of indolence and independence (see *DI* 83–5; *OC* III, 171-4). From these 'progressive' changes emerge differences of wealth and power, which enable some to prosper while others live in enforced indigence, and which result finally in the institution of unjust states

197

which reinforce such inequalities by positive law: these are among the features of human life of which Rousseau is most critical.

None the less, amendment in the affairs of man, though difficult to achieve, is not impossible. One of the main purposes of the argument of ÉMILE is to show how a human being may be brought up in such a way as not to fall into those forms of relation with others which have such harmful effects. But it is part and parcel of this upbringing that many of the products of 'progress', such as luxury, refinement and the sophisticated arts, will be eschewed, and tastes and occupations will be directed towards the simple necessities of life.

In not viewing his age as one of triumphal development liberating people from want, superstition and ignorance, Rousseau was at odds with many of his contemporaries and erstwhile friends. At the same time, he articulated some of the reservations about such developments as industrial growth and the increase in the size and influence of cities that were to find more eloquent exponents in the nineteenth and twentieth centuries.

See also CIVILIZATION; ENLIGHTENMENT.

Sources: DI
DSA

Further reading: de Jouvenel (83); Pollard (341); Wokler (149)

Project for a Constitution for Corsica   *See* CORSICA, PROJECT FOR A CONSTITUTION FOR.

Project for Perpetual Peace (*Projet de Paix Perpétuelle*)   *See* ÉCRITS SUR L'ABBÉ DE SAINT-PIERRE.

property   Part 2 of THE DISCOURSE ON THE ORIGIN OF INEQUALITY begins thus:

> The first man who, having enclosed a piece of ground, bethought himself of saying 'This is mine', and found people simple enough to believe him, was the real founder of civil society. From how many crimes, wars, and murders, from how many horrors and misfortunes might not any one have saved mankind, by pulling up the stakes, or filling up the ditches, and crying to his fellows: 'Beware of listening to this impostor; you are undone if you once forget that the fruits of the earth belong to us all, and the earth itself to nobody.' (*DI* 76; *OC* III, 164)

From this passage it would seem reasonable to infer, first, that Rousseau believes that the institution of private ownership of property was fundamental to the formation of civil society. But, second, with that institution – and, by implication, with the formation of civil society – men brought down immeasurable evil and misery on themselves. However, he goes on to say that 'the idea of property depends on many prior ideas', and that men 'must have made very considerable progress, and acquired considerable knowledge and industry which they must also have transmitted from age to age, *before* they arrived at this last point of the state of nature' (my emphasis). So it is clear that Rousseau should not be classed among those social and political theorists who claim to find in private ownership the *raison d'être* of civil society and the source of its principal ills. For him, private property represents the culmination, or crystallization, of many more basic processes and developments that have led men to form civil associations and to establish those relationships which, typically, harm and cripple human beings. Ownership, for Rousseau, plays no *fundamental* role in explaining the rise and character of civil society.

He does not, in fact, ever argue for the complete abolition of private property. Even in his most 'collectivist' political work, the *Project for a Constitution for Corsica* (*see* CORSICA), he does not argue for the common ownership of all land. And in *The Social Contract* he allows that citizens shall retain some private property. Indeed, he cites as one of the *merits* of the civil association described there that it transforms 'possession, which is merely the effect of force or the right of the first occupier' into 'property, which can be founded only on a positive title' (*SC* I, ch. 8, 178; *OC* III, 364; see also ch. 9, entitled 'Real Property'). It is ridiculous to suppose, therefore, that Rousseau saw private property as 'the root of all evil'.

In the first instance, he founds ownership on Lockean principles – 'the right of the first occupant by labour' (*E* II, 99; *OC* IV, 331, and *DI* 85; *OC* III, 173). However, he does not think that this right remains unaltered by the institution of civil society. In such society, such rights may be modified; but, primarily, their possessor will be protected in the enjoyment of them under law, so that his proprietorship becomes a positive right in the enjoyment of which he will be sustained and defended.

Where private ownership causes harm and misery it is because, in Rousseau's view, the extent of ownership by some has grown so great as to enforce servitude or dispossession on others (*see* DOMINATION). This, however, is not in the nature of private ownership as such, but only in its improper enlargement. In the *Discourse on the Origin of Inequality* he offers two reasons why people will tend to try to extend their ownership. First, with the development of metallurgy and agriculture the strong and enterprising will prosper and the weak and indolent will fail – and fail

199

all the more decisively so because of the demands on resources that the prosperity of the strong involves. One incentive that the strong and energetic have for this increase in their ownership by labour is to secure themselves more completely against hard times to come, thereby improving their own future well-being.

This line of argument now converges with another, which specifies a second, distinct, reason for this extension of possession. As men are brought into society with each other, it becomes important to them to achieve invidious personal distinction and prestige for themselves by imposing ignominy and destitution on others (*see* AMOUR-PROPRE). Property becomes one of the signal marks of this prestigious difference. By the extent of his ownership, a person is known to be a 'man of substance'. It is this meaning of, or aspect of meaning of, ownership that is, in fact, the more important for Rousseau. It is the desire to attain visible precedence over others that causes property to be regarded as so crucial to human well-being. In many cases it is not because they wish to protect themselves better against future hardship that people wish to own more than others: it is for the sake of conspicuous consumption (or possession). It is property as a sign of status, not as a necessity for survival, that is the manifestation of social evil. Rousseau observes penetratingly: 'The rich [have] feelings, if I may so express myself, in every part of their possessions' (*DI* 91; *OC* III, 179); and that 'rich and powerful men . . . prize what they enjoy only in so far as others are destitute of it . . . they would cease to be happy the moment the people ceased to be wretched' (*DI* 101; *OC* III, 189). It is inequalities in 'personal qualities' that are at the root of a state's bad constitution, and though it is not so in the beginning, wealth becomes the basis of inequality 'to which they are all reduced in the end' (*DI* 101; *OC* III, 189).

Sources: DI
            E, Bk II
            SC, Bk I

Further reading: MacAdam (264); Ryan (296); Schlatter (297)

providence   *See* LETTER TO VOLTAIRE ON PROVIDENCE.

200

R

rationalism   *See* CREED OF A SAVOYARD VICAR; CIVILIZATION; ENLIGHT-
ENMENT; REASON.

reason   Rousseau discusses the nature, scope and limits of reason in
many different contexts. Sometimes he is critical of the power of reason, at
least in so far as it has been applied to issues in which it has no proper role
– for instance, to provide a basis for religious belief or for moral principles.
Elsewhere he stresses the value of the use of reason in extending human
understanding and correcting prejudice. He recognized that he sometimes
had difficulty in making his ideas regarding reason plain. Thus he writes
in a footnote to a passage about children's reasoning: 'One time I say
children are incapable of reasoning; another time I make them reason
quite keenly. I do not believe that with that I contradict myself in my
ideas; but I cannot gainsay that I often contradict myself in my expressions' (*E* II, 108n.; *OC* IV, 345).

One area where, Rousseau says, reason has no proper application or
use has to do with seeking rational proofs of God's existence. In his view,
such a search is inappropriate and doomed to failure. At the start of the
CREED OF A SAVOYARD VICAR he argues, typically, that the reasoning of
philosophers about God's nature and existence leads only to endless
obfuscating disputes, and culminates in scepticism and confusion. We
must, he says, trust instead in the 'inner light', in those basic, simple and
incontestable convictions which, although not grounded in reasoning –
nor would they, perhaps, withstand rational scrutiny – serve none the less
to persuade an unprejudiced and honest person that there is a 'Being
which wills, and is powerful ... active in itself ... which moves the
universe and orders all things' (*E* IV, 277; *OC* IV, 581).

The second matter where, Rousseau holds, appeal to reason is both
inappropriate and useless concerns the origins of moral principles:

> Even the precept of doing unto others as we would have them do unto us has
> no true foundation other than conscience and sentiment; for where is the

precise reason for me, being myself, to act as if I were another, especially
when I am morally certain of never finding myself in the same situation? . . .
From this I conclude that it is not true that the precepts of natural law are
founded on reason alone. They have a base more solid and sure. Love of
men derived from love of self is the principle of human justice. (*E* IV, 235n.;
OC IV, 523)

Moral convictions and behaviour originate in our sentiments and attachments, as well as in CONSCIENCE; it is therefore a mistake to think that
reason alone is the source of moral understanding and action (*see* COMPAS-
SION).

A third issue concerns the education of children:

To reason with children was Locke's great maxim. It is the one most in
vogue today. Its success, however, does not appear to me such as to
establish its reputation; and, as for me, I see nothing more stupid than these
children who have been reasoned with so much. Of all the faculties of man,
reason, which is, so to speak, only a composite of all the others, is the one
that develops with the most difficulty and latest. (*E* II, 89; *OC* III, 317)

Rousseau's thought here is that 'rational' explanations are apt to exceed
the child's understanding, and not to connect with anything that he is
interested in or will pay attention to. But, also, the child is likely to see in
such explanations only the attempt to control and frustrate him, giving
rise to resentment and the determination to evade a restriction that
appears to be arbitrary. He sees only tyranny, and will be inclined never
to attend, even when there might be something valuable to be learned (*see*
EDUCATION).

It might be natural to infer from this that there is a dominant irrational-
ist or anti-rationalist theme in Rousseau's work, borne out by his making
the redirection of sentiments and loyalties, rather than the appeal to
reason, central to the foundation of society and the state; and by his
celebrating reverie and the contemplation of nature more than critical
analysis and rational inquiry. Rousseau's place as a forerunner of Romanticism is well established.

On the other hand, he often claims an essential and desirable use for
reason. If Émile – or any of us – is to be able to provide successfully for
himself in the world, to find his way about it and to utilize its resources,
then he must utilize reason in order to compare, analyse, explain and
generalize so that he can understand and predict how things will work and
change. Without ideas obtained by generalization and abstraction, a
person would be confined to what he had immediate experience of, which
would ill equip him to deal with novel circumstances or to adapt effec-

tively to change. Rousseau is wholly positive towards these functions of reason; a substantial part of Émile's life is given over to the acquisition of the knowledge and skills that they involve.

Equally, despite stating that 'reason alone' cannot be the foundation of the precepts of natural law, he says that the 'affections of the soul' must be 'enlightened by reason' (*E* IV, 235; *OC* IV, 522–3). Conscience, also, appears to require to be checked and informed by reason, if it is not to 'go astray' (*E* V, 382–3; *OC* IV, 730). So reason is not rejected here, either, as an irrelevant or obstructive capacity. But Rousseau is not very explicit about what factors fall within reason's sphere of influence here. What he appears to have in mind is knowledge of the circumstances of life, of the possible deceptions that might lead a person, however well intentioned, to make wrong choices or to mistake his situation. It requires experience and judgement to assess precisely what is happening, if inclination – even if uncorrupted – is to direct a person towards doing the right thing.

Rousseau's ideas about the power of reason might be clearer if he had specified what capacities and achievements, in his view, 'reason' comprehends. It certainly appears to signify for him the power to compare, analyse and draw inferences, thereby equipping a person, starting from his own experience and interests, to judge and understand beyond his present circumstances. Reason in its logical and scientific employment seems to meet with his approval; it exceeds its proper scope where settling the purposes of life, or grounding moral and religious conviction, are involved.

Source: DI
       E, Bks II–IV

Further reading: Grimsley, ch. 1 (26); Derathé (308); Masters, chs 1, 2 (69)

religion (civil)   It is in THE SOCIAL CONTRACT Bk IV, ch. 8, that Rousseau sets out most fully his arguments concerning the place and role of religious beliefs and institutions in a civil society. His ideas about individual religious conviction and the nature of God are most in evidence in his CREED OF A SAVOYARD VICAR.

Critics are apt to see in Rousseau's arguments concerning the need for a civil religion a very clear display of totalitarian elements in his political thinking. He maintains that an individual who does not believe in the articles of the 'civil profession of faith' is to be banished, and that he who has publicly recognized these dogmas but then behaves 'as if he does not believe them' may be put to death. (All quotations are from *SC* IV, ch. 8.) This appears to imply that, in Rousseau's view, religious observance should be enforced by sanction. Yet at the same time he insists that civil religion will contain one principal 'negative dogma', prohibiting intolerance. So the religious yoke may not be so burdensome, after all.

Rousseau's primary concern in his discussion of civil religion is the need to form, consolidate and perpetuate the bonds of union between all the members of one civil society, so that they shall bear with each other in mutual respect, care and support. He believes that religious allegiance and loyalty comprise one of the great spurs to active commitment to a cause. It is therefore essential to find out how this willingness to give of oneself shall be accommodated within a civil society – to find out whether it does, or should, sustain that society, or whether it weakens or subverts it.

In Rousseau's view, there are four possibilities here. First, religious allegiance may remain wholly unregulated by the civil powers and law. Second, it may be more or less marginalized, treated as a private or informal matter unrelated to the maintenance of the civil association. Third, it may be regulated by the civil powers; fourth, it may be so directed as to become united, in some essential repects, with the requirements of civil society and law. Rousseau inclines towards the fourth possibility. His reasons for this view are twofold: the first is to do with the positive benefits that this would procure; the second, to do with the hazards and drawbacks that the other three possibilities involve.

The positive benefits are these. If compliance with the fundamental requirements of law, which involve respecting and honouring the person and good of others, is felt to be a religious requirement also, then observance of the law will be thought to bring divine blessing and favour, and breach of it to bring retribution and damnation (in addition to any civil rewards or penalties). In this way, civil obedience becomes invested with a deeper significance, becomes more complete and dedicated.

Rousseau insists that this is not to turn an unwarranted and illegitimate demand into one that appears to have legitimacy, just because it is now invested – or so it is claimed – with the authority of God. For laws make their own, proper, claim on each citizen. But there can be no harm, and there is likely to be much good, in reinforcing that claim. However, it is only so far as religion affects the observance of morality and those duties that each citizen is bound to undertake for others that it is of proper concern to the state. 'Each man may have, over and above, what opinions he pleases, without its being the sovereign's business to take cognizance of them.'

It thus follows that when Rousseau says that one who disobeys the articles of the civil faith is to be banished it is not for *impiety* as such that he is so treated, but because he shows himself to be 'an anti-social being, incapable of loving the laws and justice'. It is in virtue of the harm that he actually (or potentially) inflicts on his fellow-citizens that he is punished, not because of his irreligion in itself. If Rousseau errs here it is not because he is making religious observance an instrument of state control, but because of his over-zealous concern with what might contribute to lawlessness.

Turning to the hazards presented by other ways of accommodating religious sentiment and commitment, Rousseau states that if these last go unregulated, they will involve an alternative object of loyalty – which may be civilly subversive or disruptive. A person may, for example, maintain that his religion exempts him from certain civil regulations. But no state can allow any individual to set himself above the law. Or, a person's religious beliefs may make him tepid in his commitment to the maintenance of the civil order and to the procurement of common well-being. Further, he argues that religious zeal is apt to divide the world into the saved and the damned, supposedly justifying the most vicious persecutions in order to rid it of noxious unbelievers. Such attitudes, plainly, breed social division and will cause civil society to disintegrate.

There are three kinds of religion, Rousseau says. The first is 'confined to the purely internal cult of the supreme God and the eternal obligations of morality'. The second is 'codified in a single country, [and] give it its gods, its own tutelary patrons'; the third is 'the religion of the priest', in which there is a 'theological system' separate from the 'political system'. To all of these Rousseau makes objection: to the first, that it makes people indifferent to earthly well-being, and hence to the security and prosperity of their fellows; to the second, that it makes men tyrannous and exclusive; and to the third, that it divides sovereignty and power, thus destroying the state by subjecting men to contradictory duties.

Rousseau's conception of the role of religious belief in society is central to his conception of the maintenance of law and order. Those who live in a climate of religious intolerance may take his views more seriously than those who enjoy complete religious freedom. Even today, there are many countries where Rousseau's arguments have evident application.

Source: *SC*, Bk IV

Further reading: Dent, ch. 7 (24); Derathé (310); Gildin (123); Grimsley (187); Masters, ch. 8 (69); Shklar, ch. 3 (36)

representation   In a famous passage about representation in The SOCIAL CONTRACT Rousseau writes:

> The people of England regards itself as free; but it is grossly mistaken; it is free only during the election of members of parliament. As soon as they are elected, slavery overtakes it, and it is nothing . . . the deputies of the people . . . are not and cannot be its representatives: they are merely its stewards, and can carry through no definitive acts. Every law the people has not ratified in person is null and void – is, in fact, not a law. . . . the moment a people allows itself to be represented, it is no longer free: it no longer exists. (*SC* III, ch. 15, 240; *OC* III, 430)

Rousseau's stand here is clear: for sovereign authority to be vested in representatives is not tolerable – is not even possible. He realizes that this will lay him open to objection – not least because it will be said that it is practically impossible for the people to assemble. To this he replies: 'Two thousand years ago it was not so'; and it is not human nature that has changed. Rather, people have lost interest in public service, and do not see that participation in sovereign affairs is their highest privilege and most dignified calling. Leisure and comfort, allied to narrow self-interest, make people unwilling to 'fly to the assemblies', little realizing that in choosing not to do so they are embracing servitude and degrading the humanity in their own person (*see* CITIZEN).

He accepts, with reservations, that popular assemblies are more feasible in small states than in larger ones, not only because of practical considerations but because the 'aggregate of common happiness furnishes a greater proportion of that of each individual, so that he has less need to seek it in private interest.' From this he extrapolates that large states are not likely to be just, nor can they realize the real good of their citizens (*see* DEMOCRACY).

It is hard to assess the applicability of Rousseau's ideas here with any precision, not least because sovereign authority and governmental (executive) powers are seldom as clearly differentiated in any actual states as Rousseau believes they should be. In most 'representative democracies' it is not merely the person of the representative, but a legislative programme, that is offered to the verdict of the people. But such programmes are seldom carried out in detail, and there are many acts promulgated as law that formed no part of any such programme. Furthermore, the procedure of submission of such programmes to the periodic vote of the people (that is, to enfranchised citizens) would be, for Rousseau, one of the most crucial acts of popular sovereign determination (and, of course, it has never been that). What is certain is that Rousseau would believe that in England today, for instance, the character and level of popular participation in civil processes is extremely limited and that, in this respect at least, liberty has been sacrificed to profit, and poverty is feared more than slavery (*SC* III, ch. 15, 241; *OC* III, 430).

For all his emphatic strictures on the impropriety of representation in *The Social Contract*, it is striking that in, for instance, his CONSIDERATIONS ON THE GOVERNMENT OF POLAND (ch. 7) he seems to allow for representatives. (They would serve only for a limited term, at the end of which their conduct would be subject to stringent public examination, particularly if they wished to present themselves for re-election.) However, there he is devising proposals for amendment and improvement (as he sees it) within an established constitutional framework, and is not setting out what might be best in abstract terms. It remains clear that he wishes to institute arrangements that will, as far as possible, keep the functions of sovereignty with the people, acting in their true office as members of the SOVEREIGN BODY. Any procedures which deviate from this will be less than satisfactory and should be amended.

Sources: GP, chs 6–14
           PCC
           SC, Bks II, III

Further reading: Fralin (64); Levine (128); Ritter (144); Rosenfeld (145); Weirich (148)

Reveries of the Solitary Walker, The (written 1776–8; published 1780) (*Les Rêveries du Promeneur Solitaire*) [21]   This, Rousseau's last work (which remained uncompleted at his death), is divided into ten brief sections entitled *Promenades*, or *Walks*. Within this framework Rousseau offers a collection of miscellaneous reflections and opinions; assessments of himself, his life, the world and the affairs of men; and any other thoughts that cross his mind. It is perhaps the most tender and moving of all his writings – though he can still note with savage precision the cruelty of men and the wrongs inflicted on him.

In the First Walk, he says that he is the victim of a plot, cast out from humanity; but, no longer tortured by hopes that everything will come right for him, he now feels calm and composed. The Second Walk describes one of his perambulations in the environs of Paris, and reveals his pleasure in flowers and other natural phenomena. He recounts the accident in which he was knocked down by a dog and injured, as he was returning home. Rumours that he had been killed circulated with indecent speed – so how can be expect that people's opinions of him and his life will be regulated by the truth? He must, he says, learn to bear his sufferings in silence.

The Third Walk returns to the events of his earlier life. He stresses how, at the age of forty, he underwent a conversion of the soul and gave up wordly pomp, dedicating himself both to expressing, and to living in, the light of a new moral vision of human justice and equality. He is speaking here of the 'illumination' that he experienced on the way to Vincennes in 1749 (described both in the LETTERS TO MALESHERBES and in THE CONFESSIONS), the after-effects of which were, in his view, to direct both his work and the rest of his life. He speaks of how the ideas in his CREED OF A SAVOYARD VICAR gave him solace and endurance, saving him from despair during his darkest miseries (especially after 1762, with the banning of *Émile* and the personal persecution that drove him, for a while, into madness).

The Fourth Walk retells the episode of the stolen ribbon (also described in *The Confessions*, Bk II). This clearly still preys on his conscience, though it was shame, he insists, and not calculating malice that forced him into lying over this and other trivialities. He upbraids himself for his need to preserve his dignity, and considers whether and to what extent he has deserved to use as his motto, *Vitam impendere vero* ('Dedicate life to truth'). (*See* LETTER TO D'ALEMBERT ON THE THEATRE.) In the Fifth Walk, wholly different in tone and matter, he recalls the solitary pleasure he enjoyed drifting in a boat on Lake Bienne during his brief stay on the island of St-Pierre in 1759. He lapsed, he says, into a trance, in which he was aware of nothing except his own existence; he became wholly absorbed in a semi-hypnotic reverie that filled him with inexpressible contentment (*see* NATURE). A similar pleasure in reverie and idle abstraction is expressed in the Seventh Walk, where he also expands on his passion for plants and his general delight in the natural world. Not everything, he stresses, should be made a matter of practical usefulness, of profit and loss; simple joy, with material interest in abeyance, is an end in itself, and one of life's redemptive possibilities. Flowers, above all, have the power to yield such joy (*see* BOTANY).

In the Sixth Walk, Rousseau offers a cutting analysis on people's motives in doing good. On the one hand there are one's spontaneous movements of love and generosity, and one's pleasure in others; on the other, the chains of duty and obligation, which kill these natural sentiments and which, while enforcing obedience, do nothing but provoke resentment. No sooner has one done a good deed, Rousseau says, than one is expected to do it again. Freedom is removed, and the pressures of demand are substituted for the immediate promptings of love. He himself has never been suited to society, because he cannot bear to have the free movements of his soul tied down by duty, and good deeds exacted from him by the constraints of obligation.

This subtle piece of psychological analysis about the sources of morality and goodness echoes ideas that find fuller expression in *Émile*. It may be that it is Rousseau's own anger at not being allowed to give rein to his own feelings that makes him experience the existence and needs of others as an aggressive imposition on him. Feeling constantly unwanted and unregarded as he does, despite protesting that he feels love for all persons he is apt to begrudge anything done for others.

In the Eighth Walk, Rousseau returns for the last time to the ravages that AMOUR-PROPRE can inflict. In making one dependent on others, it exposes one to the constant torment of their contempt and indifference. The only solution to this failure to honour one at one's own estimate is withdrawal from men, a self-sufficient self-reliance, which will make one immune from the shocks of human intercourse. He no longer feels that reciprocal care and regard between himself and others is a real possibility. But such withdrawal is only to salvage what one can from the wreckage of hope; it is not to realize what is best for man.

This same motif of reconciliation to failed hopes, and of treasuring the residual possibilities of peace, recurs in the Ninth Walk. Happiness is beyond us, he says; instead, we should seek peace of mind. He speaks of his own children, whom he abandoned, but insists that he loves giving pleasure to children. In this he finds a simple joy, in contrast with the pain and effort involved in seeking opulence and exclusive pleasures. He cannot abide the grumpy expressions that spoiled and sullen people wear when they do not get what they think are their rightful pleasures. It should be the sentiments of humanity, not the greed and privileges that money establishes, that govern the relations of men.

In the uncompleted Tenth Walk Rousseau's mind turns to his life with Mme de Warens, and his regrets over the lost happiness that he enjoyed with her. He speaks of his attempts to repay her as, he hopes, he makes his way in the world. Then the *Reveries* breaks off – it is not clear how near to death he was when he ceased work on this last Walk. He left Paris in late May 1778 to live at Ermenonville, where he died on 2 July.

Reflections on individual self-sufficiency and on human association, and the profits and losses attaching to each, recur constantly in these Walks. Despite being a collection of apparently undirected reveries, they disclose, both consciously and unconsciously, many of the preoccupations that shaped both Rousseau's adult life and his writings.

Further reading: Gossman (175); Gourevitch (174); Green (8); Grimsley (176); Williams (184)

rights Rousseau nowhere gives an exact explanation of what he takes a right to be, nor an account of the rights that he believes people have (in either the natural or civil state) and why they have them. For all that, his thought about individuals and society is permeated by the idea of rights. (*See* JUSTICE.)

A person's rights may be seen as covering those areas of his life in which he ought to be protected, or aided, for reasons that do not depend on, or derive from, the discretion or favour of others. From this might be extrapolated three kinds of rights. First, liberty rights, which demand that an individual not be interfered with or subjected to another's directions or control; rights to forbearance, which demand that he not be harmed, molested or hurt in any way; and 'welfare' rights, which demand that certain opportunities, goods or advantages be made available to the individual. Rousseau identifies rights which fall into all these categories.

Thus, he holds that all people have a 'natural' right to provide for their own preservation and to do so by whatever means they think best, according to their own judgement and free from the interference or control of others (*SC* I, ch. 2, 166; *OC* III, 352). The first comment to be made here is that by calling this right 'natural', Rousseau is making two points: that possession of this right is intrinsic to the very existence of each and every person, and that its possession does not derive from membership of society – it is a pre-social right. It may be objected that where men stand in no social relations the notion of right has no application. Such a notion only makes sense in the context of the regulation of one person's behaviour towards another. But Rousseau's second point in calling this right 'natural' is that it is not inherent in the native condition and circumstances of man to be subordinate to others, to be bound in deference or subjugation to others. To claim such a 'natural right' is to assert the common, equal independence of all – a claim that makes sense against the assumption that everyone is automatically born into relations of authority and obedience.

This right to provide for one's own preservation is the one to which Rousseau attaches most significance in *The Social Contract*, where it more or less equates with that 'liberty' which, he says, is inherent in man's nature (*see* FREEDOM). However, he also thinks that people enjoy other natural rights as and when they first form social ties with others. In particular, in our dealings with each other each of us will need and want to be acknowledged as a significant being whose life and desires count as the life and desires of a human being; whose life and desires count not just for reasons of expediency and convenience to others – because, for instance, we are being agreeable to them, or we are joining in with their projects, or we are of the 'right' colour or class. So to be acknowledged is to be recognized as a person, as a morally significant entity. The form that such acknowledgement takes is others' recognition of us as right-holders, as people whose preferences should be consulted in any matter that affects us, or whose hurt determines a limit to what is morally permissible in relation to us.

So, although Rousseau gives no systematic explanation of those rights that pertain to human standing in mutual transactions, he indicates some of the ways in which we may be disregarded or downgraded in our dealings with others.

It is in this acknoweldgement of the equal moral standing of all that Rousseau grounds his arguments about the rights that citizens (*see* CITIZEN) should enjoy in any legitimate civil society. No such society can be just and enjoy legitimate command of a person if, in any way at all, that person is afforded lesser standing than any other person (other than by their own, rational consent), or if all persons are denied their proper human standing. This will involve, for instance, citizen participation in sovereign deliberations and determinations, and equal protection by the public force of the person and goods of each individual. The civil state, in Rousseau's view, largely consolidates and secures those moral rights of humanity that are more precariously enjoyed when we need to rely on our own resources alone to obtain them from others. Thus, with regard to property: 'We must clearly distinguish natural liberty, which is bounded only by the strength of the individual, from civil liberty which is limited by the general will; and possession, which is merely the effect of force or the right of the first occupier, from property, which can be founded only on a positive title' (*SC* I, ch. 8, 178; *OC* III, 365). Here the distinction between the 'natural right' of the first occupier (which follows from the right to provide for one's own preservation) is distinguished from the civil title of possession, or ownership, which is grounded in positive law.

When in August 1789 the National Assembly drew up its Declaration of the Rights of Man and Citizens, many of its points articulated, with exemplary precision, matters central to Rousseau's thought (for all that he never spelled them out in full). And though he would have been revolted by the misapplications of the Declaration that were to ensue, he would not in all probability have dissented from it.

Rousseau's originality in making use of the idea of rights in political theory lies in his insistence on the absolute equality of right amongst all persons, and his unwillingness to countenance any social or civil arrangements that detract from such equality. Indeed, it is to the protection and celebration of the moral dignity of each and all, in his view, that the principal effort of statecraft should be dedicated. Possession of full humanity in one's own person in concord with others similarly circumstanced is not, for Rousseau, the means to some greater social or civil objective, but is in itself the end for which civil society should exist.

Sources: *DI*
    SC, Bk I, II

Further reading: Macdonald (340); Masters, chs 4, 6, 7 (69); Strauss (346); Wasserstrom (348)

Rome Rousseau recounts (*The Confessions*, Bk I) that, very early in his life, he fell under the influence of Plutarch's *Lives* and was inspired to imagine himself a partner in, a perpetrator of, the great deeds recounted in those books. This childhood experience never left him, and in his mature political writings he constantly refers to Rome as an instance of a great state which embodies, both in its institutions and in the character and attitudes of its people, some of the best principles of civil society. In ÉMILE (I, 40; *OC* IV, 249) Rousseau writes of 'good social institutions that best know how to denature man, to take his absolute existence from him in order to give him a relative one and to transport the *I* into the common unity, with the result that each individual believes himself no longer one but a part of the unity and no longer feels himself except within the whole.' Then: 'A citizen of Rome was neither Caius nor Lucius; he was a Roman ... This has little relation, it seems to me, to the men we know.'

This theme of the Roman citizen's identification with his country, of his paramount patriotic loyalty and dedication to the greatness of his nation, emerges also in the (DISCOURSE ON) POLITICAL ECONOMY: 'Everything both at Rome, and in the Roman armies, breathed that love of fellow-citizens one for another, and that respect for the Roman name, which raised the courage and inspired the virtue of everyone who had the honour to bear it' (*DPE* 133; *OC* III, 257). And Cato is praised above Socrates: Cato 'defended his country, its liberty, and its laws' – he had 'the cause of his country always at heart'. Socrates may have been the greater philosopher, but Cato was the greater citizen. Even more striking is the prominence given to Roman institutions and procedures in The SOCIAL CONTRACT. More than half of Bk IV (chs 4–6) is given over to a detailed treatment of Roman civil structures, while Rome and Romans figure frequently in the rest of his argument.

As with other political theorists, Rome continued to exert a powerful influence over Rousseau's imagination. Insight may be gained into what he disliked in current political arrangements and into what he aspired to achieve in his own political thinking, if his projects are seen as often shaped by his effort to emulate the achievements of Rome.

Sources: *C*, Bk I
    DPE
    E, Bk I
    SC, Bk IV

Rousseau Judge of Jean-Jacques: Dialogues (written 1772–6; published 1780–2) (*Rousseau Juge de Jean-Jacques*) [20]   Rousseau began this work in 1772, not long after his final return to Paris and the prohibition of private readings from THE CONFESSIONS. By early 1776 he had completed it. On 24 February, in a frenzy of distress, he attempted to place a copy of the manuscript on the high altar of Notre-Dame. Finding the choir gates closed, he wandered the streets of Paris in despair, returning home late at night in a state of collapse. He gave one copy of the manuscript to Condillac, and a copy of Bk I to Brooke Boothby, an English acquaintance from his time at Wootton in Derbyshire. (This was the first part of the work to be published, at Lichfield in 1780.) Still seized with the idea that he was the object of malicious plotting and contempt, in April of that year, in an attempt to vindicate his name, he wrote a short open letter, *To All Frenchmen who Still Love Justice and Truth* (*À tout Français Aimant encore la Justice et la Vérité*), which he tried to thrust into the hands of passers-by and sent to various acquaintances. Not long afterwards, the worst of his mental suffering seems to have abated, and he began work on his last and in many ways most tranquil and transparent work, the REVERIES OF THE SOLITARY WALKER.

Rousseau Judge of Jean-Jacques takes the form of dialogues between Rousseau appearing as a participant and a Frenchman, a representative member of the public. One of the manuscripts gives the following table of contents: 'First Dialogue: Of the System of Conduct towards Jean-Jacques adopted by the administration with public approval. Second Dialogue: Of Jean-Jacques's character and habits. Third Dialogue: Of the Spirit of his Books and Conclusions'. Rousseau uses the dialogue form to develop a debate about his (Jean-Jacques's) own character, motives, way of life and achievements, between his *alter ego*, 'Rousseau' (the writer and participant), and the Frenchman. Rousseau starts with a recital of the innumerable calumnies and vilifications that are put abroad about him. He aims gradually to establish the truth about himself: this truth will result, first, from a visit paid to Jean-Jacques by 'Rousseau' (as described in the second *Dialogue*) and, second, from a careful reading of his books made by the Frenchman (as described in the third *Dialogue*). The whole is an extended exercise in self-articulation and self-vindication on Rousseau's part against what he felt to be an entrenched vendetta against himself by 'those gentlemen' (unspecified) who wished to profit from his downfall and ignominy.

The *Dialogues* is a long, repetitive and sometimes obsessively detailed work, containing little of enduring interest or significance for the appreciation of Rousseau's major creative achievement, aside from some telling restatements of his views about the nature and effects of AMOUR-PROPRE. (And in an interesting assessment of his own works he assigns to ÉMILE a

213

primary place (*RJJ* III, 211; *OC* I, 933).) Most of the work comprises a recital of the accusations made against him (that he is a plagiarist, a liar, a hypocrite, a monster of calculating evil), and attempts to show not only that these accusations are baseless, but that Jean-Jacques is the victim of men motivated by an awareness of their own defects, which the simplicity and integrity of Jean-Jacques has rendered intolerable to them. It is true, the writer/participant Rousseau says, that Jean-Jacques has often done wrong, and it is these lapses that have been the occasion for his enemies' attacks. But these are not the wickednesses of a corrupt man, but the slips of a weak man ruled by an excessive sensibility, who cannot bear shame or trouble. Jean-Jacques is incapable of malice, if only because he finds the effort it involves too great. He craves a loving intimacy, and it is his self-exposure that has been the source of the misfortunes that have befallen him.

When studied closely, his works show Jean-Jacques not to harbour any hatred, but to be always and everywhere a believer in human goodness, and dedicated to promoting the cause of human happiness. Properly understood, his are writings of moral utility and service to mankind. If he points out other people's errors it is not to glory in their worthlessness, but to try to redirect them towards what will bring them true happiness and reward.

Further reading: Green (8); Grimsley (176); Jones (180); Kelly and Masters (181)

S

savage   *See* NOBLE SAVAGE.

science   *See* DISCOURSE ON THE SCIENCES AND THE ARTS; REASON.

Second Discourse   *See* DISCOURSE ON THE ORIGIN OF INEQUALITY.

self-estrangement   *See* ALIENATION.

sensibility   *See* CREED OF A SAVOYARD VICAR; NATURE; REVERIES OF THE SOLITARY WALKER.

sex   In the DISCOURSE ON THE ORIGIN OF INEQUALITY ROUSSEAU argues that there is a distinction to be made between 'the physical and the moral ingredients in the feeling of love' (*DI* 70; *OC* III, 157–8). Of the physical element, he says it is 'that general desire which urges the sexes to union with each other'. The moral element is 'that which determines and fixes this desire exclusively upon one particular object; or at least gives it a greater degree of energy toward the object thus preferred'.

> It is easy to see that the moral part of love is a factitious feeling, born of social usage, and enhanced by the women with much care and cleverness, to establish their empire, and put in power the sex which ought to obey. This feeling, being founded on certain ideas of beauty and merit which a savage is not in a position to acquire . . . must be for him almost non-existent . . . He follows solely the character nature has implanted in him . . . so that every woman equally answers his purpose.

A little later (*DI* 81; *OC* III, 169) he suggests somewhat coyly that jealous and exclusive sexual desire and possessiveness are two of the primary causes of the emergence of invidious inequality between persons. The desire to command the exclusive attention and desire of another incites people to denigrate and nullify competitors for that attention, and to identify marks by which they will seem to have exemplary distinction and

215

merit for the attention of the object of their desire. Rousseau makes some rather more subtle observations on this theme in *Émile* (V, 429–30; *OC* IV, 796–9).

Within sexual jealousy itself Rousseau distinguishes a natural and an artificial component. Where, in animal species, sexual potency is unlimited, jealous exclusivity is at its peak, for 'the male measures his rights according to his needs and can never see another male as anything but an intrusive competitor.' But there are also cases in nature

> in which mating produces a sort of moral bond ... the female belongs by her own choice to the male to whom she has given herself, and commonly resists all others. And the male, who has this affection founded on preference as the guarantee of her fidelity, is thus less anxious at the sight of other males and lives more peacefully with them. (*loc. cit.*)

Applying this to human sexuality, Rousseau argues that, as far as the natural component of sexuality goes, ours is more like the second sort: 'It is easy to see from the male's limited potency and the moderation of his desires that he is destined by nature to be content with one female.' However – and here he returns to the point central to his earlier argument – much sexual jealousy in humans is motived by the 'social passions more than ... primitive instinct ... In most liaisons of gallantry the lover hates his rivals far more than he loves his mistress. If he fears that he is not the only object of her attentions, it is the effect of ... *amour-propre* ... and he suffers far more out of vanity than out of love' (*E* V, 430; *OC* IV, 797–8).

Thus, Rousseau regards much human sexuality as a snare and a delusion, in which we are more tormented by anxiety about our prestige and desirability than we are moved by pleasure and affection. It is notoriously difficult to evaluate views of this sort, not least because of people's unwillingness, or inability, to acknowledge such factors. However, he does not think that sexual passion is bound to be an 'unbridled ardour which intoxicates ... with the chimerical attractions of an object which [one] no longer sees as it really is' (*E* V, 430; *OC* IV, 797–8). It is both possible and desirable that it forms part of affection and constancy, which furthers and fosters the 'moral bond' between persons – a 'sort of marriage', as he describes it, even in the case of certain animals (*see* LOVE).

Rousseau's own sexual career was a mostly unhappy one (described at length, in sometimes painful detail, in THE CONFESSIONS). Quite early on he found erotic pleasure in punishments (Bk I, 25ff.; *OC* I, 15), and this shaped his sexual preferences – often to the astonishment, but at the same time saving the virtue, of several of the later targets of his sexual interest.

He appears to have enjoyed a fully confident and ample sexual relationship only once in his life (with Mme de Larnarge; *C* VI, 239–42; *OC* I, 251–5); for the rest, he seems to have been unable to focus both his sexual desires and his admiration and esteem on to one woman. Although Thérèse Levasseur bore his children, it would seem that he felt no passion for her; and the object of his deepest passion, 'the first and only love in all my life', Sophie d'Houdetot (*C* IX, 408; *OC* I, 439), was apparently spared any sexual liaison with him. His sexual initiation by Mme de Warens (*C* V, 186ff.; *OC* I, 193ff.) clearly brought him little pleasure, and, as he recounts in an episode with a Venetian prostitute, his ardour was subject to the most crippling vagaries (*C* VII, 301; *OC* I, 321).

Few writers have been as candid as Rousseau about their sexual ineptitude. Those who are explicit about their sexuality tend to concentrate on their exceptional prowess – perhaps, thereby, neatly illustrating Rousseau's claim regarding the influence of the 'social passions'.

Sources: *C*, Pt 1
          DI, Pt 1
          E, Bks IV, V

Further reading: Schwartz (35)

sin (original) Rousseau discusses the doctrine of original sin at length only in his LETTER TO CHRISTOPHE DE BEAUMONT (although he alludes to it also in JULIE OU LA NOUVELLE HÉLOÏSE), in which he defends himself against the strictures passed on ÉMILE by the Archbishop of Paris. In *Émile* Rousseau argues that men are by nature good (*see* NATURAL GOODNESS), and it was to this claim – or, rather, to what he took to be the implication in it, that man is not responsible for his own evil being and doing – that de Beaumont took exception.

Principal among the many objections that Rousseau levels at the Archbishop's view is that whereas he, Rousseau, explains how man has become wicked, the Archbishop simply asserts that he is, and by his own fault – but without explanation. The rite of baptism is supposed, Rousseau argues, to cleanse this sin; yet we do not find that all Christians are angels. And it is absurd to say that everyone requires wise and vigilant teachers, since it is precisely the tyranny of such persons that induces the wicked dispositions and acts that are then identified as the ills that call for cure: 'I have proved that the education which you call the soundest is the most senseless, that the education which you call the most virtuous gives children all their vices . . . I have proved that all the errors of youth, which you complain cannot be repressed by these means, are really the result of them' (*OC* IV, 941).

217

Underlying Rousseau's objections to the Archbishop's claims lies, perhaps, a deeper source of his resistance to the doctrine of original sin. Although he agrees that man's highest duty is to follow God and to do His works, he thinks that the most powerful counter-incentive to our carrying this duty out is the insistence that each of us is under an obligation to do so. Throughout his moral writings (particularly in *Émile*) Rousseau argues that the imposition of obligations produces only resentment and aggression, and that the desire for good and for God can come only out of love and creative freedom. It is not natural to man to be commanded and judged by others, the temporal custodians of right and justice. Men learn to be good only because they find in goodness the realization of their own best aspirations, not because they fear punishment and damnation should they do wrong. To place man under command is to govern him only by threat and fear, and right-doing becomes a hated burden. It is this perversion that Rousseau believes the doctrine of original sin induces; his diagnosis of the pathology of moral disposition is extraordinarily penetrating.

Rousseau held not that men were not capable of evil-doing and evil dispositions, or that these were not their own responsibility, but that the idea of original sin not only did not explain such matters but actually served to arouse the very aggressive impulses that are taken to be proof of its existence.

Rousseau's consideration of original sin, of this idea of the original perversion of human will, has its role in the context of a French debate extending over the seventeenth and eighteenth centuries. Pascal had argued that human nature is irrevocably divided, and that our own power of reason and our will are impotent to equip us to know ourselves and to lead a good life. We depend ultimately not on ourselves, but on God, for our redemption. So far from being self-sufficient and self-dependent, we constantly fall into evil and contradiction through our weakness and incompleteness. If the integrity of human nature is to be asserted, then to uncover the formative forces within the personality of man becomes the central issue, so that the origin of evil and suffering may be identified and understood independent of any theory of human duality.

Rousseau's careful account (principally in *Émile*) of the empirical conditions giving rise to such emotions as envy, malice and spite in human relationships dispenses with any need to think of man as having a dual character, part perverse beast and part dependent on the divine (although there are residues of this in the CREED OF A SAVOYARD VICAR). Human's are not, *qua* creatures of the earth, necessarily evil; nor do they need spiritual redemption given only by the grace of God if they are to become whole and good. Although Rousseau finds signs of God's providence in this possibility of recovering intact and creative life, for oneself and for others, he sees it as a providence that shows itself in the deep harmony of our nature, not in our having the possibility of overcoming the world as dross.

Source: *Letter to Christophe de Beaumont*

Further reading: Cassirer, ch. 4 (239); Grimsley (189); Horowitz, chs 2, 8 (27)

slavery Rousseau devotes ch. 4 of Bk I of *The Social Contract* to a discussion of slavery; but he also uses the idea of slavery in a somewhat metaphorical sense extensively throughout his works.

He is uniformly critical of slavery in all its forms. He attacks as groundless and ridiculous Grotius' view that an individual can alienate his liberty to a master and become the latter's 'living tool'. To alienate, Rousseau says, is to give or to sell. If a man sells his liberty in return, for instance, for his subsistence, how shall he gain his subsistence, since his master secures what he has only from the labour of his slave? Rousseau applies this to the case of a people enslaved to a king: 'Do subjects then give their persons on condition that the king takes their goods also?' On the other hand, 'to say that a man gives himself gratuitously, is to say what is absurd and inconceivable; such an act is null and illegitimate, from the mere fact that he who does it is out of his mind' (*SC* I, ch. 4, 169; *OC* III, 356).

Slavery is 'incompatible with man's nature', since it reduces a person to a thing and prevents there being any moral relations between master and slave, making possible only a one-way relation of absolute disposal at will. It is proper to man to act and to be recognized as a moral agent, a possessor of moral consciousness, whose life and being require acknowledgement as having moral significance. Enslavement entirely nullifies that character in a man. However, then, a master stands in regard to his slaves, it cannot be on the basis of right on one side and obligation on the other (*see* DOMINATION). Nor, Rousseau continues, does victory in war bestow on the conqueror a right to enslave. In WAR, people encounter each other as defenders of their own country, and when hostilities have ceased each person resumes his character and standing as a moral agent in his own right. War 'does not give the conqueror the right to massacre the conquered peoples'; and, therefore, it cannot give him the right to enslave them, since, as conquered, they no longer serve as defenders of their nation.

Extrapolating from these – surely, wholly convincing – ideas, he then goes on to say that any legitimate authority over men must depend on a convention that acknowledges the like moral character and standing of all persons. Otherwise, some persons will stand under that power not as under any justifiable obligation of obedience to it, but merely as compelled to comply (*see* GENERAL WILL).

It is in this connection that Rousseau's extended use of the idea of slavery comes into play. He is apt to regard any human relationship in which one person is denied full and equal acknowledgement as a human being, vested with rights and moral standing, as a relationship in which that person is 'enslaved' by those who deny him that acknowledgement. Such relationships of subordination and ignominy can have many origins and forms. Some arise because of economic inequalities: the poor become so dependent on the grace and favour of the rich for their subsistence that their continued survival comes to be at the rich man's disposal. Then, also, the inequalities in rank, honour and distinction which AMOUR-PROPRE demands and sustains require that many be denied any proper recognition or standing in society or in the state. Their full humanity is not granted to them:

> Civilised man . . . pays his court to men in power, whom he hates, and to the wealthy, whom he despises; he stops at nothing to have the honour of serving them; he is not ashamed to value himself on his own meanness and their protection; and, proud of his slavery, he speaks with disdain of those who have not the honour of sharing it. (*DI* 104; *OC* III, 192)

Those who are moved by (excessive) *amour-propre* elect for a form of enslavement, by participating in a relationship in which human significance and honour are granted only to those who gain ascendancy and invidious superiority. However, they thereby purchase for themselves a social and spiritual condition that is both miserable and degrading.

Rousseau also uses the idea of slavery in talking of self-mastery over the passions and irrational desires. Thus, when Émile first falls in love, he becomes tormented by jealousy and by the fear of displeasing his beloved:

> A new enemy is arising which you have not learned to conquer and from which I can no longer save you. This enemy is yourself . . . You were bound to nothing other than the human condition, and now you are bound to all the attachments you have given to yourself. In learning to desire, you have made yourself the slave of your desires. (*E* V, 443; *OC* IV, 815–16)

Compare *SC* I, ch. 8, 178 (*OC* III, 365), where Rousseau speaks of 'the mere impulse of appetite' as 'slavery'.

Sources: *DI*, Pt 2
E, Bk V
SC, Bk I

Further reading: Masters, ch. 6 (69); Shklar, chs 3, 4 (36)

Social Contract, The (1762) (*Du Contrat Social*) [14]   Early in the 1750s, following the publication of the *Discourse on the Sciences and the Arts* and when he was serving as secretary to the French ambassador in Venice, Rousseau conceived the project of writing a work of political theory, to be called 'Political Institutions'. But although his article on political economy (1755) for the *Encyclopaedia* shows something of how his ideas were developing, he had not got far with the project by the time he moved to Montmorency in 1756. Its completion was one of his objectives when he settled at the Hermitage, but he became side-tracked by other work (principally *La Nouvelle Héloïse* and *Émile*). About 1758–9 he resolved to abandon the project and to put together some extracts to make a shorter work. This shorter work is *The Social Contract*.

Given this complex genesis, it is not surprising that there are numerous rough drafts of different sections – in particular, one extensive early manuscript, usually called the Geneva MS, which encompasses about half of the final version as well as some interesting passages that Rousseau, in the end, omitted. (One of these, originally intended as ch. 2 of Bk I, 'The General Society of the Human Race', is normally included in modern editions of *The Social Contract*.) The organization of each of the books in this earlier version is somewhat tighter and clearer. Rousseau gives titles to each of them – Bk I: The Basic Idea of a Civil Body; Bk II: The Establishment of Laws; Bk III: The Institution of Government (there is no Bk IV in this draft). And in Bk V of *Émile* Rousseau gives a short summary of many of the principal ideas of *The Social Contract* (*E* V, 458–67; *OC* IV, 836–49), purportedly as part of Émile's political education, but also providing a succinct digest of the larger work.

The Social Contract was finished in 1761 and published (not without distribution difficulties) in April 1762. Although this essay has subsequently become Rousseau's most famous and widely read work, it was in fact ÉMILE, published a few weeks later, that brought the censure and condemnation down on him. Both books were burned in Geneva, but *The Social Contract* was seen as the less significant work at the time. Hume thought that Rousseau's own high estimate of it was ridiculous; in his view, *La Nouvelle Héloïse* was incomparably the better work.

The Social Contract is now generally regarded as his greatest achievement and as one of the classic texts of political theory. Book I is principally concerned with identifying the rightful basis for a civil society and some of the principal characteristics of that society. Book II deals with the nature and functions of, and the conditions necessary for establishing, an effective sovereign body for a civil society. In Bk III Rousseau discusses government, its place in the state, forms of government, and its powers and limits. Book IV treats further issues concerning the form and organization of a just society, discussing the Roman polity at length, and civil religion.

At the start of Bk I, Rousseau's purpose is to discover whether there can be 'any sure and legitimate rule or administration' for a civil order. 'Man is born free; and everywhere he is in chains' – but, he asks, is this change in man's position legitimate? Neither paternal right nor the right of the strongest – which he denies, in fact, creates any right – can justify the enslavement of men. SLAVERY is, indeed, absolutely contrary to the nature and rights of man: 'To renounce liberty is to renounce being a man, to surrender the rights of humanity and even its duties ... such a renunciation is incompatible with man's nature' (see FREEDOM). Even the right of a majority to command the actions of all must have come from unanimous agreement of all to establishing this 'law of majority voting' (see CONVENTION).

Having thus cleared the ground, Rousseau turns to the question of how rightful authority should be instituted. He asks what makes human association necessary to men, and concludes that it is material want and weakness. They must, then, 'aggregate' their forces so that they can act in concert. But how can each man pledge his 'force and liberty' to the common cause without 'harming his own interests, and neglecting the care he owes to himself?' 'The problem is to find a form of association which will defend and protect with the whole common force the person and goods of each associate, and in which each, while uniting himself with all, may still obey himself alone, and remain as free as before' (SC I, ch. 6, 174; OC III, 360).

The 'social contract' provides the solution to this problem. In it, each member transfers all his force and rights 'to the whole community', and 'puts his person and all his power in common under the supreme direction of the general will' (see GENERAL WILL). By this act, a corporate body is created which may be called a city or republic. Each member is at once a citizen, as sharing in the sovereign authority, and a subject, as being under the laws of the state (see CITIZEN; DEMOCRACY).

The SOVEREIGN BODY in the state, the supreme authority, is 'formed wholly of the individuals who compose' the state. Every adult member of that association is indivisibly a member of the sovereign body. Rousseau admits that individuals will retain particular, or private, interests, apart from their interests as citizens. But the whole contract would be empty unless they were compelled to obey the general will of the citizens as sovereign. In being so compelled, they are being forced to be free, being dependent not on the protection or favour of individuals, but only on the general laws applicable alike to all. The assumption of the rights and duties of citizenship better protects a person both in himself and in his possessions, as a being enjoying the support of the whole common force.

In Bk II, Rousseau clarifies the character of the general will and the conditions under which it can emerge and carry its due authority. First, he argues that sovereignty is inalienable and indivisible, but also that it must confine itself to general conventions, not laying 'more charges on one subject than another'. What is not regulated by these general conventions or laws (see LAW) remains under the individual's own discretion: 'Every man may dispose at will of such goods and liberty as these conventions leave him.'

How are we to achieve laws that will tend to justice and equality alike for all, and be properly concerned with general preservation and well-being? The answer is that each member must place the common interests that he shares alike with all above his own private interests, which he might seek in indifference to, or to the detriment of, others (see PARTICULAR WILL). Each person must be transformed 'into part of a greater whole from which he in a manner receives his life and being', so that his primary identity becomes that of member, of citizen, among others of the same kind, not that of a 'complete and solitary whole' (see DENATURING). This 'transformation' is partly the work of a LEGISLATOR who, calling on divine authority, engenders in people a dominant sense of common life and destiny. But it requires, equally, the happy coincidence of many factors to render an aggregate of persons ready to live and function as one people for the common good of all.

> What people, then, is a fit subject for legislation? One which, already bound by some unity of origin, interest, or convention, has never yet felt the real yoke of law ... one in which every member may be known to every other, and there is no need to lay on any man burdens too heavy for a man to bear. (SC II, ch. 10, 203; OC III, 390)

Rousseau here names CORSICA as a country where good laws may still be introduced.

In Bk III he turns to the function and forms of GOVERNMENT, making a sharp distinction between the legislative power, which belongs to the sovereign body alone, and executive or administrative power, which belongs to the government. Government is an office or function which, in Rousseau's eyes, is wholly derivative in its power and activities from the sovereign body: 'It is simply and solely a commission, an employment, in

223

which the rulers, mere officials of the sovereign, exercise in their own name the power of which it makes them depositaries.' Such a function is required to provide for the daily administration of the affairs of the state, and to apply laws to particular people or cases. The sovereign body, concerning itself as it must only with general issues, cannot properly (or effectively) determine such matters.

Rousseau stresses that establishing governmental office introduces pressures towards inequality and enslavement in the state (*see* CORPORATE WILL). He lays down some general rules about how best to check the usurpation of sovereign power by governmental officers, whilst yet leaving them with the resources they require to discharge the necessary tasks. But there is no one form for government to take that will best meet this concern, and at the same time adequately serve the material, geographical and other needs of a people. He briefly considers some familiar 'pure' forms of governement – democratic, aristocratic and monarchic – as well as mixed forms, but in each case there are notable drawbacks as well as advantages. Most of all, he insists that sovereign authority must not be usurped or bypassed, and he is scornful of the habits and weaknesses that make men unwilling to assemble as a people and declare the law by their general will. 'The people in assembly, I shall be told, is a mere chimera. It is so to-day, but two thousand years ago it was not so. Has man's nature changed?' (*SC* III, ch. 3, 236; *OC* III, 425); *see* REPRESENTATION. Here he cites the Roman republic as an instance of a great state, in which, although there were 400,000 citizens, 'few weeks passed without the Roman people being in assembly, and even being so several times.' In contrast: 'The people of England regards itself as free; but it is grossly mistaken; it is free only during the election of its members of parliament. As soon as they are elected, slavery overtakes it, and it is nothing' (*SC* III, ch. 15, 240; *OC* III, 430).

Rousseau spends several chapters of Bk IV discussing the elements and functions of the various authoritative bodies in the Roman polity (*see* ROME). He describes 'the methods of giving and counting opinions in the assembly of the people' as a means of determining the general will. But how to ensure that just laws will be passed and that obedience to them will be willing and safeguarded? Here he introduces civil religion (*see* RELIGION (CIVIL)), as adding to the force of law and creating one of the great bonds of unity in society. The dogmas of the civil religion 'ought to be few, simple, and exactly worded ... [They are] the existence of a mighty, intelligent, and beneficent Divinity ... the sanctity of the social contract and the laws', and the prohibition of intolerance (*SC* IV, ch. 8, 276; *OC* III, 468). Anyone who does not accept, in deed if not in heart, these

224

dogmas, should be banished, not as impious but as an 'anti-social being, incapable of truly loving the laws and justice'.

The significance of *The Social Contract* lies in its attempt to articulate the legitimate basis of political authority in the rule of the people over themselves, and in its account of the manner in which the people authorize their own terms and conditions for association through the acts of the general will. There is continuous controversy over the interpretation of many points, especially over whether Rousseau, while professing to be concerned with the freedom and dignity of the individual, does not in fact make him a slave of the whole community. But in its absolute affirmation of the equal rights of all citizens, of their standing as members one with another of the sovereign body, it remains a work of radical import.

Further reading: Althusser (110); Cranston (116); Crocker (117); Dent ch. 5 (24); Lemos (68); Levine (128); McManners (133); Masters, chs 6–8 (69); Noone (140); Shklar, ch. 5 (36)

society   A young man should 'know that man is naturally good; let him feel it; let him judge his neighbour by himself. But let him see that society depraves and perverts men' (*E* IV, 237; *OC* IV, 525). That society is corrupt and corrupting is a recurrent theme throughout Rousseau's writings. In what ways, exactly, did he think this was so?

One pervasive interpretation of Rousseau's thought is this: as soon as social contact of any settled kind is established between persons, each competes with the others for invidious ascendancy and comes to measure his own value and significance only in terms of his having prestigious superiority over the others (*see* AMOUR-PROPRE). 'Society' corrupts people, in this sense, not as an agent of corruption but as the forum in which corrupt tendencies emerge and take over in human beings, dominating and deforming their relationships when social intercourse takes place.

In one respect this interpretation seems correct: namely, in its refusal to treat 'society' as if it were a collective entity (other people) which, by accident or design, works against the individual and deforms and harms him. However deep Rousseau's own paranoid delusions may have been, and however widespread may be, in his view, paranoid attitudes in society, these did not extend as far as his reifying 'society' and regarding it as a malign agency inflicting undeserved hurt on the hapless and innocent individual. 'Society' merely signifies 'human association'. It is *associating* with other people that 'depraves and perverts', not they that cause the depravity and perversion, which is more likely to originate in our own dispositions and attitudes.

225

In another respect, this interpretation is mistaken: namely, in its supposition that it is Rousseau's view that associating with others *unavoidably* brings with it depravity and perversion. Certainly, he thinks that this is what most commonly occurs, and that social processes and institutions codify and consolidate those forms of invidious relationship that are so humanly damaging. But it was never his view that this is bound to occur. One of the central purposes of the argument in ÉMILE is to show how it can be avoided – by preventing the development of resentment and aggression – and to show what possibilities for individual and social existence would be achieved if it were avoided. If COMPASSION can be introduced into human association as the primary basis for encounter and relationship, then bonds of mutual care and respect can unite people in society, instead of hatred and malice dividing them.

Rousseau is not one of those political theorists who think that between the STATE OF NATURE, in which humans have no settled association and live as isolated beings, and civil society or the state, there are no significant intermediate modes of human association. Indeed, he criticizes Plato's *Republic* for, in effect, abolishing intermediate societies that stand between the individual and the state:

> I speak of that subversion of the sweetest sentiments of nature, sacrificed to an artificial sentiment which can only be maintained by them – as though there were no need for a natural base on which to form conventional ties: as though the love of one's nearest were not the principle of the love one owes the state; as though it were not by means of the small fatherland which is the family that the heart attaches itself to the large one; as though it were not the good son, the good husband, and the good father who make the good citizen. (*E* V, 363; *OC* IV, 699–700)

In other words, it is only in the context of smaller associations than the state that we can learn the meaning and value of caring for others, sharing a life with them and making common cause – which sentiments any state needs to draw on and enlarge on, but cannot create *ex nihilo*. Accordingly, it is not simply any people, let alone a mere aggregate of persons, that is a 'fit subject for legislation': there must be some pre-existing 'unity of origin, interest or convention', if those persons are to be able to receive and accept law that will make for their true liberty and prosperity (*SC* II, ch. 10, 203; *OC* III, 390–1).

It may be objected that Rousseau says elsewhere that the existence of 'partial societies' within the state – including, presumably such 'societies' as families, united by close bonds – obstructs the determination of the general will or gives rise to its usurpation (compare *SC* II, ch. 3, 185; *OC* III, 371). However, although in practice difficulties often enough arise, there is in fact no contradiction of principle here. His complaint is against 'partial associations', which are 'formed *at the expense* of the great association' (my emphasis). The family, on the other hand, is an 'association' out of which loyalty and commitment to the 'great association' can grow; the family need not exist in opposition to, or at the expense of, that greater association. The sentiments that are learned in the family – those of sharing with and caring for others – do not cause people to seek profit at others' expense, as do those people who form the partial societies that subvert the general will. Rather, such 'family sentiments' are naturally extensible enough to take in concern for others who are not related by any immediate blood tie, but who have some other 'unity of origin'. It is in actuality, though, just as common for AMOUR-PROPRE to work by vaunting the precedence of families, as it does the precedence of individuals. So Rousseau's ideas here may seem a little optimistic.

Sources: *DI*, Pt 2
       E, Bks IV, V
       SC, Bks I, II

Further reading: Charvet (23); Masters, ch. 4 (69); Perkins (31); Shklar, chs 1, 2
       (36)

Sophie *See* ÉMILE; ÉMILE ET SOPHIE; WOMEN.

sovereign body Rousseau does not attribute any special sense to the notion of the sovereign body; he uses it in its familiar meaning of the bearer of supreme and final authority in the state. What is distinctive is his account of the *composition* and the characteristics of the sovereign body and its powers.

It is, perhaps, Rousseau's most famous political doctrine that the sovereign body in a state shall be composed of all the adults who comprise that civil association for which this is the supreme authority. In being, and functioning as, a member of the sovereign body, each person attains the status and character of CITIZEN, which is a different status and character from those that he enjoys as a separate and particular individual (*see* PARTICULAR WILL). So it is only by assuming a certain specific 'character' that each individual comes to comprise one member of the sovereign body – which is not a mere aggregation of individuals in their particularity. In being a member of the sovereign body, each individual should consider only the common interest that he shares alike with other individuals; he should consider himself, and judge and decide, only as 'one of the people'.

The declaration of the sovereign will in legislation is by means of the GENERAL WILL, which alone makes legitimate LAW. As a subject, each

227

individual is subordinate to a law which he has participated in devising as a member of the sovereign body. In Rousseau's view, no other basis of law can be legitimate. Law which is declared by only a few in a state forces servitude upon those who are compelled to conform to it, and establishes no obligation of obedience upon them.

No guarantees need be given by the sovereign body to the subject, because 'the Sovereign, being formed wholly of the individuals who compose it, neither has nor can have any interest contrary to theirs' (*SC* I, ch. 7, 176; *OC* III, 363) – this interest being 'their common preservation and general well-being' (*SC* IV, ch. 1, 247; *OC* III, 437). But the common interest, which is the interest that each person has as a citizen, is not the only interest each person has: his particular interest 'may speak to him quite differently'. In order, therefore, that the acts of the sovereign body shall not be 'empty', it must have at its disposal sufficient power to enforce compliance on anyone who attempts to place his private interest above the public interest. The individual is compelled by this to obey the general will, and so is 'forced to be free' (*SC* I, ch. 7, 177; *OC* III, 364: *see* FREEDOM).

Sovereign power is not, however, unlimited – because, in Rousseau's assessment, it is not the case that all aspects of a person's actions and goods bear decisively upon common preservation and the general well-being. Thus: 'Each man alienates ... by the social compact, only such part of his powers, goods, and liberty as it is important for the community to control' (*SC* II, ch. 4, 186; *OC* III, 373). When Rousseau adds that 'it must also be granted that the Sovereign is the sole judge of what is important', what he means is this: if it lay at the discretion not of the whole sovereign body, but of an individual or subgroup in the state to exempt their powers, goods and so on from the control of the community, then the rest would thereby, in effect, be subjugated to the will of this individual or subgroup and suffer tyrannical abuse by them. In that the portion of life that is unregulated by law remains so only at the discretion of the sovereign body, it is perhaps after all true in a way to say that sovereign power is unlimited.

Rousseau argues (*SC* II, ch. 1, 182; *OC* III, 368) that sovereignty cannot be alienated – that is, the powers and rights that the whole body of the people enjoy in their capacity as citizens cannot be transferred to one person or to a subgroup. For it is not 'incumbent on any will to consent to anything that is not for the good of the being who wills', and this agreement between the general will (as the sovereign will) and any other will cannot be 'lasting and constant'. Perhaps more tendentiously, Rousseau contends that sovereignty is 'indivisible':

Sovereignty, for the same reason as makes it inalienable, is indivisible; for will either is, or is not, general; it is the will either of the body of the people, or only of a part of it. In the first case, the will, when declared, is an act of Sovereignty and constitutes law: in the second, it is merely a particular will, or act of magistracy – at most a decree. (*SC* II, ch. 2, 183; *OC* III, 369)

Moreover, he then inveighs against those who divide sovereignty 'according to its object': for example, into legislative power and executive power, or into internal administration and foreign negotiation. These, he says, are not 'parts' of sovereign authority, but only 'emanations' from it. But it may be argued that there can exist in a state a separation of authority, powers and functions between several distinct bodies – familiarly, the legislative, executive and juridical – which operate harmoniously by balance and compromise where their functions impinge upon one another. And there need certainly be no single 'assembly of the people' which bears, uniquely, the power of sovereign action (compare *SC* III, ch. 12, 236; *OC* III, 425). It is precisely such separation of powers that appears to prevent abuse of sovereign authority which can happen when the exercise of that authority is concentrated in a single body (however large). It remains true, formally, that there must be, if and when there is a conflict of claims, one single decisive resolution. But it does not follow, materially, that there must be a single body that declares that resolution.

body – that is, to be capable both of effectively identifying and of willing what makes for their common preservation and general well-being – needs, in Rousseau's view, the most careful attention and maintenance. The growth and preservation of the 'social spirit' must be of central concern in any state in which a properly general will is to emerge and possess its appropriate dominance. The function of the LEGISLATOR in forming 'a people' is at the same time his function of bringing into existence a properly constituted and effective sovereign legislative body which will, so to say, 'take over' from him (see *SC* II, ch. 4, 187; *OC* III, 373; and *SC* II, ch. 7, 194; *OC* III, 381–4).

Finally: Rousseau also discusses 'sovereign states', meaning states in which there are sovereign bodies legislating for the members of those states, but for which there is no common sovereign power or authority over their relations with each other.

Sources: DPE
        SC Bks I, II

Further reading: Derathé (311); Gildin (123); Hinsley (335); de Jouvenel (337); Masters, ch. 7 (69); Rosenfeld (145); Shklar (146)

state (civil) Rousseau nowhere gives any comprehensive definition of the factors that entitle a human association properly to be counted as a state, or civil and political association. None the less, it may be conjectured that he held that a state exists when a number of persons are subject to a common set of rules (laws) for the governance of their conduct, these rules being promulgated by some centralized and supreme authority, and their observance of them being enforced, if necessary, by the imposition of sanctions or penalties. This being the case, it must be essential to consider, about any state, how these common rules originate, who formulates them, how they are to have proper authority over individuals, why enforcement of them is rightful, and so on. All these questions, and more, preoccupy Rousseau when he considers the character of civil society, particularly in THE SOCIAL CONTRACT. It is reasonable, therefore, to infer that it is his view that these questions are fundamental to the principal aspects of a human association that make it a civil state.

Concerning the legitimacy of these common rules, Rousseau invokes his notion of the GENERAL WILL; in regard to their claim on our obedience, he analyses the notions of AUTHORITY and of the SOVEREIGN BODY. To study the foundation and nature of the civil state is to study Rousseau's political theory in its entirety. But one aspect of the matter deserves special attention here.

Book I, ch. 8, of *The Social Contract* is entitled 'The Civil State'. What Rousseau argues here is that it is only in virtue of becoming a member of a (just and well constituted) civil association, and by identifying themselves with the role of CITIZEN, that human beings acquire the full range of powers and capacities that are proper to them and to the completion of their humanity. In becoming a citizen, a person knows himself to be the bearer of certain rights and titles, to be owed a certain honour and respect by his fellows. Equally, he knows he owes cognate responsibilities and duties. Thus it is that in his own actions and forbearances, and in his expectations and demands of others, a citizen is not merely expressing his feelings and desires, but acting from a moral understanding of the significance of his own needs and good and of the character of his relationship to others. The character of his self-understanding, and the footing of his actions and purposes, have been transformed by the assumption of the persona of citizen:

> The passage from the state of nature to the civil state produces a very remarkable change in man, by substituting justice for instinct in his conduct, and giving his actions the morality they had formerly lacked. Then only, when the voice of duty takes the place of physical impulses and right of appetite, does man, who so far had considered only himself, find that he is

forced to act on different principles and to consult his reason before listening to his inclinations. (*SC* I, ch. 8, 178; *OC* III, 365)

In virtue of this change, 'his faculties are so stimulated and developed, his ideas so extended, his feelings so ennobled, and his soul so uplifted, that ... he would be bound to bless continually the happy moment which ... instead of a stupid and unimaginative animal, made him an intelligent being and a man.'

It may appear that Rousseau is following Aristotle's lead here, arguing that man is, by nature, a 'political animal' – that is, a creature who can attain and enjoy the fullness of truly human possibility only by living and being as a member of a *polis*, a civil association properly ordered and regulated. What he is claiming – and it is a claim that he does not, apparently, maintain elsewhere – is that it is only in and from the character that a person is invested with as a member of a *civil* association that he acquires the ideas, capacities and dispositions which enable him to transcend instinct and act as a morally aware and conscientious being. This, apart from being false, is not what Rousseau maintains in, for instance, Bk IV of ÉMILE. There is, in fact, a certain crudity and oversimplification in some of the arguments of *The Social Contract* which betray that Rousseau formulated its principal ideas *before* he undertook the more penetrating analysis that he proffers in *Émile*. He continues to deploy in *The Social Contract* some of the uncritical contrasts that mar, for instance, the *Discourse on the Origin of Inequality* but that he transcends in his most mature work. In style, content and composition *The Social Contract* is closer to his earlier essays in social and political theory.

In *Émile* Rousseau argues that a child enters the 'moral order' first through personal encounters with others mediated by COMPASSION or by AMOUR-PROPRE. It is in virtue of relationships established through these sentiments that he first obtains and begins to use the idea of himself, and of others, as bearers of moral titles and responsibilities (*see* MORALITY). There is no suggestion here that it is only in and from the civil order that such ideas can be derived; indeed, he argues in *Émile* that we shall only understand the proper character that a just and legitimate civil order should take if we appreciate that it must incorporate and consolidate the moral relationships that have their origin and meaning in other, earlier, modes of human engagement. Although the assumption of the character of citizen effects many important changes in a person's self-understanding and modes of possible action, we should not suppose that it is only from having a place in the civil order that all such moral ideas and modes of action are derived.

231

Sources: *DI*, Pt 2
        E, Bks IV, V
        SC, Bks I, II

Further reading: Horowitz, ch. 5 (27); Masters, chs 4, 7 (69); Melzer (136); Shklar,
        chs 1, 5 (36)

state of nature   Most political philosophers describe a pre-civil (and
sometimes pre-social) condition of man which they call a 'state of nature'.
Of the many reasons for having recourse to such an idea, one is the desire
to present civil and political arrangements as having a purpose, particularly that of remedying drawbacks or limitations which people suffered in
this state of nature. Another is the desire to argue that political arrangements must meet certain conditions – for example, that of respecting and
protecting certain rights which individuals (supposedly) enjoyed in the
state of nature. There is no consensus of opinion among political philosophers about what that state was like, about what characteristics people
in it possessed, nor about what the circumstances of life in that state might
have been. They do not even agree as to whether such a state ever existed,
or whether appeal to the idea of it is a mere explanatory or interpretative
device.

In making significant use of the idea of a state of nature, especially in
the Discourse on the Origin of Inequality, Rousseau firmly dissents
from the views of certain of his predecessors, particularly Hobbes, about
the character of that state. Indeed, he complains that

> [while] philosophers . . . have all felt the necessity of going back to a state of
> nature . . . not one of them has got there . . . Every one of them, in short,
> constantly dwelling on wants, avidity, oppression, desires, and pride, has
> transferred to the state of nature ideas which were acquired in society; so
> that, in speaking of the savage, they described the social man. (*DI*, 45; *OC*
> III, 132)

What, then, were Rousseau's views?

First, he considers the state of nature to be a wholly pre-social condition
of man, reflected not only in the character of his environment but also,
most significantly, in the characteristics of man himself (*see* NOBLE SAV-
AGE). Such an environment comprises untamed nature, on which humans
are largely dependent for food, shelter and safety. Rousseau suggests that
those who find their way to, or are born into, harsh northern climes are
caused more rapidly to abandon the state of nature than those who live
where the climate is mild and food naturally plentiful. It is the hardships
of life that force people to join with others in some form of society or

shared life, in order to provide the material necessities for survival (*see* ORIGIN OF LANGUAGES).

Man in the state of nature is motivated by AMOUR DE SOI, but is also susceptible to pity (*see* COMPASSION). He has the capacity for PERFECTIBIL-ITY and for the exercise of free will (*see* FREEDOM) – but these may remain undeveloped and unexercised unless environmental changes require him to employ them for self-advantage. (Rousseau sometimes suggests that when these last two are in evidence, then man is already moving away from his primitive, natural state.) Being a stranger to all social inter-course, man in his natural state is devoid of all those concerns, attitudes and passions that depend on his recognizing the existence of others and on standing in some relationship to them (with the exception of pity, which is evoked just as much by the suffering of beasts as by that of humans). Man in the natural state is not aggressive and combative; rather, he is fearful and peaceable (*see* WAR). If there should be a dispute between two persons in the state of nature over, say, some item of food, then each will 'consider these acts of violence as mere natural occurrences, without the slightest emotion of insolence or despite, or any other feeling than the joy or grief of success or failure' (*DI* 66 n. 2; *OC* III, 219–20 n. 15).

Of the character of man in his natural state, the 'savage', Rousseau writes: 'His soul, which nothing disturbs, is wholly wrapped up in the feeling of its present existence, without any idea of the future, however near at hand; while his projects, as limited as his views, hardly extend to the close of day (*DI* 56; *OC* III, 144). He describes natural man as 'carrying [his] self, as it were, perpetually whole and entire about [him]' – rather as a snail carries its house (*DI*, 48; *OC* III, 136). And again:

> [Men in the state of nature] maintained no kind of intercourse with one another, and were consequently strangers to vanity, deference, esteem, and contempt; they had not the least idea of 'mine' and 'thine', and no true conception of justice; they looked upon every violence to which they were subjected, rather as an injury that might easily be repaired than as a crime that ought to be punished; and they never thought of taking revenge. (*DI* 69; *OC* III, 157)

Rousseau's depiction of man's natural condition and character, in its innocence, simplicity and peaceableness, exercises a powerful hold on many people's imagination. But what good reason has he for describing matters as he does? He does not hold that he is obliged to undertake historical or anthropological investigations to determine what evidence there might be for his contentions; apparently his views should be regarded as 'mere conditional and hypothetical reasonings, rather calculated to explain the nature of things, than to ascertain their actual origin' (*DI* 45; *OC* III, 133). But in his opinion, his is the best account of what we now find to be true about the characteristics of men in society. Since he makes no serious attempt to eliminate, or even to consider, alternative hypotheses, though, acceptance of his views must depend not on his account of the state of nature taken in isolation, but on the cogency and persuasiveness of his entire social theory.

Rousseau agrees that man in the state of nature, in his most 'pure' character, is hardly different from the beasts. Devoid of language, foresight, practical skills and application, he leads his life at the direction of impulse and with little conscious purpose. This image of man gives rise to the view that according to Rousseau, he either remains in this natural condition, innocent, free and happy but scarcely human; or else he acquires human characteristics, but leaves nature behind and becomes evil, enslaved and miserable. But, although there are traces of this view in the *Discourse on the Origin of Inequality*, it does not represent Rousseau's mature opinion. For although processes of socialization often do corrupt and pervert human beings even as they are acquiring their properly human capabilities and attributes, it is possible, in his view, for human development to keep faith with man's natural powers and dispositions even when his original circumstances are left behind (*see* NATURAL GOODNESS).

When Rousseau contrasts man's 'natural' and his 'civilized' states he is, in fact, contrasting those powers and dispositions of men that do not involve relations with others with those that do, thus showing how much in human beings depends on and derives from intercourse with others. Making this distinction is important for Rousseau, not least because he believes that once we can determine what in us derives from the character of our relations with others we can, in principle, change ourselves by changing the nature of our relations with others, at all levels – individual, social and civil. And making this distinction in no way implies that man's social relations are not part of, and proper to, his nature, just as much as are those of his powers and dispositions which conduce to his survival and well-being as if he were a wholly independent, separate, and self-contained creature.

Sources: *DI*
        E, Bks I, II

Further reading: Aldridge (77); Dent, ch. 3 (24); de Jouvenel (83); Lovejoy (92); Masters, ch. 3 (69); Plattner (99)

subject Most of what is significant in Rousseau's understanding of what it is to be a subject is contained in his discussions concerning the CITIZEN and the SOVEREIGN BODY. He precisely defines the term when in Bk I, ch. 6, of *The Social Contract* he writes about that 'corporate and collective body' that is formed by the act of association: 'Those who are associated in it take collectively the name of *people*, and severally are called *citizens*, as sharing in the sovereign authority, and *subjects*, as being under the laws of the State' (*SC* I, ch. 6, 175; *OC* III, 362).

Thus, the notions of subject and citizen are strictly complementary: a subject is merely a citizen in his character (or role) of one living under the law, which, in his character of citizen, he has taken part in authorizing. To be a subject, in Rousseau's sense, is to be bound by a law of which one is indirectly also the author.

It follows, then, that the civil position of many people who are subjected to law in actual states should not be described in terms of their being subjects. For, in most cases, both in Rousseau's time and now, these laws have not been authorized by the people acting as citizens. Rather, the people are under the control of monarchic, aristocratic or some other rule which does not express the GENERAL WILL. They are not so much subjects of, as subjugated by, LAW, in its character as dominant force, not as legitimate authority.

In departing from ordinary usage and giving the term 'subject' this specific meaning, Rousseau has identified a principal idea of his political theory.

Sources: *DI*, Pt 2
            SC, Bk I

Further reading: Gildin (123); Jimack (168); Mason (134); Masters, chs 2, 6 (69); Shklar, chs 1, 5 (36)

T

theatre [26] Rousseau's plays are of limited interest. The only one to receive public performance was *Narcissus* (or *L'Amant de Lui-Même* ('The Lover of Himself')), staged by the Comédie Française in December 1752 on the strength of the recent success of *Le Devin du Village* (*see* MUSICAL COMPOSITION).

It was with *Narcissus* (probably written *c*. 1732) and his *Project for a New Musical Notation* (*see* MUSIC: WRITINGS ON) that Rousseau had set off for Paris in 1742, hoping to make a name. The play, which he himself thought mediocre, was taken off after only two or three performances. For its publication in 1753 he wrote an extensive preface, which concerns not so much the content of the play itself but the controversy surrounding the recent publication of his DISCOURSE ON THE SCIENCES AND THE ARTS. His only other play to be performed at all, though privately, was *L'Engagement Téméraire* ('The Rash Promise'), which he wrote for the Dupin family for performance at their summer home at Chenonceaux in 1747. It was also staged once or twice by Mme d'Épinay and her circle, and in one performance Rousseau himself played, ineptly, the part of the valet Carlin. His other plays, *Arlequin Amoureux Malgré Lui* ('Harlequin in Love Despite Himself') (unfinished), *Les Prisonniers de Guerre* ('The Prisoners of War') and *La Mort de Lucrèce* ('The Death of Lucretius'), all date from the 1740s and 1750s, and have never been performed. They are of interest only as the incidental writings of a famous philosopher.

The plot of *Narcissus* concerns the hero, Valère, who is engaged to Angélique, falling in love with a person depicted in a portrait. He does not realize that he is being shown a picture of himself, disguised as a woman. Instantly, he wishes to break off his engagement to Angélique. In the subplot his sister Lucinde, who is engaged to Angélique's brother Léandre, is smitten with someone she knows as Cléonte, and no longer wishes to marry Léandre. But Léandre and Cléonte are one and the same person. Valère and Lucinde's gruff father, Lisimon, has no time for these youthful frivolities. In the end, all comes out happily. Vanity, self-absorption and the fickleness of lovers are satirized in a simple vein. Some

236

critics have claimed to see in the play undertones of sexual deviation – Valère (Rousseau) finding sexual satisfaction in self-union – as well as veiled allusions to masturbation.

In the preface to *Narcissus* Rousseau attacks those who say that he does not seriously mean all the things that he said against the arts and sciences in his *First Discourse*. His own literary works cannot, he says, be set against him, for he did not always think as he now does, and his dramatic and musical efforts are merely the amusements of his youth. In any event, he has never argued that arts and letters are thoroughly vicious. His point was that a taste for them arises from idleness, and that they encourage a craving for fashionable distinction, diverting people from their primary human duties. In the position we are now in, virtue has already been lost. Letters and the arts do now exist to distract people from committing worse evils, for they had better be scoundrels than bandits. His own involvement with music and theatre is, in any case, shallow. When his play failed, he was not shamed and devastated, for he has never been mad to succeed. His soul is not, therefore, corrupted by the desire for invidious supremacy; he does not want to do others down, to have the better of them. He may write poems and music for amusement, and those works may alleviate a little the incurable illness of society, but he has no personal investment in them. Whether what Rousseau says about himself here is the total truth is debatable.

L'Engagement Téméraire, written in rhyming couplets, is another slight piece concerning the tangled affairs of the heart (the plot is modelled on several plays by Marivaux). The hero, Dorante, promises his beloved, the widow Isabelle, that he will refrain from making any more protests of love, a promise heedlessly given and received in the same vein. Much of the plot is borne by two comic servants, Carlin, Dorante's valet, and Lisette, Isabelle's maid. The subplot concerns the love of Dorante's friend Valère for Isabelle's cousin Éliante. The action depends on the exchange of false letters which purport to disclose that each has fallen in love with someone else. After much toing and froing, all is resolved.

The plot of *Les Prisonniers de Guerre*, a one-act comedy written in 1743, concerns a French officer, another Dorante, held prisoner by the Hungarians. Dorante has fallen in love with Sophie, the daughter of a Hungarian gentleman, Goterniz, who has a violent prejudice against the French. She is betrothed to Maker, the gross old man who is Dorante's jailer. Dorante's freedom is procured in exchange for Frederick, Sophie's brother, who has been held captive by the French. Frederick overcomes his father's hostility to the French, and ensures that Dorante and Sophie are united.

Arlequin Amoureux Malgré Lui is an unfinished fragment of a comedy, probably written at Chenonceaux in 1746 or 1747. *La Mort de Lucrèce* is the unfinished tragedy that Rousseau wrote during his stay at Geneva in 1754 when he went there to reclaim his citizenship. Inspired, no doubt, by his sense of mission, he felt he must tackle a severe subject with austere political oratory.

Rousseau deals with the moral and social issues raised, in his view, by the establishment of theatres and by playgoing in his LETTER TO D'ALEMBERT ON THE THEATRE.

Further reading: Cranston, vol. I, chs 11–14 (17); Ellrich (206); Rex (209)

V

vanity Vanity, conceit grounded in the idea of oneself as better than others, is a sentiment most closely associated in Rousseau's discussions with (excessive) AMOUR-PROPRE. Indeed, many critics of Rousseau have said that 'vanity' is the closest English equivalent to *amour-propre*. But this is both to mistake the significance of *amour-propre*, taking what are its distorted or excessive manifestations for the thing itself, and to be unfaithful to Rousseau, who always uses the term *vanité* as a distinct notion.

The vainglorious desire to measure oneself in relation to others and to congratulate oneself for one's precedence over them is, in his view, one of the most pervasive of human desires in society, for all that it is deeply hurtful to both the perpetrator and the recipient of the attitude. Vanity not only shapes social processes and institutions, inducing people to seek grounds for invidious distinction just for the sake of being able to think that they have got the better of others, but it also moulds and colours people's other, most intimate, concerns.

Thus Rousseau argues that rare and refined foods are seldom chosen with a view only, or even mainly, to gustatory pleasure, but rather with the idea uppermost in one's mind that others are not able to enjoy them, and that it is the mark of wealth or connoisseur status that one can (*see* LUXURY). Similarly, sexual conquest is seldom the outcome of sexual ardour, but, rather, of the wish to consider oneself as having enjoyed a pleasure denied to others, which will make one an object of envy or admiration (*see* SEX).

Rousseau is not saying that we should not think well of ourselves, take pleasure in our excellences; nor that these excellences will not sometimes involve doing better than others (*see* COMPARISON). Nor, again, does he say we should pay no regard to what others think of us. There is every difference between superior achievement in a meritorious activity, and the invention of differences between persons for the sake of being able to be contemptuous towards and dismissive of those who lack the distinguishing marks. (For all their moral and human distinctness, though, these two attitudes tend to merge in actual life.) The essential point is made clear in

239

this passage from *Émile*:

> Although [Émile's] desire to please does not leave him absolutely indifferent to the opinion of others, he will concern himself with their opinion only insofar as it relates immediately to his person, and he will not worry about arbitrary evaluations whose only law is fashion or prejudice. He will have the pride to want to do everything he does well, even to do it better than another. He will want to be the swiftest at running . . . the most competent at working . . . But he will hardly seek advantages which are not clear in themselves and which need to be established by another's judgement, such as being more intelligent than someone else, talking better . . . still less will he seek those advantages which are not at all connected with one's person, such as being of nobler birth, being esteemed richer . . . or making an impression by pomp.
>
> . . . he will be quite gratified to be approved in everything connected with good character. He will not precisely say to himself, 'I rejoice because they approve of me', but rather, 'I rejoice because they approve of what I have done that is good.' (*E* IV, 339; *OC* IV, 670)

The hurt that a vain person inflicts on those around him is plain enough. More subtle is Rousseau's account of the hurt he suffers in himself, which is principally of two kinds. Since his good opinion of himself, his idea of himself as worthy of acknowledgement, is dependent upon his ability to see himself as superior to others, he is particularly vulnerable to any indifference or contempt directed towards him, having no independent basis for the preservation of his self-respect and sense of self-worth in the face of public humiliation. In addition, should those others change their preferences, he is rendered nothing. Not least, a vain person may find that he is outstripped in the very respects that he thought he excelled in, or that he lacks other fashionable attributes that now command more attention. The vainglorious person 'seems to receive the consciousness of his own existence merely from the judgement of others concerning him' (*DI* 104; *OC* III, 193), and, as such, he is an alienated and dispossessed being (*see* ALIENATION).

Sources: *DI*, Pt 2
             E, Bks IV, V

Further reading: Plamenatz (70); Shklar, chs 3, 4 (36)

virtue   Rousseau makes a distinction between the possession of virtue and the possession of amiable or good feeling (see NATURAL GOODNESS). Virtue, in his view, requires will and commitment to principle over and above following the promptings of inclination, however benevolent such inclination may be. Someone who is guided by his feelings alone will easily be deflected from his purpose if other concerns intervene; or he will abandon their object if it ceases to appeal to those feelings. The same will not be true of a virtuous person. He will have a resolute commitment to securing good, which will make him hold fast to his purpose even when difficulties or contrary inclinations arise. This passage from *Émile* illustrates Rousseau's ideas here:

> My child, there is no happiness without courage nor virtue without struggle. The word *virtue* comes from *strength*. Strength is the foundation of all virtue. Virtue belongs only to a being that is weak by nature and strong by will. It is in this that the merit of the just man consists; and although we call God good, we do not call Him virtuous, because it requires no effort for Him to do good ... I have made you good rather than virtuous. But he who is only good remains so only as long as he takes pleasure in being so. Goodness is broken and perishes under the impact of the human passions. The man who is only good is good only for himself.
>
> Who, then, is the virtuous man? It is he who knows how to conquer his affections; for then he follows his reason and his conscience, he does his duty; he keeps himself in order, and nothing can make him deviate from it. (*E* V, 444; *OC* IV, 817–18)

It is with this definition in mind that Rousseau often says of himself that, being a creature of inclination governed by overactive sensibility, he is devoid of virtue (see, for example, *Rousseau Judge of Jean-Jacques*, second Dialogue). On the same basis he says that he has no vices, not having the determination to carry through an evil deed.

He assigns to the possession and exercise of virtue an important place in the maintenance of a good and just society. He is adamant that good laws cannot be enacted, nor will they be well administered or obeyed, unless the citizens are already quite strongly disposed to act in the ways prescribed and to cherish the objectives which the laws are intended to achieve. Where law does not build on established virtues, it will be evaded or abused. This is a theme that looms large in, for example, his *Letter to d'Alembert on the Theatre* and in the (*Discourse on*) *Political Economy*. Attention not merely to the behaviour of citizens, but also to the cultivation of their loyalties and dispositions, must then be a central concern of any legislator or statesman. Systems of education that are intended to develop the attachments by which alone the integrity and well-being of a state can be sustained must be of paramount significance in any satisfactory state (*see* CONSIDERATIONS ON THE GOVERNMENT OF POLAND).

Rousseau is inclined to say that individual virtue will 'take the place of positive law' (compare *E* V, 473; *OC*, IV, 857). This claim, together with his ideas about public education in virtue, have been criticized. It is argued, first, that he arrogates to himself (or to those who claim perfected virtue) a standing above the law, the right to judge the fitness of what is required of him by law, rather than accepting the common duty of obedience to law; and, second, that for a state to inculcate virtue in its citizens is for it to play an altogether too invasive and controlling role in directing human lives, whereas it should more properly confine itself primarily to regulating harmful behaviour. Neither of these criticisms appears just. It is precisely because, for Rousseau, each citizen plays a crucial role in devising sovereign legislation that he requires that loyalty, justice and commitment to the common good be the paramount virtues of each citizen. For, without these, legislation will embody only factional interests and will be potentially hurtful to many. It is not that the virtuous man stands above the law, but that good law can only come from those who have strong and clear moral commitments. To such persons, positive law is not so much the cause of their good behaviour as a further expression of the attitudes and responsibilities that generate it.

It is also a mistake to suppose that virtues such as commitment to justice and to the common good spring from nowhere: they need to be inculcated and cultivated. Laws which require abstention from behaviour hurtful to others can only secure certain obedience if respect for others and care for their good are widespread dispositions. Any state, however minimal the demands that it places on its citizens, sows the seeds of its own destruction if it does nothing to develop the attitudes necessary to maintain its basic principles. The neglect of public education in virtue is only admissible where it is developed and sustained by other agencies in the community, such as the family. Rousseau thought that this did not often happen – and we have little reason to disagree with him with respect to our own society, either.

Sources: DPE
E, Bks IV, V

Further reading: Blum (21); Grimsley (187); Hamilton (86); Masters, chs 1, 2, 6 (69); Shklar, ch. 2 (36)

Virtue of Heroes, The (1751) (*Discours sur cette question: Quelle est la vertu la plus nécessaire au héros?*) In 1751 the Corsican Academy set a prize essay title: What virtue is most necessary to heroes? Rousseau began to write in response, but left the work uncompleted. When, in 1768, it was illicitly published, Rousseau, annoyed, attempted to persuade his publisher Marc-Michel Rey to produce an authorized version. Nothing came of this, however, and the fragment did not appear officially until 1782, in the complete edition of his works prepared by P. Moultou and P. A. Du Peyrou. Rousseau himself says, in a short preface to it, that it is a very poor piece of writing.

He begins by contrasting the qualities of sages and heroes, taking Diogenes and Alexander as examples. Sages, he says, purport to show people the way to happiness; but it requires the talents of heroes to enable people to live well. Heroes are not always virtuous. Their excellence lies in inspiring the people, arousing their admiration and thus uniting them. Heroism requires charisma: to be just, temperate and equitable is not essential, but to manifest a personal glory and force is. It is this powerful energy of soul that is the true foundation of heroism, and that alone can lend itself to great deeds.

Some have seen in Rousseau's failure to complete this work his recognition that the admiration for heroic virtue expressed in it was incompatible with his new role of defender of the 'quiet' civic virtues of justice, equity and peaceableness as the prerequisites for a secure and prosperous society; and it is undeniable that there is real incompatibility here. On the other hand, he did not then abandon the issue of the attributes that make a person fit to be a leader of men, able to unite them in common cause. The role he assigns to the LEGISLATOR, an essential figure with regard to the creation of a state, clearly requires extraordinary personal qualities, although he would certainly not expect such a person to be cruel and brutal, actively vicious, doing whatever might be needed to form 'a people'.

Further reading: Cameron (216)

W

war Rousseau never wrote systematically on war. However, from 1756 onwards he drafted numerous notes on such themes as the character of war and the relations between individuals in wars, particularly after reading the *Project for Perpetual Peace* by the Abbé de Saint-Pierre (*see* ÉCRITS SUR L'ABBÉ DE SAINT-PIERRE). None of these notes was published in his lifetime, though some have survived, including a substantial fragment normally known as *L'État de Guerre* ('The State of War'; precise date unkown; *OC* III, 601–12); another brief discussion, now entitled *Guerre et État de Guerre* ('War and the State of War'; *OC* III, 1899–1904, probably originating from 1757; and a number of jottings (*OC* III, 613–16). There are also some remarks on these topics in *The Social Contract* (for instance, *SC* I, ch. 4, 171; *OC* III, 356–7) and elsewhere. It seems likely that the two named fragments belong together.

Rousseau considers, first, whether the STATE OF NATURE should be regarded as a state of war, as it was so famously held to be by Hobbes (*Leviathan*, Part I, ch. 13). Rousseau denies this, on two grounds. First, he maintains that man is naturally peaceable and fearful; at the slightest danger, he is apt to flee, not to stand and fight. He contends that Hobbes has 'transferred to the state of nature ideas which were acquired in society; so that, in speaking of the savage, [he] described the social man' (*see DI* 45; *OC* III, 132). But, even if it is true that men naturally take up arms against danger, against other men, Rousseau denies that this amounts to war between them. Even in 'civilized' society, where men do consistently attack and harm each other, this does not signify a state of war. For war is not a condition of conflict between individuals, but an encounter in which persons as representatives of states are in struggle.

Rousseau is not making an empty verbal point here. Rather, he is beginning a profound analysis of the footing on which people engage with each other when fighting in wars: 'War . . . is a relation, not between man and man, but between State and State, and individuals are enemies only accidentally, not as men, nor even as citizens, but as soldiers; not as members of their country, but as its defenders' (*SC* I, ch. 4, 171; *OC* III, 357). Those who encounter each other in battle are those who have 'combat status' (the soldiery), and such status neither swallows up all aspects of their humanity nor extends to all members of the state that they represent. As soon as a soldier lays down his arms or is disarmed, he ceases to be a threat and resumes his rights to be unmolested as no longer posing a danger. Again, those who do not stand as defenders of their state, those with no intent to resolve such disputes as there may be with the opposing state by means of arms – for instance, children – do not have combat status and therefore may not properly be regarded as having forfeited any of their rights to just and humane treatment.

Rousseau is arguing here very much in the tradition of reasoning about 'the just war', although he does not allude to this. Rather, he is primarily concerned to oppose the doctrines of Grotius, who supposed, apparently, that there were no limits to the just titles of the victor in any conflict with the vanquished. Rousseau's ideas may be considered as both morally sound and humane.

War itself, he thinks, will remain a more or less inevitable aspect of human experience so long as conquest and superior power can contribute to the aggrandizement of princes – which will continue to be so until there is a proper federation of states where each is so dependent on the others that it could not be to the advantage of any to attempt to subdue or conquer another. In parallel with his argument in *The Social Contract* regarding the position of individuals under law, Rousseau argues that in such a confederation princes would be exchanging the 'dangerous power' of being able to seize by force – but also, of course, the liability of being deprived by force – for real right to jurisdiction and control, and so would gain from such a restructuring of the basis of their sovereign power in relation to other states.

See also SLAVERY.

Sources: DI
        L'État de Guerre
        Guerre et État de Guerre
        SC, Bk I

Further reading: Carter (219); Hinsley (221); Hoffman (222); Hoffman (223); Perkins (226); Roosevelt (228); Roosevelt (229); Waltz (231)

will *See* CORPORATE WILL; FREEDOM; GENERAL WILL; PARTICULAR WILL; WILL OF ALL.

will of all

> There is often a great deal of difference between the will of all and the general will; the latter considers only the common interest, while the former takes private interest into account, and is no more than a sum of particular wills: but take away from these same wills the pluses and minuses that cancel one another, and the general will remains as the sum of the differences. (*SC* II, ch. 3, 185; *OC* III, 371)

Few other passages in Rousseau, or in any works of political theory, have aroused as much perplexity and provoked as much comment as this one.

If sense is to be made of Rousseau's thought it is necessary, first, to understand what he means by the GENERAL WILL and by a PARTICULAR WILL; then, to see how, out of the 'pluses and minuses' of particular wills, the general will might emerge.

Rousseau's meaning can be construed as follows. A person's 'particular will' comprises what he wants for himself alone, giving no weight or consideration to the desires or interests of others, except to the extent to which he can make use of these to advance his own interest as an individual, self-concerned person. Suppose that he envisages as his particular interests, first, the enjoyment of security and material comfort obtained with a minimal expenditure of effort, and, second, a command of others such that their labour can be directed to serve his own personal good. (It should not be supposed that a person's particular will concerns only his good in isolation: he can bring his particular will to bear on social relations with others, aiming to 'milk' them for his own private benefit (see, for instance, *SC* I, ch. 7, 177; *OC* III, 363).)

Others will have similar objectives. Therefore, since not everyone can enjoy command of others, and since if material goods are not readily available an effort to produce or obtain them must be made, it is clear that each individual's wants are not realizable along with everyone else's. What does Rousseau mean by saying that we must then 'take away' from these particular wills 'the pluses and minuses that cancel one another'? A plus for me is my enjoying material plenty with minimal labour, but this is cancelled out by the fact that others also want this for themselves, and if no one is prepared to work no plenty will be available. Another plus for me would be having command of others; but the minus is that others want to command also, not to be commanded. Does anything remain? What remains are residues, in each of our schemes of private interest, that are compossibly achievable. These residues comprise projects for the benefit of each that can be realized while like projects are being pursued by others. If we sum these residues we shall have a set of objectives that will

246

be in the interest of each person alike. Advancing such objectives may, then, be said to be a good in common to all and to coincide, at least approximately, with the objective of the general will, which is 'the common interest'.

This explanation leaves much unexplained. In particular, it does not explain why any one individual should be willing to set aside those elements in his private interest that conflict with the private interests of others while being willing to be content with and to work for those goods that advantage each and all in similar measure. He may, for instance, be prepared to fight others for superior advantage over them, or to trick or deceive them for the sake of private benefit. What is completely missing from this putative explanation of the coincidence of the 'sum of particular wills' and the general will is any account of common loyalty and shared destiny – those sentiments that make it seem desirable to each individual to advance those projects that are to the like advantage of all those with whom he lives in one association. Rousseau sees the cultivation and maintenance of such sentiments as crucial, if a just, equitable and prosperous civil society is to exist. Although, by some abstract calculation, we may work out the objective of the general will from a study of all individuals' particular wills, it would be absurd to think that there was any real equivalence between them.

This conclusion should not surprise. Rousseau does not expand on the comment (quoted above) concerning the will of all. He goes on to talk about the importance of checking the influence of 'partial associations' in the formation of law and rule in the state, insisting that if there are to be 'partial societies' (which it would be better that there should not be) 'it is best to have as many as possible and to prevent them from being unequal' (*SC* II, ch. 3, 185; *OC* III, 371) (*see* CORPORATE WILL). These remarks help to confirm the present interpretation of Rousseau's meaning regarding the will of all. This interpretation represents, at best, an idealized case where each individual's interest is evenly balanced against every other's, and what is extracted as the residue is some common policy that will be of like advantage to everyone. Where unequal 'partial societies' grow up, this 'cancellation' of differences will not occur, and a rule for all will be arrived at which really only expresses the good of a few.

Kant discusses this matter in his essay, *Perpetual Peace*, stating that a 'good organization for the state' may be achieved if it is arranged so that men's 'self-seeking energies are opposed to one another, each thereby neutralizing or eliminating the destructive effects of the rest . . . And as far as reason is concerned, the result is the same as if man's selfish tendencies were non-existent, so that man, even if he is not morally good in himself, is nevertheless compelled to be a good citizen.' In this, as so often, Kant is the best interpreter of Rousseau.

Source: SC, Bks I, II

Further reading: Allen (109); Barry (112); Dent, ch. 5 (24); Gildin (123); Masters, ch. 7 (169); Melzer (137); Rosenfeld (145); Shklar, ch. 5 (36)

women   Rousseau discusses the nature, education, habits and position of women most extensively in ÉMILE where, under the heading of 'Sophie, or the Woman', he introduces these issues as a prelude to Émile's falling in love and forming an affectionate, sexual and marital union with his betrothed, Sophie (*E* V, 357ff.; *OC* IV, 692ff.).

'In everything not connected with sex, woman is man. She has the same organs, the same needs, the same faculties.' However, the sexual differences of men and women 'have a moral influence'. Man's merit lies in his power; he ought to be active and strong. Women, made 'specially to please man', should be passive and weak. Rousseau appears to think that these differences stem from differences between male and female sexual desire, males being easily roused and ardent while it is the role of the female merely to resist or accommodate this desire.

It is in regard not only to the character of sexual desire, but also to the consequences of sexual intercourse, that 'the physical leads us unawares to the moral'. If a man is to care for his children, Rousseau holds, he must be assured that they are his. 'It is important, then, not only that a woman be faithful, but that she be judged to be faithful by her husband, by those near her, by everyone.' Thus, what is thought of a woman is no less important to her than what she actually is: 'Opinion is the grave of virtue among men and its throne among women.' The education proper to woman should, Rousseau thinks, take these points into account, and so cannot be the same as the education appropriate to man. Women, he thinks, depend more on men than men on women. From men women derive not only the satisfaction of desire and affection, but their station in life.

Since what is thought of them is so central to women's situation, their education must be appropriate to that. A taste for embellishment is natural in girls, and in all things it is a pleasing grace of manner and execution that should be striven for. Not that Rousseau wishes to encourage indulgence in artificial finery and ostentation; such affectations derive from 'vanity of rank', and have nothing to do with true refinement of one's person. Despite this emphasis on pleasing, he is insistent that women have, and should exercise, a power of independent moral judgement, and that they are not obliged to accept men's notions of the just and beautiful:

Let us not bring so low the sex that governs us and honours us when we have not abased it. A rule prior to opinion exists for the whole of the human species . . . This rule judges prejudice itself, and only insofar as the esteem of men accords with it ought this esteem to be authoritative for us . . . As soon as she depends on both her own conscience and the opinions of others, she has to learn to compare these two rules, to reconcile them . . . She becomes the judge of her judges; she decides when she ought to subject herself to them and when she ought to take exception to them . . . None of this can be done well without cultivating her mind and reason. (*E* V, 382–3; *OC* IV, 730–1)

Women's and men's different moral constitutions and roles complement each other, and each benefits from this:

The social relationship of the sexes is an admirable thing. This partnership produces a moral person of which the woman is the eye and the man is the arm . . . in the harmony which reigns between them, everything tends to the common end; they do not know who contributes more. Each follows the promptings of the other; each obeys, and both are masters. (E V, 377; *OC* IV, 720)

Even allowing for the very different customs and expectations of his time (not that these limited his imagination in other areas of his work), Rousseau assigns to women a peculiarly derivative and subservient existence in relation to men. Even when he depicts women as having the power to judge and as possessing independent moral understanding, they still appear to be dependent on men's permission rather than acting in their own indisputable right. It is hardly without warrant that Rousseau has become a target for much current feminist criticism. On the other hand, as the intimacy and affection between Émile and Sophie develops, it is Sophie who is represented as the more perceptive, morally and emotionally more stable person from whom Émile has something to learn. It is he who falls into patterns of feeling which, if unchecked, would destroy their relationship, and Sophie who is depicted not only as free from these perverse dispositions but as providing a possible corrective.

Source: *E*, Bk V

Further reading: Canovan (217); Graham (220); Lloyd (274); Okin (225); Rapaport (227); Wexler (232)

Bibliography

The Bibliography is divided into two principal parts: Part I, Works by Rousseau; and Part II, Works on Rousseau.

Each item (book, chapter, article) is assigned a round-bracketed number which cross-refers to the citation given in the *Further reading* at the end of each entry in the Dictionary. The secondary literature on Rousseau is vast. It would be impracticable to cite even a quarter of possibly relevant items, but I hope that I have made a useful selection.

Annales: *Annales de la Société Jean-Jacques Rousseau*
SVEC: *Studies in Voltaire and the Eighteenth Century*

USING THE BIBLIOGRAPHY

Part I: Works by Rousseau

These are referred to either as entry heads (in the case of major works), or in the body of the entries. Where they occur as entry heads, the number in square brackets indicates where in the list of individual works by Rousseau (p. 254) information about any given major work is to be found.

If the work occurs in the body of an entry, it is either specified by its full title or (if it is a major work) by an abbreviation – for instance, *DI* (see list of abbreviations, p. 26). Reference to the entry head for that work gives the square-bracketed number used in the list of individual works, or the Index may be consulted. All references to particular passages, and quotations, are followed by book, chapter and page numbers (as appropriate) in the translation used, followed by the volume and page numbers in the

Oeuvres Complètes, ed. B. Gagnebin and M. Raymond (Bibliothèque de la Pléiade, 1959–), which has become standard. Since this edition is not yet complete, reference to it has not been possible in every case, so alternative editions are occasionally cited.

Example: *DI* 57; *OC* III, 169 signifies *A Discourse on the Origin of Inequality*, p. 57 in the translation used here (by G. D. H. Cole, revised by J. H. Brumfitt and J. C. Hall); *Oeuvres Complètes*, vol. III, p. 169. The *Discourse on Inequality* is item [2] in the list of individual works by Rousseau.

Part II: Works on Rousseau

The *Further reading* at the end of each entry gives for each work mentioned the author's name followed by a round-bracketed number, which is the number that precedes that work as listed here. I have attempted to group these secondary works roughly according to the topics that they concern, so that if a spread of material on a particular topic is required then this may be open to survey. But these groupings are at best only a guide.

In citing those secondary works that cover a large range of Rousseau's ideas, I have, for reasons of economy, been quite selective. I have most frequently referred to Charvet (23), Horowitz (27), Masters (69), Shklar (36), and to my own Dent (24). Clearly, other works with a general compass could equally well be consulted. Such works are listed in sections 2 (19)–(38) and 3 (55)–(76). Many of the works listed in section 1 also have a general compass.

PART I: WORKS BY ROUSSEAU

PRIMARY TEXTS

1   TRANSLATIONS CITED IN THE TEXT

(For details of French-language editions and alternative translations of these works, see below, pp. 254–9.)

A Discourse on the Sciences and the Arts (*DSA*) [1]
    In *The Social Contract and Discourses*, Jean-Jacques Rousseau, trans. and ed. G. D. H. Cole, rev. and augmented J. H. Brumfitt and J. C. Hall (London: Dent, 1973)

A Discourse on the Origin of Inequality (*DI*) [2]
    In *The Social Contract and Discourses*, Jean-Jacques Rousseau, trans. and ed. G. D. H. Cole

(A Discourse on) Political Economy (DPE) [3]
In *The Social Contract and Discourses*, Jean-Jacques Rousseau, trans. and ed. G. D. H. Cole

Émile, or On Education (E) [11]
Trans., with intro. and notes, Allan Bloom (New York: Basic Books, 1979)

The Social Contract (SC) [14]
In *The Social Contract and Discourses*, Jean-Jacques Rousseau, trans. and ed. G. D. H. Cole

Project for a Constitution for Corsica (PCC) [16]
In *Political Writings*, Jean-Jacques Rousseau, trans. and ed. F. Watkins (Edinburgh: Nelson, 1953)

The Confessions (C) [18]
Trans., with intro., J. M. Cohen (Harmondsworth: Penguin Books, 1954)

Considerations on the Government of Poland (GP) [19]
In *Political Writings*, Jean-Jacques Rousseau, trans. and ed. F. Watkins

Rousseau Judge of Jean-Jacques: Dialogues (RJJ) [20]
In *The Collected Writings of Rousseau*, trans. J. R. Bush, C. Kelly and R. D. Masters, ed. R. D. Masters and C. Kelly (Hanover, New Hampshire: University Press of New England for Dartmouth College, 1990), vol. I

The Reveries of the Solitary Walker (RSW) [21]
Trans., with intro., P. France (Harmondsworth: Penguin Books, 1979)

Where no translation has been specified, I have used my own. I have also sometimes used, and indicated my use of, *A Discourse on (the Origin of) Inequality*, trans. and ed. M. Cranston (Harmondsworth: Penguin Books, 1984) which has all of Rousseau's notes to the *Discourse*.

2 COMPLETE EDITIONS IN FRENCH

The edition referred to throughout this book is:

Jean-Jacques Rousseau: Oeuvres Complètes, ed. B. Gagnebin and M. Raymond, (Paris: Gallimard, Bibliothèque de la Pléiade, 1959 –) 4 vols to date
This edition has established itself as standard for modern use. Volume V, to contain Rousseau's *Essai sur l'Origine des Langues*, his *Lettre à M. d'Alembert sur les Spectacles* and other works principally concerned with music, has yet to appear.

Other collected editions of importance include:

Collection Complète des Oeuvres de Jean-Jacques Rousseau, ed. P. Moultou and P.A. Du Peyrou, 17 vols (Geneva: Société Typographique de Genève, 1782–9)
Oeuvres Complètes de Jean-Jacques Rousseau, 13 vols (Paris: Hachette, 1905)

Oeuvres et Correspondance Inédites de Jean-Jacques Rousseau, ed. G. Streckeisen-Moultou (Paris: Michel Levy, 1861)

Oeuvres Complètes, ed. M. Launay, 3 vols (Paris: Éditions du Seuil, 1967–71)

3 SELECTIONS IN FRENCH

The Political Writings of Jean-Jacques Rousseau, ed. C. E. Vaughan, 2 vols (Cambridge University Press, 1915), contains all Rousseau's major political writings, with allied material from letters and other sources, and substantial introductions by the editor.

Rousseau: Religious Writings, ed. Ronald Grimsley (Oxford: Clarendon Press, 1970), collects Rousseau's writings on religious themes, with editor's introductions.

4 SELECTIONS IN ENGLISH

The Social Contract and Discourses, trans. and ed. G. D. H. Cole, rev. and augmented J. H. Brumfitt and J. C. Hall (London: Dent, 1973).

The Indispensable Rousseau, ed. John Hope Mason (London: Quartet Books, 1979), contains a brief selection from the total range of Rousseau's writings.

There is no comprehensive English translation of Rousseau's total output. The most far-reaching is in progress. Volume 1 of *The Collected Writings of Rousseau* has appeared: *Rousseau Judge of Jean-Jacques: Dialogues*, ed. R. D. Masters and C. Kelly (Hanover, New Hampshire: University Press of New England for Dartmouth College, 1990).

5 INDIVIDUAL WORKS

[1] *Discours qui a Remporté le Prix a l'Académie de Dijon en l'année 1750.* A Genève, chez Barrilot, novembre 1750

Normally known as *Un Discours sur les Sciences et les Arts*, or the *First Discourse*. Published in *OC* III. Translation used in this text: *The Social Contract and Discourses*, trans. and ed. G. D. H. Cole, J. H. Brumfitt and J. C. Hall (London, 1973).

Other translations include *First and Second Discourses*, ed. R. D. Masters (New York, 1964); *The First and Second Discourses together with the Replies to Critics*, ed. V. Gourevitch (New York, 1986). Another modern French edition: *Discours sur les Sciences et les Arts*, ed. G. R. Havens (New York, 1946).

[2] *Un Discours sur l'Origine et les Fondemens de l'Inégalité parmi les Hommes.* A Amsterdam, chez Marc-Michel Rey, 1755

Normally known as *Un Discours sur l'Origine de l'Inégalité*, or *Discours sur l'Inégalité*, or the *Second Discourse*. Published in *OC* III. Translation used in this text (except when otherwise specified): *The Social Contract and Discourses*, G. D. H. Cole, J. H. Brumfitt and J. C. Hall (London, 1973).

Other translations include *First and Second Discourses*, ed. R. D. Masters (New York, 1964); *The Social Contract and the Discourse on Inequality*, ed. L. G. Crocker (New York, 1967); *A Discourse on Inequality*, ed. M. Cranston (Harmondsworth, 1984); *The First and Second Discourses together with Replies to Critics*, ed. V. Gourevitch (New York, 1986).

[3]   *Discours sur l'Oeconomie Politique*. A Genève, chez Emanuel du Villard Fils, 1758

The first separate edition; first appeared as an article, 'De l'économie politique', in vol. V of the *Encyclopédie ou Dictionnaire Raisonné des Sciences, des Arts et des Métiers . . . par M. Diderot . . . et M. d'Alembert*, Paris, 1755. Published in *OC* III. Translation used in this text: *The Social Contract and Discourses*, G. D. H. Cole, J. H. Brumfitt and J. C. Hall (London, 1973).

Other translations include *The Social Contract*, ed. C. M. Sherover (New York, 1974); *On the Social Contract with Geneva Manuscript and Political Economy*, ed. R. D. Masters (New York, 1978).

[4]   The *Écrits sur l'Abbé de Saint-Pierre* covers two works (and allied material): *Extrait du Projet de Paix Perpétuelle* (Paris, 1761); and *La Polysynodie*, vol. XXIII of the *Oeuvres Complètes*, ed. P. Moultou and P. A. Du Peyrou (Geneva, 1782). (Rousseau's own *Jugement sur la Paix Perpétuelle* and *Jugement sur la Polysynodie* also first appeared in vol. XXIII of Moultou and Du Peyrou's *Oeuvres Complètes*.) Published in *OC* III. Parts of these works translated in *The Indispensable Rousseau*, John Hope Mason (London, 1979).

Originating with this material are also Rousseau's fragmentary works dealing with war, including *Que l'État de Guerre Naît de l'État Social*, and *Guerre et État de Guerre*; also published in *OC* III. No current translations of these works.

[5]   *Lettre de Jean-Jacques Rousseau à M. de Voltaire, 18 Août 1756*

First appeared in *Lettre sur l'État Présent des Sciences et des Moeurs*, ed. J. L. S. Formey (Berlin, 1759), an unauthorized publication. First authorized edition: *Lettre à Voltaire* (Paris: Duchesne, 1764). Published in *OC* IV.

Parts of this letter translated in *The Indispensable Rousseau*, John Hope Mason (London, 1979).

[6]   *Lettres Morales*

Letters 2, 3 and 4 first appeared as *Lettres sur la Vertu et le Bonheur*, ed. G. Streckeisen-Moultou, in *Oeuvres et Correspondance Inédites* (Paris, 1861). Letters 1, 5 and 6 first appeared as *Lettres Inédites de Jean-Jacques Rousseau à Madame d'Houdetot*, in

Verhandlung der neununddreissigsten Versammlung Deutscher Philologen . . ., ed. E. Rittei (Leipzig, 1888). Published in *OC* IV.

No current translations.

[7]   *Lettre à M. d'Alembert sur les Spectacles*

Full title of original edition: *Jean-Jacques Rousseau, Citoyen de Genève, à M. d'Alembert . . . sur son article Genève dans le VIIe volume de l'Encyclopédie et particulièrement sur le projet d'établir un Théâtre de Comédie en cette ville.* A Amsterdam, chez Marc-Michel Rey, 1758. Not yet included in *OC*. Translation used in this text: *Politics and the Arts: Rousseau's Letter to d'Alembert*, trans. and ed., with intro., Allan Bloom (Ithaca, NY, 1960).

Modern French editions: M. Fuchs (ed.) (Geneva and Lille, 1948); M. Launay (ed.) (Paris, 1967).

[8]   *Essai sur l'Origine des Langues*

First published in a collection of miscellaneous works by Rousseau concerned with music; *Traités sur la Musique* (Geneva, 1781). Not yet included in *OC*. English translations include *On the Origin of Languages*, ed. J. H. Moran and A. Gode (New York, 1966); *The First and Second Discourses . . . and The Essay on the Origin of Languages*, ed. V. Gourevitch (New York, 1986).

Best modern French edition: *Essai sur l'Origine des Langues*, ed. C. Porset (2nd edn Bordeaux, 1970). Also, an edition ed. A. Kremer-Marietti (Paris, 1974); and an *Index-Concordance de l'Essai*, D. Bourdin and M. Launay (Paris, 1989).

[9]   *Julie, ou La Nouvelle Héloïse*; subtitle: *Lettre de deux amans, habitants d'une petite ville au pied des Alpes.* A Amsterdam, chez Marc-Michel Rey, 1761

The sequel: *Les Amours de Milord Édouard Bomston* first appeared in the *Oeuvres Complètes*, ed. P. Moultou and P.A. Du Peyrou (Geneva, 1782).

Published in *OC* II. Translations include *La Nouvelle Héloïse*, trans. Judith H. McDowell (Philadelphia, 1968) (heavily abridged); *Eloisa, or a Series of Original Letters*, reprint of 1803 translation (Oxford, 1989) (includes *The Adventures of Lord B—— at Rome*, a complete but archaic translation).

Other French editions include D. Mornet (ed.), 4 vols (Paris, 1925); R. Pomeau (ed.) (Paris, 1960).

[10]   *Lettres à Malesherbes*

First published as notes to eleventh verse of J.-A. Roucher's poem, *Les Mois* (Paris: Quillau, 1779); unauthorized. First authorized edition: *Oeuvres Posthumes*, ed. P. A. Du Peyrou, vol. VIII (Geneva, 1782). Published in *OC* I.

Letters translated in *Citizen of Geneva*, trans. and ed. C. W. Hendel (Oxford, 1937). Parts included in *The Indispensable Rousseau*, John Hope Mason (London, 1979).

[11]   *Émile, ou de l'Éducation.* A La Haye, chez Jean Néaulme, 1762

Published in *OC* IV (includes MS Favre). Translation used in this text: *Émile, or On Education*, Allan Bloom, with intro. and notes (New York, 1979).

Other translations include *Émile, or Education*, trans. B. Foxley (London, 1911). Modern French editions include F. and P. Richard (eds) (Paris, 1951).

[12]   *La Profession de Foi du Vicaire Savoyard*

Originally appeared in Bk IV of *Émile*, 1762. Published in *OC* IV. Other translations include *The Creed of a Priest of Savoy*, trans. A. H. Beattie (New York, 1956).

A modern French edition: P.-M. Masson (ed.) (Fribourg and Paris, 1914).

[13]   *Émile et Sophie*

First published in *Collection Complète des Oeuvres de Jean-Jacques Rousseau*, ed. P. Moultou and P. A. Du Peyrou (Geneva, 1782). First separate edition: *Émile et Sophie, ou les Solitaires*. Geneva, chez la Société Typographique, 1781. Published in *OC* IV.

No current English translations, but a summary account given in J. Shklar, *Men and Citizens* (Cambridge, 1969)

[14]   *Du Contrat Social, ou Principes du Droit Politique.* Normally known as *Du Contrat Social.* A Amsterdam, chez Marc-Michel Rey, 1762

Published in *OC* III. Translation used in this text: *The Social Contract and Discourses*, G. D. H. Cole, J. H. Brumfitt and J. C. Hall (London, 1973).

Other translations include *On the Social Contract with Geneva Manuscript and Political Economy*, ed. R. D. Masters (New York, 1978); *Political Writings*, ed. F. Watkins (Edinburgh, 1953); *The Social Contract*, ed. M. Cranston (Harmondsworth, 1968); *The Social Contract*, ed. C. M. Sherover (New York, 1974); *The Social Contract and Discourse on Inequality*, ed. L. G. Crocker (New York, 1967).

French editions include E. Dreyfus-Brisac (ed.) (Paris, 1896); G. Beaulavon (ed.) (Paris, 1903; 5th edn, 1938); C. E. Vaughan (ed.) (Manchester, 1918); M. Halbwachs (ed.) (Paris, 1943); B. de Jouvenel (ed.) (Geneva, 1947); R. Grimsley (ed.) (Oxford, 1972); J.-L. Lecercle (ed.) (Paris, 1956).

[15]   *Jean-Jacques Rousseau, Citoyen de Genève, à Christophe de Beaumont.* A Amsterdam, chez Marc-Michel Rey, 1763

Normally known as *Lettre à Christophe de Beaumont*. Published in *OC* IV. No current English translations, but parts included in *The Indispensable Rousseau*, John Hope Mason (London, 1979).

[16]   *Projet de Constitution pour la Corse*

First published in *Oeuvres et Correspondance Inédites*, ed. G. Streckeisen-Moultou (Paris, 1861). Published in *OC* III.

Translation used in this text: *Political Writings*, ed. F. Watkins (Edinburgh, 1953). Parts included in *The Indispensable Rousseau*, John Hope Mason (London, 1979).

[17]   *Lettres Écrites de la Montagne*. A Amsterdam, chez Marc-Michel Rey, 1764

Published in *OC* III. No currently available English translation, but parts included in *The Indispensable Rousseau*, John Hope Mason (London, 1979).

A modern French edition: H. Guillemin (ed.) (Neuchâtel, 1962).

[18]   *Les Confessions*

Part 1, comprising Bks I–VI, first appeared in *Oeuvres Posthumes*, ed. P. A. Du Peyrou (Geneva, 1782), vols VIII, IX. Part 1 also published in 1782 in separate edition in Geneva. Part 2, comprising Bks VII–XII, first appeared in *Second Supplément à la Collection des Oeuvres de Jean-Jacques Rousseau*, eds P. Moultou and P. A. Du Peyrou (Geneva, 1789). First edition of whole work published by Poincot, Paris, 1796. Published in *OC* I. Translation used in this text: *The Confessions*, J. M. Cohen (Harmondsworth, 1954).

Other English translations include *The Confessions* (London, 1913). Other French editions include A. van Bever (ed.) (Paris, 1913).

[19]   *Considérations sur le Gouvernement de Pologne*

First published in *Collection Complète des Oeuvres de Jean-Jacques Rousseau*, eds P. Moultou and P. A. Du Peyrou (Geneva, 1782). Separate edition published in 1782, in Geneva. Published in *OC* III. Translation used in this text: *Political Writings*, ed. F. Watkins (Edinburgh, 1953).

Other English translations include *The Government of Poland*, trans. and ed. W. Kendall (New York, 1972).

[20]   *Rousseau Juge de Jean Jacques: Dialogues*

First Dialogue: *Rousseau Juge de Jean-Jacques: Dialogues*, d'après le manuscrit de M. Rousseau, laissé entre le mains de M. Brooke Boothby. A Lichfield, chez J. Jackson, 1780.

First complete edition: *Collection Complète des Oeuvres de Jean-Jacques Rousseau*, eds P. Moultou and P. A. Du Peyrou (Geneva, 1782). Published in *OC* I. Translation used in this text: *Rousseau Judge of Jean-Jacques: Dialogues*, in *The Collected Writings of Rousseau*, vol. I, eds R. D. Masters and C. Kelly (Hanover, New Hampshire, 1990).

[21]   *Les Rêveries du Promeneur Solitaire*

First published in *Oeuvres Posthumes*, ed. P. A. Du Peyrou (Geneva, 1780). Separate edition appeared in 1780, Geneva. Published in *OC* I. Translation used in this text: *Reveries of the Solitary Walker*, P. France (Harmondsworth, 1979).

Other English translations include *Reveries of the Solitary Walker*, trans. and ed. C. E. Butterworth (New York, 1979); *Reveries of the Solitary Walker*, trans. and ed. J. G. Fletcher (New York, 1971).

Other French editions include J. S. Spink (ed.) (Paris, 1948); M. Raymond (ed.) (Geneva, 1948); J. Voisine (ed.) (Paris, 1964).

6   GROUPS OF WORKS

Note: Where two dates are given in this section, the first refers to date of composition and the second to date of publication.

[22]   Botanical writings
Two principal works:

> *Lettres Élémentaires sur la Botanique à Madame de L* . . ., and *Fragments pour un Dictionnaire des Termes d'Usage en Botanique*. Both first appeared in the *Collection Complète des Oeuvres de Jean-Jacques Rousseau*, ed. P. Moultou and P. A. Du Peyrou (Geneva, 1782).

Published in *OC* IV. Translation used in this text: *Botany: A Study of Pure Curiosity*, ed. K. Ottevanger, illus. P. J. Redouté (London, 1979).

[23]   Musical composition
Eight works of significance:

> *Iphis et Anaxarette* (1737?), in *Oeuvres Mêlées*, ed. de Boubers (London, 1776); and in *Supplément à la Collection des Oeuvres*, ed. P. Moultou (Geneva, 1782). *La Découverte du Nouveau Monde* (1740–1), in *Supplément*. *Les Muses Galantes* (1745), in *Oeuvres Posthumes*, ed. P. A. Du Peyrou (Geneva, 1781). *Les Festes de Ramire* (1745), *Annales*, 1 (1905). *Le Devin du Village*, Intermède représenté à Fontaine-bleau . . . Avec Privilège du Roy (1752) (Paris: Pissot, 1753); translated as *The Cunning Man*, ed. C. Burney T. Becket and P. A. de Hondt (London, 1766). *Pygmalion* (1762–3), in *Mercure de France*, 1771. *Daphnis et Chloé* (1774), ed. Corancez, A Paris, chez Espril Libraire, 1779. *Les Consolations des Misères de ma Vie* (1770–8) (Paris, 1781).

Published in *OC* II (without music).

[24]   Music: writings on
Five works of significance:

> *Dissertation sur la Musique Moderne* (Paris: Quillau, 1743); trans. L. Hewitt (ed.),

Project Concerning New Symbols for Music (Kilkenny, 1982). *Lettre sur la Musique Françoise* (Paris: Pissot, 1753) trans. in part in *Source Readings in Music History*, ed. O. Strunk (New York, 1950). *Dictionnaire de Musique* (Paris: Duchesne, 1767); trans. W. Waring, *The Complete Dictionary of Music* (London, 1771). *Traités sur la Musique* (Geneva, 1781) (contains *Projet Concernant de Nouveaux Signes pour la Musique*; *Dissertation sur la Musique Moderne*; *Essai sur l'Origine des Langues*; *Lettre à M. l'Abbé Raynal*; *Examen de Deux Principes Avancés par M. Rameau*; *Lettre à M. Burney*). *Oeuvres Complètes* (Paris: Hachette, 1905) contains the foregoing, and also *Lettre d'un Symphoniste*; *Observations sur l'Alceste de Gluck*; *Lettre à M. Grimm au Sujet d'Omphale*.

None of these is yet included in *OC*.

[25]   Poetry and miscellaneous prose
Ten works of significance:

Le Verger de Madame la Baronne de Warens (London: Jacob Tonson, 1739, actually published in Chambéry or Annecy). *Épître à M. Bordes, Journal de Verdun*, 1743. *Épître à M. Parisot* (1741–2), in *Oeuvres Mêlées*, ed. de Boubers (London, 1776). *L'Allée de Sylvie* (1746), *Mercure de France*, 1750. *La Reine Fantasque* (1756), illicit edition 1758; authorized edition in *Oeuvres de Jean-Jacques Rousseau* (Amsterdam: Marc-Michel Rey, 1769). *Les Amours de Claire et de Marcellin* (1756), in *Oeuvres et Correspondance Inédites*, ed. G. Streckeisen-Moultou (Paris, 1861). *Le Petit Savoyard* (1756), in *Oeuvres et Correspondance Inédites*, ed. Streckeisen-Moultou. *Le Lévite d'Éphraïm* (1762), *Oeuvres Posthumes* (Geneva, 1781). *La Vision de Pierre de la Montagne* (Geneva, 1765). *Discours sur la Vertu du Héros* (1751), illicit edition, *L'Année Littéraire*, 1768; authorized edition, *Oeuvres de Jean-Jacques Rousseau* (Amsterdam: Marc-Michel Rey, 1769).

All published in *OC* II.

[26]   Theatre
Five works of significance:

Les Prisonniers de Guerre (1743), *Supplément à la Collection des Oeuvres Complètes* (Geneva, 1782). *Arlequin Amoureux Malgré Lui* (1746–7), *Annales*, 2 (1906). *L'Engagement Téméraire* (1747), *Oeuvres Posthumes* (Geneva, 1781). *Narcisse, ou l'Amant de Lui-Même* (1732?), (Paris: Pissot, 1753). *La Mort de Lucrèce* (1754), *Annales*, 2 (1906).

All published in *OC* II.

BIBLIOGRAPHICAL WORKS

Courtois, L. J., 'Chronologie critique de la vie et des oeuvres de Jean-Jacques Rousseau', *Annales*, 15 (1923)

Dufour, T., *Recherches Bibliographiques sur les Oeuvres Imprimées de Jean-Jacques Rousseau*, 2 vols (Paris, 1925)

Aubert, F., *Manuscrits de Jean-Jacques Rousseau qui se trouvent à Genève* (Geneva, 1938)

Schinz, A., *État Présent des Travaux sur Jean-Jacques Rousseau* (New York, 1941)

Sénelier, J., *Bibliographie Générale des Oeuvres de Jean-Jacques Rousseau* (Paris, 1950)

Leigh, R.A., 'Les manuscrits disparus de Jean-Jacques Rousseau', *Annales*, 34 (1956–8)

CORRESPONDENCE

Dufour, T., and P.-P. Plan (eds), *Correspondance Générale de Jean-Jacques Rousseau*, 20 vols (Paris, 1924–34)

Hendel, C. W. (trans. and ed.), *Citizen of Geneva: Selections from the Letters* (Oxford, 1937)

Leigh, R. A. (ed.), *Correspondance Complète de Jean-Jacques Rousseau*, 49 vols (Geneva, 1965–71; Banbury, 1972–89) One of the greatest achievements of modern scholarship.

PART II: WORKS ON ROUSSEAU

1 LIFE AND WORKS

Many of these books include substantial discussions of Rousseau's works as well as narrating his life. These references are given in order of publication so that the reader can see at a glance which are the modern biographies, which in general are more comprehensive and reliable than earlier ones.

(1) Bernardin de Saint-Pierre, *Études de la Nature*, 3 vols (Paris, 1784)

(2) Morley, J., *Rousseau* (London, 1873)

(3) MacDonald, F., *Jean-Jacques Rousseau: A New Study in Criticism*, 2 vols (London, 1906)

(4) Wright, E. H., *The Meaning of Rousseau* (Oxford, 1929)

(5) Hendel, C. W., *Jean-Jacques Rousseau, Moralist*, 2 vols (London, 1934)

(6) Mowat, R. B., *Jean-Jacques Rousseau* (Bristol, 1938)

(7) Cassirer, E., *The Question of Jean-Jacques Rousseau*, trans. P. Gay (Indiana, 1954; 2nd edn 1989)

(8) Green, F. C., *Jean-Jacques Rousseau: A Critical Study of his Life and Writings* (Cambridge, 1955)

(9) Grimsley, R., *Jean-Jacques Rousseau: A Study in Self-Awareness* (Cardiff, 1961)

(10) Broome, J. H., *Rousseau: A Study of his Thought* (London, 1963)

(11) Guéhenno, J., *Jean-Jacques Rousseau*, 2 vols, trans. J. and D. Weightman (London, 1966)

(12) Einaudi, M., *The Early Rousseau* (New York, 1967)

(13) Crocker, L. G., *Jean-Jacques Rousseau: The Quest (1712–58)*, vol. I (New York, 1968); *Jean-Jacques Rousseau: The Prophetic Voice (1758–78)*, vol. II (New York, 1973)
(14) de Beer, G., *Rousseau and his World* (London, 1972)
(15) Huizinga, J. H., *Rousseau: The Making of a Saint* (London, 1975)
(16) Grimsley, R., *Jean-Jacques Rousseau* (Brighton, 1983)
(17) Cranston, M., *Jean-Jacques*, vol. I (London, 1983); *The Noble Savage*, vol. II (London, 1991)
(18) Miller, J., *The Dreamer of Democracy* (New Haven, Conn., 1984)

2 ASPECTS OF ROUSSEAU'S WORK

BOOKS

(19) Babbit, I., *Rousseau and Romanticism* (New York, 1919)
(20) Berman, M., *The Politics of Authenticity* (New York, 1970)
(21) Blum, C., *Rousseau and the Republic of Virtue* (Ithaca, NY, 1986)
(22) Cameron, D., *The Social Thought of Rousseau and Burke* (London, 1973)
(23) Charvet, J., *The Social Problem in the Philosophy of Rousseau* (Cambridge, 1974)
(24) Dent, N. J. H., *Rousseau* (Oxford, 1988)
(25) Ellrich, R. J., *Rousseau and his Reader* (Chapel Hill, NC, 1969)
(26) Grimsley, R., *The Philosophy of Rousseau* (Oxford, 1973)
(27) Horowitz, A., *Rousseau, Nature and History* (Toronto, 1987)
(28) Kavanagh, T. M., *Writing the Truth* (Berkeley, Calif., 1987)
(29) Melzer, A. M., *The Natural Goodness of Man: On the System of Rousseau's Thought* (Chicago, 1990)
(30) O'Neal, J. C., *Seeing and Observing* (Saratoga, Calif., 1985)
(31) Perkins, M. L., *Jean-Jacques Rousseau on the Individual and Society* (Lexington, Ky., 1974)
(32) Riley, P., *Will and Political Legitimacy* (Cambridge, Mass., 1982)
(33) Riley, P., *The General Will before Rousseau* (Princeton, NJ, 1986)
(34) Roche, K.F., *Rousseau: Stoic and Romantic* (London, 1974)
(35) Schwartz, J., *The Sexual Politics of Jean-Jacques Rousseau* (Chicago, 1984)
(36) Shklar, J., *Men and Citizens* (Cambridge, 1969)
(37) Starobinski, J., *Jean-Jacques Rousseau: la Transparence et l'Obstacle* (Paris, 1971), *Transparency and Obstruction*, trans. A. Goldhammer (Chicago, 1988)
(38) Viroli, M., *Jean-Jacques Rousseau and the 'Well-Ordered Society'* (Cambridge, 1988)

COLLECTIONS OF ARTICLES (IN ORDER OF PUBLICATION)

(39) *Yale French Studies*, 28 (1961–2)
(40) *Jean-Jacques Rousseau*, Université Ouvrière et Faculté des Lettres de l'Université de Genève (Neuchâtel, 1962)
(41) 'Entretiens sur Jean-Jacques Rousseau', *Annales*, 35 (1959)

(42) *Études sur le Contrat Social de Jean-Jacques Rousseau*, Actes des journées d'étude organisées à Dijon (Paris, 1964)
(43) *Jean-Jacques Rousseau et son Oeuvre: Problèmes et Recherches* (Paris, 1964)
(44) 'Rousseau et la philosophie politique', *Annales de la Philosophie Politique*, 5 (1965)
(45) Cranston, M., and R. S. Peters (eds), *Hobbes and Rousseau* (New York, 1972)
(46) Launay, M. (ed.), *Rousseau et Voltaire en 1978* (Geneva, 1981)
(47) 'Rousseau for our time', *Daedalus*, 107 (1978)
(48) MacAdam, J., M. Neumann and G. LaFrance (eds), *Trent Rousseau Papers* (Ottawa, 1980)
(49) Harvey, S., M. Hobson, D. Kelly, and S. S. B. Taylor (eds), *Reappraisals of Rousseau* (Manchester, 1980)
(50) Leigh, R. A. (ed.), *Rousseau after 200 Years* (Cambridge, 1982)
(51) Terrasse, J. (ed.), *Studies on Rousseau's Discourses* (Ottawa, 1988)
(52) Bloom, H. (ed.), *Jean-Jacques Rousseau* (New York, 1988)
(53) Lively, J., and A. Reeve (eds), *Modern Political Theory from Hobbes to Marx* (London, 1989)
(54) LaFrance, G., *Studies on the Social Contract* (Ottawa, 1989)

3 ROUSSEAU'S POLITICAL PHILOSOPHY (AND RELATED SUBJECTS)

GENERAL

(55) Burns, J. H., 'Du côté de chez Vaughan: Rousseau revisited', *Political Studies*, 12 (1964)
(56) Cell, H. R., and J. I. MacAdam, *Rousseau's Response to Hobbes* (New York, 1988)
(57) Chapman, J. W., *Rousseau – Totalitarian or Liberal?* (New York, 1956)
(58) Cobban, A., *Rousseau and the Modern State* (London, 1934; rev. edn 1964)
(59) Cobban, A., 'New light on the political thought of Rousseau', *Political Science Quarterly*, 66 (1951)
(60) Cobban, A., and J. H. Burns, 'Rousseau's *Du Contrat Social*: some problems of translation', *Political Studies*, 10 (1962)
(61) Colletti, L., *From Rousseau to Lenin* (New York, 1972)
(62) della Volpe, G., *Rousseau and Marx* (London, 1978)
(63) Ellenburg, S., *Rousseau's Political Philosophy: An Interpretation from Within* (Ithaca, NY, 1976)
(64) Fralin, R., *Rousseau and Representation* (New York, 1978)
(65) Hall, J. C., *Rousseau: An Introduction to his Political Philosophy* (London, 1973)
(66) de Jouvenel, B., 'Rousseau's theory of the forms of government', in (45)
(67) Kateb, G., 'Aspects of Rousseau's political thought', *Political Science Quarterly*, 66 (1951)
(68) Lemos, R., *Rousseau's Political Philosophy* (Athens, Georgia, 1977)
(69) Masters, R. D., *The Political Philosophy of Jean-Jacques Rousseau* (Princeton, 1968)
(70) Plamenatz, J., *Man and Society*, vol. I (London, 1963)

(71) Rapaczynski, A., *Nature and Politics* (Ithaca, NY, 1987)
(72) Shklar, J., 'Rousseau's two models: Sparta and the Age of Gold', *Political Science Quarterly*, 76 (1961)
(73) Strauss, L., 'On the intention of Rousseau', in (45)
(74) Talmon, J., *The Rise of Totalitarian Democracy* (Boston, 1952)
(75) Vaughan, C. E., *Studies in the History of Political Philosophy Before and After Rousseau* (Manchester, 1939)
(76) Wokler, R., 'Rousseau and Marx', in *The Nature of Political Theory*, ed. D. Miller and L. Seidentop (Oxford, 1983)

THE *DISCOURSES*

(77) Aldridge, A. O., 'The state of nature', *SVEC*, 198 (1982)
(78) Allers, U. S., 'Rousseau's *Second Discourse*', *Review of Politics*, 20 (1958)
(79) Benda, H., 'Rousseau's early Discourses', Part I, Part II, *Political Science*, 5, 6 (1953, 1954)
(80) Cook, M., 'Rousseau and the negro', *Journal of Negro History*, 21 (1936)
(81) Crocker, L. G., 'The relation of Rousseau's *Second Discourse* and the *Social Contract*', *Romanic Review*, 51 (1960)
(82) Dent, N. J. H., 'Rousseau and respect for persons', in *Justifying Toleration*, ed. S. Mendus (Cambridge, 1988)
(83) de Jouvenel, B., 'Rousseau évolutionniste pessimiste', *Annales de la Philosophie Politique*, 5 (1965)
(84) Gourevitch, V., 'Rousseau on the arts and sciences', *Journal of Philosophy*, 69 (1972)
(85) Hamilton, J. F., 'Parallel interpretations ... of Rousseau's *Discours sur l'inégalité*', *SVEC*, 94 (1972)
(86) Hamilton, J. F., 'Virtue in Rousseau's First Discourse', *SVEC*, 98 (1972)
(87) Havens, G. R., *Voltaire's Marginalia on the Pages of Rousseau* (Columbus, 1933)
(88) Havens, G. R., 'Diderot and the composition of Rousseau's First Discourse', *Romanic Review*, 30 (1939)
(89) Havens, G. R., 'Diderot, Rousseau and the *Discours sur l'inégalité*', *Diderot Studies*, 3 (1961)
(90) Havens, G. R., 'The road to Rousseau's *Discours sur l'inégalité*', *Yale French Studies*, 42 (1968)
(91) Levin, M., 'Rousseau on independence', *Political Studies*, 18 (1970)
(92) Lovejoy, A. O., 'Rousseau's supposed primitivism', in *Essays on the History of Ideas*, A. O. Lovejoy (Baltimore, 1948)
(93) MacAdam, J. I., 'The *Discourse on Inequality* and the *Social Contract*', *Philosophy*, 50 (1975)
(94) Manuel, F. E., 'Sketch for a natural history of paradise', *Daedalus*, 101 (1972)
(95) Mason, J., 'Reading Rousseau's First Discourse', *SVEC*, 249 (1987)
(96) Meek, R., *Social Science and the Ignoble Savage* (Cambridge, 1976)
(97) Peled, Y., 'Rousseau's inhibited radicalism', *American Political Science Review*, 74 (1980)

(98)   Perkins, M. L., 'Liberty and the concept of legitimacy in the *Discours sur l'inégalité*', *SVEC*, 89 (1972)

(99)   Plattner, M. F., *Rousseau's State of Nature: An Interpretation of the Discourse on the Origin of Inequality* (DeKalb, 1979)

(100) Powers, R. H., 'Rousseau's useless science: dilemma or paradox?', *French Historical Studies*, 2 (1961–2)

(101) Skillen, A., 'Rousseau and the fall of social man', *Philosophy*, 50 (1975)

(102) Winch, P., 'Man and society in Hobbes and Rousseau', in (45)

(103) Wokler, R., 'The influence of Diderot on the political theory of Rousseau', *SVEC*, 132 (1975)

(104) Wokler, R., 'Tyson and Buffon on the orang-utan', *SVEC*, 155 (1976)

(105) Wokler, R., 'Perfectible apes in decadent culture: Rousseau's anthropology revisited', *Daedalus*, 107 (1978)

(106) Wokler, R., 'The *Discours sur les Sciences et les Arts* and its offspring', in (49)

(107) Wokler, R., and C. Frayling, 'From orang-utan to vampire', in (50)

(108) Wokler, R., *Social Thought of Jean-Jacques Rousseau* (New York, 1987)

THE SOCIAL CONTRACT

(109) Allen, G. O., ' "La volonté de tous" and "la volonté générale" ', *Ethics*, 73 (1962)

(110) Althusser, L., 'Sur le *Contrat Social*', in *Politics and History*, L. Althusser (London, 1972)

(111) Barnard, F. M., 'Will and political rationality in Rousseau', *Political Studies*, 32 (1984)

(112) Barry, B. M., 'Preferences and the common good', *Ethics*, 73 (1962)

(113) Cell, H., 'Breaking Rousseau's chains', in (48)

(114) Charvet, J., 'Rousseau and the ideal of community', *History of Political Thought*, 1 (1980)

(115) Cohen, J., 'Reflections on Rousseau and democracy', *Philosophy and Public Affairs*, 15 (1980)

(116) Cranston, M., 'Rousseau's *Social Contract*', in *The Mask of Politics*, M. Cranston (London, 1973)

(117) Crocker, L. G., *Rousseau's Social Contract: An Interpretive Essay* (Cleveland, 1968)

(118) Dagger, R., 'Understanding the general will', *Western Political Quarterly*, 34 (1981)

(119) Echeverria, D., 'The pre-revolutionary influence of Rousseau's *Social Contract*', *Journal of the History of Ideas*, 34 (1972)

(120) Fetscher, I., 'Rousseau's concepts of freedom', *Nomos* (1962)

(121) Friedrich, C. J., 'Law and dictatorship in the *Social Contract*', *Annales de la Philosophie Politique*, 5 (1965)

(122) Gardiner, P., 'Rousseau on liberty', in *Conceptions of Liberty in Political Philosophy*, Z. A. Pelczynski and D. Gray (London, 1984)

(123) Gildin, H., *Rousseau's 'Social Contract'* (Chicago, 1983)

(124)   Jones, W. T., 'Rousseau's general will and the problem of consent', *Journal of the History of Philosophy*, 25 (1987)

(125)   Kelly, C., 'To persuade without convincing', *American Journal of Political Science*, 31 (1987)

(126)   King, P., 'Towards a theory of the general will', *History of Philosophy Quarterly*, 4 (1987)

(127)   Leigh, R. A., 'Liberté et autorité dans le *Contrat Social*', in (43)

(128)   Levine, A., *The Politics of Autonomy* (Amherst, Mass., 1976)

(129)   Lough, J., 'The *Encyclopaedia* and the *Contrat Social*', in (49)

(130)   MacAdam, J. I., 'Rousseau and the friends of despotism', *Ethics*, 74 (1963)

(131)   MacAdam, J. I., 'What Rousseau meant by the general will', *Dialogue*, 5 (1967)

(132)   McKenzie, A., 'Rousseau's debate with Machiavelli in the *Social Contract*', *Journal of the History of Ideas*, 43 (1982)

(133)   McManners, J., 'The *Social Contract* and Rousseau's revolt against society', in (45)

(134)   Mason, J. H., 'Individuals in Rousseau's republican vision', *History of Political Thought*, 10 (1989)

(135)   Matthews, R., and D. Ingersoll, 'The therapist and lawgiver', *Canadian Journal of Political and Social Theory*, 4 (1930)

(136)   Melzer, A., 'Rousseau and the problem of bourgeois society', *American Political Science Review*, 74 (1980)

(137)   Melzer, A., 'Rousseau's moral realism: replacing natural law with the general will', *American Political Science Review*, 77 (1983)

(138)   Nesbit, R., 'Rousseau and equality', *Encounter*, 43 (1974)

(139)   Nisbet, A. R., 'Rousseau and the general will', in *The Social Philosophers*, A. R. Nisbet (London, 1974)

(140)   Noone, J. B., *Rousseau's Social Contract* (London, 1980)

(141)   Plamenatz, J., 'On le forcera d'être libre', in (45)

(142)   Remple, H. D., 'On forcing people to be free', *Ethics*, 87 (1976–7)

(143)   Riley, P., 'A possible explanation of Rousseau's general will', *American Political Science Review*, 67 (1970)

(144)   Ritter, G., 'Direct democracy and totalitarianism', *Diogenes*, 3 (1954–5)

(145)   Rosenfeld, D., 'Rousseau's unanimous contract and the doctrine of popular sovereignty', *History of Political Thought*, 8 (1987)

(146)   Shklar, J., 'Rousseau's images of authority', in (45)

(147)   Waldmann, T., 'Rousseau on the general will and the legislator', *Political Studies*, 8 (1960)

(148)   Weirich, P., 'Rousseau on proportional majority rule', *Philosophy and Phenomenological Research*, 47 (1986–7)

(149)   Wokler, R., 'Rousseau's perfectible libertarianism', in *The Idea of Freedom*, ed. A. Ryan (Oxford, 1979)

(150)   Wokler, R., 'Rousseau's two concepts of liberty', in *Lives, Liberties and the Public Good*, ed. G. Feaver and F. Rosen (London, 1987)

OTHER POLITICAL WRITINGS

(151) Barnard, F. M., 'National culture and political legitimacy: Herder and Rousseau', *Journal of the History of Ideas*, 44 (1983)
(152) Cohler, A., *Rousseau and Nationalism* (New York, 1970)
(153) Fralin, R., 'Rousseau and community: the role of *moeurs* in social change', *History of Political Thought*, 1 (1980)

4 *JULIE, OU LA NOUVELLE HÉLOÏSE*

(154) Anderson, D. L., 'Abélard and Héloïse: eighteenth-century motif', *SVEC*, 84 (1971)
(155) Crocker, L. G., 'Julie: ou la nouvelle duplicité', *Annales*, 34 (1963–5)
(156) Ellis, M. B., *Julie or La Nouvelle Héloïse: A Synthesis of Rousseau's Thought* (Toronto, 1949)
(157) Frayling, C., 'The composition of *La Nouvelle Héloïse*', in (49)
(158) Gossman, L., 'The worlds of *La Nouvelle Héloïse*', *SVEC*, 41 (1966)
(159) Howells, R. J., *La Nouvelle Héloïse* (London, 1980)
(160) Jimack, P. D., 'The paradox of Sophie and Julie', in *Women and Society in Eighteenth-Century France* (London, 1979)
(161) Jones, J. F., *La Nouvelle Héloïse: Rousseau and Utopia* (Geneva, 1977)
(162) Tanner, T., 'Julie and "La Maison Paternelle" ', *Daedalus*, 162 (1976)

5 *ÉMILE*

(163) Bloom, A., 'Introduction', in *Émile, or On Education*, A. Bloom (New York, 1979) (rev. edn of 'The education of democratic man', A. Bloom, *Daedalus*, 107 (1978))
(164) Burgelin, P., 'The second education of Émile', *Yale French Studies*, 28 (1961–2)
(165) Carr, D., 'The free child and the spoiled child', *Journal of the Philosophy of Education*, 19 (1985)
(166) Dent, N. J. H., 'The basic principle of Émile's education', *Journal of the Philosophy of Education*, 22 (1988)
(167) Jimack, P. D., 'La genèse et la rédaction de l'*Émile*', *SVEC*, 13 (1960)
(168) Jimack, P. D., '*Homme* and *citoyen* in Rousseau's *Émile*', *Romanic Review*, 56 (1965)
(169) Jimack, P. D., *Rousseau–Émile* (London, 1983)
(170) Mercken-Spaas, G., 'The social anthropology of Rousseau's *Émile*', *SVEC*, 132 (1975)
(171) Meyer, P. H., 'The individual and society in Rousseau's *Émile*', *Modern Language Quarterly*, 19 (1958)

6   *THE CONFESSIONS* AND OTHER AUTOBIOGRAPHICAL WRITINGS

(172)   Ellis, M. B., *Rousseau's Venetian Story: An Essay on Art and Truth in Les Confessions* (Baltimore, 1966)
(173)   France, P., *Rousseau: Confessions* (Cambridge, 1987)
(174)   Gourevitch, V., 'Rousseau on lying. A provisional reading of the Fourth Reverie', *Berkshire Review*, 16 (1980)
(175)   Gossman, L., 'The innocent art of confession and revery', *Daedalus*, 107 (1978)
(176)   Grimsley, R., *Jean-Jacques Rousseau: A Study in Self-Awareness* (Cardiff, 1961)
(177)   Hamilton, J. F., *Rousseau's Theory of Literature* (York, S. Carolina, 1979)
(178)   Hartle, A., *The Modern Self in Rousseau's Confessions* (Indiana, 1983)
(179)   Jimack, P. D., 'Rousseau and the primacy of self', *SVEC*, 32 (1965)
(180)   Jones, J. F., 'The *Dialogues* as autobiographical truth', *Eighteenth-Century Studies*, 14 (1965)
(181)   Kelly, C., and R. D. Masters, ' "Rousseau on reading Jean-Jacques" – *The Dialogues*', *Interpretation*, 17 (1989)
(182)   Palmer, R. R., 'A clash with democracy: Geneva and Jean-Jacques Rousseau', in *The Age of Democratic Revolution*, R. R. Palmer (Princeton, 1959)
(183)   Pascal, R., *Design and Truth in Autobiography* (Cambridge, Mass., 1960)
(184)   Williams, H., *Rousseau and Romantic Autobiography* (Oxford, 1983)

7   RELIGION

(185)   Dickstein, M., 'The faith of a vicar: reason and morality in Rousseau's religion', *Yale French Studies*, 28 (1961–2)
(186)   Goldbery, R., 'Voltaire, Rousseau and the Lisbon earthquake', *Eighteenth-Century Life*, 13 (1989)
(187)   Grimsley, R., *Rousseau and the Religious Quest* (Oxford, 1968)
(188)   de Man, P., 'The timid god: a reading of Rousseau's *Profession*', *Georgia Review*, 29 (1975)
(189)   Masson, P.-M., *La formation religieuse de Rousseau*, 3 vols (Paris, 1916)
(190)   Thomas, J. F., *Le pélagianisme de Jean-Jacques Rousseau* (Paris, 1956)

8   MUSIC

(191)   Blom, E., 'The philosopher, the actress and the boy', in *Stepchildren of Music*, E. Blom (London, 1923)
(192)   Cucuel, G., *La Pouplinière et la Musique de Chambre au 18e Siècle* (Paris, 1913)
(193)   Duchez, M.-E., '*Principe de la Mélodie* et *Origine des Langues*', *Revue de Musicologie*, 60 (1974)
(194)   Jansen, A., *Jean-Jacques Rousseau als Musiker* (Berlin 1884; repr. Geneva, 1971)
(195)   Kisch, E., 'Rameau and Rousseau', *Music and Letters*, 22 (1941)

(196) Launay, D. (ed.), *La Querelle des Bouffons*, 3 vols (Paris, 1973)
(197) Oliver, A. R., *The Encyclopedists as Critics of Music* (Columbus, 1947)
(198) Pougin, A., *Jean-Jacques Rousseau Musicien* (Paris, 1940)
(199) Robinson, P. E. J., *Jean-Jacques Rousseau's Doctrine of the Arts* (Berne, 1984)
(200) Strauss, J. F., 'Jean-Jacques Rousseau, musician', *Music Quarterly* (1978)
(201) Strunk, O. (ed.), *Source Readings in Music History* (New York, 1950)
(202) Weber, S. M., 'The aesthetics of Rousseau's *Pygmalion*', *Modern Language Notes*, 83 (1986)
(203) Wokler, R., 'Rousseau on Rameau and revolution', *Studies in the Eighteenth Century*, 6 (1979)
(204) Wokler, R., *Social Thought of Jean-Jacques Rousseau* (New York, 1987)

9 THEATRE, POETRY, MISCELLANEOUS PROSE

(205) Bloom, A., 'Introductory essay', in *Politics and the Arts: Letter to M. d'Alembert on the Theatre*, A. Bloom (Ithaca, NY, 1960)
(206) Ellrich, R., 'Rousseau's androgynous dream: the minor works 1752–62', *French Forum*, 13 (1988)
(207) Kavanagh, T., 'Rousseau's *Le Lévite d'Éphraïm*', *Eighteenth-Century Studies*, 16 (1982–3)
(208) Polizer, R. L., 'Rousseau on the theatre and the actors', *Romanic Review*, 46 (1955)
(209) Rex, W. R., 'Sexual metamorphoses ... Rousseau's *Narcisse*', *SVEC*, 278 (1990)

10 THE *ESSAY ON THE ORIGIN OF LANGUAGES*

(210) Derrida, J., 'Genesis and structure of the *Essay*', in *Of Grammatology*, J. Derrida (Baltimore, 1976)
(211) Grimsley, R., 'Rousseau and the problem of "original" language', in *The Age of Enlightenment: Studies Presented to Th. Besterman*, ed. W. H. Barber, (Edinburgh, 1967)
(212) Lovejoy, A. O., 'Monboddo and Rousseau', in *Essays in the History of Ideas*, A. O. Lovejoy (Baltimore, 1948)
(213) Wokler, R., 'Rousseau, Rameau and the *Essai*', *SVEC*, 117 (1974)
(214) Wokler, R., '*L'Essai* en tant que fragment du *Discours sur l'inégalité*', in (46)
(215) Wokler, R., *Social Thought of Jean-Jacques Rousseau* (New York, 1987)

11 BOTANY; WRITINGS OF THE ABBÉ DE SAINT-PIERRE; WAR; WOMEN

(216) Cameron, D. R., 'The hero in Rousseau's political thought', *Journal of the History of Ideas*, 45 (1984)
(217) Canovan, M., 'Rousseau's two concepts of citizenship', in *Women in Western Political Thought*, ed. E. Kennedy and S. Mendus (Brighton, 1987)

(218) Cantor, P. A., 'The metaphysics of botany: Rousseau and the new criticism of plants', *Southwestern Review*, 70 (1985)

(219) Carter, C. J., *Rousseau and the Problem of War* (New York, 1987)

(220) Graham, R., 'Rousseau's sexism revolutionised', in *Women in the Eighteenth Century*, ed. P. Fritz and R. Morton (Toronto, 1976)

(221) Hinsley, F. H., *Power and the Pursuit of Peace* (Cambridge, 1967)

(222) Hoffman, S., 'Rousseau on war and peace', *American Political Science Review*, 57 (1963)

(223) Hoffman, S., *The State of War* (London, 1965)

(224) Lloyd, G., 'Rousseau on reason, nature and women', *Metaphilosophy*, 11 (1983)

(225) Okin, S. M., *Women in Western Political Thought* (Princeton, 1979)

(226) Perkins, M. L., *The Moral and Political Philosophy of the Abbé de Saint-Pierre* (Geneva, 1959)

(227) Rapaport, E., 'On the future of love: Rousseau and the radical feminists', in *The Philosophy of Sex*, A. Soble (Totowa, NJ, 1980)

(228) Roosevelt, G., *Reading Rousseau in a Nuclear Age* (Philadelphia, 1988)

(229) Roosevelt, G., 'The role of Rousseau's writings on war and peace in the evolution of the *Social Contract*', in (54)

(230) Scott, D., 'Rousseau and flowers', *SVEC*, 182 (1979)

(231) Waltz, K. N., *Man, the State and War* (New York, 1959)

(232) Wexler, V. G., 'Made for man's delight: Rousseau as anti-feminist', *American Historical Review*, 81 (1976)

12 THE ENLIGHTENMENT; THE *ENCYCLOPAEDIA*; AND RELATED SUBJECTS

(233) Baczko, B., 'Rousseau and social marginality', *Daedalus*, 107 (1978)

(234) Becker, C., *The Heavenly City of the Eighteenth-Century Philosophers* (New Haven, Conn., 1932)

(235) Blanchard, W. H., *Rousseau and the Spirit of Revolt* (Ann Arbor, 1967)

(236) Bloom, A., 'Rousseau', in *The History of Political Thought*, ed. L. Strauss and J. Cropsey, (Chicago, 1963)

(237) Boswell, J., *Boswell on the Grand Tour: Germany and Switzerland 1764*, ed. F. Pottle (London, 1953)

(238) Bowler, P., 'Evolutionism in the Enlightenment', *History of Science*, 12 (1974)

(239) Cassirer, E., *The Philosophy of the Enlightenment* (Princeton, 1951)

(240) Cassirer, E., *Rousseau, Kant and Goethe* (Princeton, 1970)

(241) Crocker, L. G., 'Rousseau et "l'opinion"', *SVEC*, 40 (1967)

(242) Darnton, R., *The Great Cat Massacre* (New York, 1984)

(243) Darnton, R., *The Business of Enlightenment* (Cambridge, Mass., 1979)

(244) Durkheim, E., *Montesquieu and Rousseau* (Ann Arbor, 1960)

(245) Ellis, H., 'Mme de Warens', *Virginia Quarterly*, 9 (1933)

(246) Ellis, M. B., 'Jean-Jacques Rousseau – biographical problems', *Romanic Review*, 38 (1948)

(247) Gay, P., *The Enlightenment – An Interpretation*, 2 vols (New York, 1966, 1969)

(248) Gay, P., *The Party of Humanity* (New York, 1971)

(249) Grimsley, R., 'Rousseau and the problem of happines', in (45)

(250) Gossman, L., 'Time and history in Rousseau', *SVEC*, 30 (1964)

(251) Hall, R. W., 'Plato and Rousseau', *Aperion*, 16 (1982)

(252) Hampson, N., *The Enlightenment* (Harmondsworth, 1968)

(253) Hampson, N., *Will and Circumstance* (Norman, Okla., 1983)

(254) Hazard, P., *European Thought in the Eighteenth Century* (Harmondsworth, 1965)

(255) Howells, R. J., 'The metaphysic of nature: basic values . . . in Rousseau', *SVEC*, 60 (1968)

(256) Hubert, R., *Rousseau et l'Encyclopédie* (Paris, 1928)

(257) de Jouvenel, B., 'Rousseau', in *Western Political Philosophers*, ed. M. Cranston (London, 1974)

(258) Kedourie, E., *Nationalism* (New York, 1972)

(259) Kelly, G. A., 'Rousseau, Kant and history', *Journal of the History of Ideas*, 29 (1968)

(260) Keohane, N. O., 'The masterpiece of policy in our time: Rousseau on the morality of the Enlightenment', *Political Theory*, 6 (1978)

(261) Kontos, A., 'Domination: metaphor and political reality', in *Domination*, A. Kontos (Toronto, 1965)

(262) Leigh, R. A., 'Jean-Jacques Rousseau and the myth of antiquity in the eighteenth century', in *Classical Influences on Western Thought 1650–1870*, R. R. Bolgar (Cambridge, 1979)

(263) Lough, J., *The Encyclopaedia* (New York, 1971)

(264) MacAdam, J. I., 'The moral dimensions of property', in *Theories of Property – Aristotle to the Present*, ed. A. Parel and T. Flanagan (Waterloo, Ontario, 1979)

(265) MacNeil, G. H., 'The cult of Rousseau and the French Revolution', *Journal of the History of Ideas*, 50 (1945)

(266) MacNeil, G. H., 'The anti-revolutionary Rousseau', *American Historical Review*, 58 (1953)

(267) McDonald, C. V., 'J. Derrida's reading of Rousseau', *The Eighteenth Century*, 2 (1979)

(268) McDonald, J., *Rousseau and the French Revolution* (London, 1965)

(269) de Man, P., 'The rhetoric of blindness: Derrida's reading of Rousseau', in *Blindness and Insight*, P. de Man (London, 1983)

(270) Manser, A., 'Rousseau as philosopher', *Royal Institute of Philosophy Lectures*, vol. V (London, 1971)

(271) Marshall, T E., 'Rousseau and the Enlightenment', *Political Theory*, 6 (1978)

(272) Martin, K., *French Liberal Thought in the Eighteenth Century* (New York, 1963)

(273) O'Mara, P., 'Jean-Jacques and Geneva', *The Historian*, 20 (1957–8)

(274) Orwin, C., 'Compassion', *The American Scholar*, 49 (1980)

(275) Palmer, R. R., *The Age of Democratic Revolution, 1760–1800* (Princeton, 1979)

(276) Sabine, G. H., *History of Political Thought* (London, 1963)

(277) Spink, J. S., *Jean-Jacques Rousseau et Genève* (Paris, 1934)
(278) Taylor, S. S. B., 'Rousseau's contemporary reputation in France', *SVEC*, 27 (1963)
(279) Taylor, S. S. B., 'Rousseau's Romanticism', in (49)
(280) Trilling, L., *Sincerity and Authenticity* (London, 1972)
(281) Williams, D., 'The influence of Rousseau on political opinion', *English Historical Review*, 48 (1933)

13 OTHER WORKS IN ENGLISH

(282) Barnard, F. M., *Self-Direction and Political Legitimacy* (Oxford, 1988)
(283) Chadwick, O., *The Secularization of the European Mind in the Nineteenth Century* (Cambridge, 1975)
(284) Green, T. H., 'On the different senses of "freedom" . . .', in *Lectures on the Principles of Political Obligation*, T. H. Green (London, 1924)
(285) Hegel, G. W. F., *Hegel's Philosophy of Right*, trans. T. M. Knox (Oxford, 1957)
(286) Hirsch, F., *Social Limits to Growth* (London, 1977)
(287) Hofstader, R., *The Paranoid Style in American Politics* (London, 1966)
(288) Kant, I., *Kant's Political Writings*, ed. H. Reiss (Cambridge, 1977)
(289) Kant, I., *Religion within the Limits of Reason Alone*, trans. T. M. Greene and H. Hudson (New York, 1960)
(290) Klein, M., *Envy and Gratitude and Other Works, 1946–63* (London, 1975)
(291) Laing, R. D., *The Divided Self* (Harmondsworth, 1965)
(292) MacPherson, C. B., *The Political Theory of Possessive Individualism* (Oxford, 1962)
(293) Marx, K., 'Introduction to a critique of political economy', in *The German Ideology*, ed. C. J. Arthur (London, 1970)
(294) Pateman, C., *Participation and Democratic Theory* (Cambridge, 1970)
(295) Paul, E. F., F. D. Miller, and J. Paul (eds), *Liberty and Equality* (Oxford, 1985)
(296) Ryan, A., *Property and Political Theory* (Oxford, 1984)
(297) Schlatter, R., *Private Property: The History of An Idea* (London, 1957)
(298) Skinner, Q., 'The idea of negative liberty: philosophical and historical perspectives', in *Philosophy in History*, ed. R. Rorty, J. Schneewind, and Q. Skinner (Cambridge, 1984)
(299) Taylor, C., 'What's wrong with negative liberty?', in *The Idea of Freedom*, ed. A. Ryan (Oxford, 1979)
(300) Tonnies, F., *Community and Association* (London, 1955)
(301) Veblen, T., *Theory of the Leisure Class* (London, 1970 (1899))

14 OTHER WORKS IN FRENCH

(302) Ansart-Dourlen, M., *Dénaturation et Violence* (Klincksieck, 1975)
(303) Baczko, B., *Rousseau: Solitude et Communauté* (Paris, 1974)

(304) Burgelin, P., *La Philosophie de l'Existence de Jean-Jacques Rousseau* (Paris, 1952)

(305) Burgelin, P., 'Le social et la politique chez Rousseau', in (42)

(306) Château, J., *Jean-Jacques Rousseau: Sa Philosophie de l'Éducation* (Paris, 1962)

(307) Clément, P.-P., *Jean-Jacques Rousseau: de l'Éros Coupable à l'Éros Glorieux* (Neuchâtel, 1976)

(308) Derathé, R., *Le Rationalisme de Rousseau* (Paris, 1948)

(309) Derathé, R., 'Les réfutations du *Contrat Social* au XVIIIe siècle', *Annales*, 32 (1950–2)

(310) Derathé, R., 'La religion civile selon Rousseau', *Annales*, 35 (1959–62)

(311) Derathé, R., *Rousseau et la Science Politique de son Temps* (2nd edn Paris, 1970)

(312) Eigeldinger, M., *Jean-Jacques Rousseau et la Réalité de l'Imaginaire* (Neuchâtel, 1962)

(313) Eigeldinger, M., *Univers Mythique et Cohérence* (Neuchâtel, 1978)

(314) Faÿ, B., *Jean-Jacques Rousseau, ou le Rêve de la Vie* (Paris, 1974)

(315) Goldschmidt, V., *Anthropologie et Politique: Les Principes du Système de Rousseau* (Paris, 1974)

(316) Gouhier, H., *Les Méditations Métaphysiques de Jean-Jacques Rousseau* (Paris, 1970)

(317) Groethuysen, B., *Jean-Jacques Rousseau* (Paris, 1949)

(318) Kryger, E., *La Notion de Liberté chez Rousseau* (Paris, 1979)

(319) Lanson, G., 'L'unité de la pensée de Jean-Jacques Rousseau', *Annales*, 8 (1912)

(320) Launay, M., *Jean-Jacques Rousseau: Écrivain Politique* (Grenoble, 1971)

(321) Lecercle, J., *Rousseau et l'Art du Roman* (Paris, 1962)

(322) Lévi-Strauss, C., 'Jean-Jacques Rousseau: fondateur des sciences de l'homme', in (40)

(323) May, G., *Rousseau par Lui-Même* (Paris, 1961)

(324) Pizzorusso, A., 'La comédie de *Narcisse*', *Annales*, 35 (1961–2)

(325) Polin, R., *La Politique de la Solitude* (Paris, 1971)

(326) Proust, J., *Diderot et L'Encyclopédie* (Paris, 1962)

(327) Raymond, M., *Jean-Jacques Rousseau: La Quête de Soi et la Rêverie* (Paris, 1962)

(328) Schinz, A., *La Pensée de Jean-Jacques Rousseau* (Paris, 1929)

(329) Vernes, P. M., *La Ville, la Fête, la Démocratie: Rousseau et les Illusions de la Communauté* (Paris, 1978)

15 SUPPLEMENT

(330) Berlin, I., 'Two concepts of liberty', in *Four Essays on Liberty*, I. Berlin (Oxford, 1969)

(331) Charvet, J., 'The idea of equality as a substantive principle of society', in *Contemporary Political Theory*, A. de Crespigny and A. Wertheimer (London, 1970)

(332) Clark, S. R. L., *Aristotle's Man* (Oxford, 1975)

(333)   Fromm, E., *Fear of Freedom* (London, 1942)

(334)   Harding, D. W., *The Impulse to Dominate* (London, 1941)

(335)   Hinsley, F. H., *Sovereignty* (London, 1966)

(336)   Hume, D., 'Account of the controversy between Hume and Rousseau' (*The Concise Account*), in *Philosophical Works*, D. Hume, vol. I (Edinburgh, 1826 (1766))

(337)   de Jouvenel, B., *Sovereignty* (London, 1957)

(338)   Leigh, R. A., 'Rousseau's letter to Voltaire on optimism', *SVEC*, 30 (1964)

(339)   Lukes, S., *Power* (London, 1974)

(340)   MacDonald, M., 'Natural rights', *Proceedings of the Aristotelian Society*, 48 (1946–7)

(341)   Pollard, S., *The Idea of Progress* (Harmondsworth, 1977)

(342)   Perelman, C., *The Idea of Justice and the Problem of Argument* (London, 1963)

(343)   Reisman, D., *The Lonely Crowd* (Chicago, 1967)

(344)   Solomon, R., *History and Human Nature* (Brighton, 1979)

(345)   Spink, J. S., 'La première rédaction des *Lettres Écrites de la Montagne*', *Annales*, 20 (1931)

(346)   Strauss, L., *Natural Right and History* (Chicago, 1953)

(347)   Walzer, M., *Spheres of Justice* (Oxford, 1983)

(348)   Wasserstrom, R., 'Rights, human rights, and racial discrimination', *Journal of Philosophy*, 61 (1964)

(349)   Williams, B. A. O., 'The idea of equality', in *Philosophy, Politics and Society*, P. Laslett and W. G. Runciman, 2nd series (Oxford, 1962)

Index

The Index is principally intended to equip the reader to find material on topics and works located in places other than in the specific entries on these topics and works. The page numbers of the entries are printed in bold. Reference to other information has been made sparingly.

I have given multiple entries in the Index to works, using both French and English titles (except where these are very similar, as with *Lettre* and *Letter*), and also using alternative leading words. Thus references are given to the *Social Contract* not only under that title, but also under *Du Contrat Social* and under *Contrat Social, Du*. The hope is that using the Index will be less like going on a treasure hunt.

275